TELEVISED
PRESIDENTIAL
DEBATES
AND PUBLIC POLICY

TELEVISED PRESIDENTIAL DEBATES
AND PUBLIC POLICY

SIDNEY KRAUS
Cleveland State University

1988
LAWRENCE ERLBAUM ASSOCIATES, PUBLISHERS
Hillsdale, New Jersey   Hove and London

Cover photos reprinted by permission of The Plain Dealer
and the League of Women Voters of the United States.

Lawrence Erlbaum Associates, Inc., Publishers
365 Broadway
Hillsdale, New Jersey 07642

Library of Congress Cataloging-in-Publication Data
Kraus, Sidney.
　Televised presidential debates and public policy / Sidney Kraus.
　　p.　　cm.
　Bibliography: p.
　Includes indexes.
　ISBN 0-8058-0007-7. ISBN 0-8058-0008-5 (pbk.)
　1. Presidents—United States—Election.　2. Campaign debates—
United States.　3. Television in politics—United States.
I. Title.
JK524.K73 1988
324.7—dc19　　　　　　　　　　　　　　　　　88-3744
　　　　　　　　　　　　　　　　　　　　　　　CIP

Printed in the United States of America
10　9　8　7　6　5　4　3　2　1

In memory of Neddie Masters, my mother-in-law,
who knew which candidate won a debate
and
In memory of Jess Yoder, my friend and colleague,
who cared about the rhetoric and the process of debating

CONTENTS

PREFACE

When John F. Kennedy and Richard N. Nixon agreed to debate on television in 1960, I had just begun my career as an assistant professor in the department of radio and television at Indiana University. My initial response to that political historical event was to investigate how voters reacted to the candidates' stands on issues and to their personalities. Realizing that the event was of major significance, I anticipated that other researchers would also rush to examine a number of variables. And indeed, I soon learned that some studies had been initiated and a few others were being contemplated. However, what was in the research mix was not comprehensive. Moreover, these few isolated studies would enter journals and chapters without an overall context about the political, social, and cultural background of the event. Worse still, perhaps, was the fact that most scholarly research ignored or gave short shrift to professional opinion in the field. This significant event, I thought, would present an opportunity to combine theory and effects with application and policy, an objective that had impressed me after reading Carl I. Hovland's "Effects of the Mass Media of Communication" in the *Handbook of Social Psychology* (Addison-Wesley Publishing Co., 1954):

> The stress on theory must not preclude study of applied phases of communication. Coupled with the lack of theory there is also insufficient knowledge of how to apply basic research to practical problems. (vol. II, p. 1099)

What was needed was a single volume assembling analyses of the many activities that would come about because two *presidential candidates* decided to debate publicly. Such an event had never been anticipated before. And television would make it possible for voters in their living rooms to see the candidates discuss issues together. Seen in that light, the event was innovative and of historical significance: *great* debates.

Great or not, the resulting volume of studies, *The Great Debates,* covered a variety of the activities and consequences of the televised confrontations. To my knowledge, that publication marked the first time that interdisciplinary studies and critiques about *one* communication event were included in a single volume. Three years later another such volume was published. In their book, *The Kennedy Assassination and the American Public: Social Communication in Crisis* (Stanford University Press, 1965) the editors, Bradley S. Greenberg and Edwin B. Parker, noted that:

> No previous single event has generated as much empirical social science research. The only comparable body of data about any one event came from studies of the televised debates between Kennedy and Nixon, for which a similar claim was made three years ago. It is ironic that Kennedy was a central figure in both these research efforts, which may have ushered in a new era in the use of behavioral research methods to study significant contemporary events. (p. 361)

It is clear now that both volumes had paved the way for interdisciplinary studies in mass and political communication concentrating on "significant contemporary events." But the initial conceptualization of investigating an event *in the making* as a study worthy of scholarly attention belongs to Gladys Engel Lang and Kurt Lang, the wife and husband team who in 1951 studied the way in which television covered Chicago's welcome home parade for General McArthur, and subsequently have contributed studies to several debate books. "Firehouse" research or critical events research continues today as an important method for understanding the role of the media in our political system.

Following the next set of presidential debates, another volume of interdisciplinary studies (*The Great Debates: Carter vs. Ford, 1976*) was published. It is evident today that televised presidential debates have gained the attention of scholars, survey researchers, and pollsters, as well as voters, media, and politicians. This attention has generated a considerable bibliography which is appended to this book.

The purpose of this book is to review and explore what we have learned about televised presidential debates, consider the impact of such encounters on the election process, and apply that knowledge to questions of policy. In addition to published accounts, I have relied on my observations and interviews with participants and other significant people involved in or with televised presidential debates.

The field research for this book began in 1976 when I was invited by the League of Woman Voters Education Fund (the League) to attend each of the presidential debates in the general election. Since then I have attended all of the general election debates in 1980 and 1984. Throughout those years I have observed and interviewed individuals involved with the debates and media personnel. I had been given press access at locations where primary debates were held, and at the Democratic and Republican parties' conventions, where I conducted additional interviews. For these activities during the 1976, 1980 and 1984 elections I received press credentials, and in many instances was a participant-observer of the media as they covered political events, especially the presidential debates. I reported on the presidential debates for television, radio stations and newspapers, and was a resource person to the media generally.

In a book of this size, it is difficult, if not impossible, to treat with reasonable attention all elements of these debates. I have attempted to review and analyze those aspects of the debates that have relevance for the academic and public sectors, and its import for public policy. An exception to following those parameters is a thorough discussion of the legal aspects of initiating, managing, and funding these debates. Throughout the chapters, those legal concerns are discussed only in relation to salient events impinging on debates.

The first chapter briefly introduces the discussion, and characterizes debate observers in terms of their criticisms. Some parts of this chapter appeared in the June, 1987 issue of *Critical Studies in Mass Communication,* (pp. 214–216) under the title of "Voters Win."

Chapter two discusses television and presidential elections from an historical view of that relationship. Scholars and practioners familiar with that development over four decades will probably want to skim this chapter for their particular interests. Students may wish to spend more time acquiring the background information necessary to appreciate many of the issues discussed later on.

Chapter three is a substantially revised and updated discussion from that which first appeared in a Cleveland State University publication: Sidney Kraus and Dennis Davis, "Televised Political Debates: the Negotiated Format," *The Gamut: A Journal of Ideas and Information,* Winter, 1982, pp. 102–112. That chapter along with subsequent chapters ought to be read sequentially, though aspects of each may be particularly pertinent for certain interests. For example, while reference is made to the Lincoln-Douglas debates throughout, Chapter four has a section on *The Myth of the Lincoln-Douglas Debates*. Similarly, references to election polling appear in several chapters, but chapter five devotes a section to *Polls*.

Research of this kind does not come easily. It takes a lot of time, not only in real time waiting for presidential elections, but in research time, others' time, and time for reactions and criticisms of events and issues. So in a true sense I want to thank many people for *their* time.

I must begin with my family. My wife, Cecile, a reading amd language arts educator, was a superb editor. She read every word, and changed many of them. She will be pleased when the boxes of documents I have used are filed and disposed of. Our eldest son, Ken, a former journalist, now a lawyer, helped me by discussing several issues of media and law. Pam, an advertising researcher, was always ready to share her social science and computer applications skills. Jody, who recently completed his doctorate in philosophy and just began his studies in law, provided excellent analyses of current affairs. His concern about the research and writing process, and his word processing expertise were much appreciated.

The John and Mary R. Markle Foundation provided research and travel funds for the election and presidential debates research in 1976, 1980 and 1984. I am indebted to them, and especially its president, Lloyd Morrisett for his support and patience. I also appreciate the 1980 professional leave given to me by Cleveland State University.

I am most grateful to the following individuals who have given me interviews, documents and tapes, credentials, and/or access to events and restricted areas:

Joseph Angotti, executive vice president, NBC News; Charles Benton, President, Benton Foundation; Art Bloom, director, CBS; Thomas J. Brazaitis, Washington bureau chief, Cleveland *Plain Dealer;* Hal Bruno, political analyst, ABC; Elliot Bernstein, producer, ABC News; Bill Carruthers, television debate consultant to Ford and Reagan; Robert Chandler, vice-president, CBS News; Wayne Chappell, executive director, Baltimore Convention Bureau; Ruth C. Clusen, President (1976), the League; Betsy Dribben, director, public relations (1976), the League; Rep. Dennis Eckert, D 11, Mentor; Stuart Eizenstat, special assistant to the President (Carter) for domestic affairs; Charles Frey, producer, ABC News; James Gannon, executive editor, *Des Moines Register;* Henry Geller, former general counsel to the Federal Communication Commission (FCC); Jeff Greenfield, media analyst, ABC; Lee and Ed Hanna, debate project co-directors (1980), the League; Harriet Hentges, executive director (1980), the

League; Ruth Hinerfield, President (1980), the League; Barry Jagoda, special assistant to President Carter; James Karayn, debate project director (1976), the League; Jack Kelly, producer, CBS News; Peggy Lampl, executive director (1976), the League; Karen Liebowitz, director, public relations (1984), the League; Elmer Lower, former President, ABC News; Newton Minow, former chairman, FCC, partner, Sidley and Austin; Warren Mitofsky, director, election and survey unit, CBS News; Michael Raoul-Duval, special counsel to President Ford; Richard Reeves, syndicated columnist; Dorothy Ridings, President (1984), the League; Howard Rosenberg, television critic, *Los Angeles Times;* Richard S. Salant, former President, CBS News, vice-chairman of the Board, NBC; Stephen A. Sharp, former counsel, FCC; Howard K. Smith, journalist; Jim Smithers, former executive director, Baltimore Convention Center, director, Kansas City Convention Center; Nicholas Zapple, former chief counsel of the Senate Communications Subcommittee.

The staff of the Newberry Library and the Chicago Historical Society were very helpful in locating documents and newspaper reports relating to the Lincoln-Douglas debates. I appreciate their time and the use of their facilities.

Two former graduate students, Tom O'Toole and Christine Fehlner, deserve credit—Tom for the coding and content analysis of selected network coverage, and Christine for her precision in sifting through, coding, and categorizing hundreds of newspaper articles on the primaries, general elections, and debates of 1980 and 1984. She also initiated the first draft of the bibliography.

I also appreciate the supportive comments of Jennings Bryant, Reagan Professor of Broadcasting at the University of Alabama, after he read each chapter.

Finally, I want to acknowledge the enormous contribution of two institutions. The media (the working press and the three broadcasting networks—ABC, CBS, and NBC) and the League of Women Voters. Often adversaries, these two institutions are complex and bureaucratic. They are difficult to penetrate, suspicious of outsiders, and often annoyed with scholarship. Professional in their daily tasks, they are driven by the best intentions to serve principles they feel are beneficial to their organizations and to the public at large.

The media, for the most part, have permitted me to observe them as they covered the debates. They have been criticized, herein and elsewhere, but overall they have done a credible job.

The League, its Education Fund, sponsor of three series of general election debates (1976, 1980, 1984), and many presidential primary debates, has been key actors in bringing candidates together for voters to "see for themselves." As I travelled to major cities hosting debates, some individuals demeaned the League's role in the election process. I have always resented the pernicious depiction of the League as "little old ladies." Some of the League's actions also have been criticized in this book, but it deserves this nation's thanks for extraordinary public service.

Many of the following pages could not have been written without these institutions' cooperation, and the participation and cooperation of the individuals noted above. However, this book is my interpretation of events and people's actions. Any errors of commission or omission are my fault and not that of others.

I hope that this enterprize will contribute to the public dialogue of how to better inform voters about issues and candidates. If it does, then what is important is not the adoption of suggestions made herein, but the recognition that televised debates offer a unique opportunity to improve the presidential election process.

Sidney Kraus

1

INTRODUCTION

We have had four presidential elections in which leading candidates have debated on television.[1] In two of those elections vice-presidential candidates have also debated. The presidential election of 1988 marks 130 years since the Lincoln–Douglas debates,[2] and 28 years since the first televised presidential debates between John F. Kennedy and Richard M. Nixon. This event will most certainly include televised debates between the two nonincumbents.[3]

These televised debates have been examined closely in scientific studies conducted by social scientists; textual examinations by rhetoricians; reviews of studies by political writers; event recording by historians; and discussions by politicians, political experts, broadcasters, sponsors, and debate participants. These assessments were presented in a variety of formats: books; articles in academic journals, newspapers, magazines and pamphlets; television public affairs programming; meetings of academic associations; and "think-tank" conferences. Topics examined included: debate effects on voters; candidate performance in terms of issues and images; formats; television production; sponsorship; legal and political aspects; political socialization; campaign advisers; debate consultants; polls and pollsters; and to a limited degree, public policy considerations.

As with elections generally, debates should be continually examined as political history, and as part of the studies of several disciplines in the humanities and the social sciences. Monitoring presidential elections and debates may provide policymakers with the data and insight to improve televised debates. Although changes in the election process are difficult to come by—alterations and innovations usually defer to tradition—the improvement of televised debates offers the opportunity to strengthen the presidential election process. That assumes, of course, that the debate assessments persuade the public and policymakers of their value.

Acting on the recommendations offered in debate assessments will, in part, depend on the predisposition of evaluators. Three "classes" of presidential debate evaluators can be identified—proponents, conditionals, and opponents.

Proponents see debates as an important contributing factor to the democratic process of electing a president. Their positive assessments are arrived at by the impact the debates have had on the American public, and the image of democracy conveyed to citizens of countries around the globe.[4] Reviewing studies of the 1976 debates, Sears and Chaffee,[5] noted several latent functions for the political system. Among these were "the political socialization of pre-adults, the legitimization of institutions, and the international credibility of an incoming . . . president of the most powerful nation in the world."[6] Their appraisal was that "a variety of indicators converge[d] on the conclusion that the political system at large was positively served by the debates [and] voters seem to have profited from [them]."[7] Proponents often are not supporters of the status quo. They may suggest particular improvements, but they want debates to continue in presidential elections despite their faults. Some would make debates mandatory in presidential elections.

Conditionals will not settle for "flawed" debates. They demand specific repair of televised debates as a prerequisite for their support. Their conditions vary: a genuine, traditional, classical debate format; removal of the press as panelists; inclusion of minor party candidates; nonmandatory candidate participation; incumbents should not debate lest they inadvertently jeopardize national security; removal of third-party sponsors; inclusion of third-party sponsors; and issues predominating candidate image.

Opponents argue that presidents are not required to debate in office; debates fail to reveal the candidates' qualifications for the presidency; personality and image of the candidates eclipse the discussion of issues; candidate gaffes are blown out of proportion in subsequent media reports; and the formats of debates have been glorified press conferences, contributing little that the voters have not heard before on the campaign trail.

These evaluator categories are not entirely mutually exclusive. For example, an evaluator might be located as a proponent for most debates and suddenly appear as a conditional. There are others, *critics,* who can live with or without televised debates, and approach them as just another event worthy or unworthy of their attention. Critics roam (from debate to debate, or election to election) among the three evaluator categories.

The following selected 14 reviews and assessments provide an historical record and a mixture of support for, and criticism of, televised presidential debates (listed chronologically):[8]

1. (1962, reissued in 1977) Kraus, Sidney, (Ed.). *The Great Debates: Background, Perspective, Effects.* A compendium of studies about the John F. Kennedy and Richard M. Nixon debates in 1960, debate preparations, legal aspects of televising debates, formats, finance, media, polls, nationwide review of effects on voters, and debate texts.
2. (1962) Mazo, Earl, Malcolm Moos, Hollock Hoffman, and Harvey Wheeler. *The Great Debates: An Occasional Paper on the Role of the Political Process in the Free Society.* Discusses the Kennedy–Nixon debates as part of the process of electing a president.
3. (1976) Kraus, Sidney (Ed.). *Presidential Debates De-Briefing.* Unpublished transcription of a 1976 Carter–Ford debate conference with Carter and Ford representatives, League of Women Voters Education Fund representatives, and broadcasters. Debate preparations, formats, legal, finance, media, polls, and effects.
4. (1978) Bishop, George, Robert G. Meadow, and Marilyn Jackson-Beeck, (Eds.). *The Presidential Debates: Media, Electoral, and Policy Perspectives.* A series of studies about the Carter–Ford 1976 debates, preparations, formats, legal, finance, media, voter effects, and debate texts.
5. (1979) Kraus, Sidney, (Ed.). *The Great Debates: Carter vs. Ford, 1976.* Primary forums, debate preparations, formats, legal, finance, media, polls, nationwide review of effects, and debate texts.
6. (1979) Mitchell, Lee. *With the Nation Watching: Report of the Twentieth Century Fund Task Force on Televised Presidential Debates.* A review of televised debates, preparations, formats, finance, and minor parties.
7. (1979) Ranney, Austin, (Ed.). *The Past and Future of Presidential Debates.* A series of articles based on a 1977 debate conference sponsored by the American Enterprise Institute with political columnists, political scientists, legal experts, communication specialists, and pollsters. Preparations, formats, legal, finance, media, polls, and voter effects.
8. (1979) U. S. Government Printing Office. *The Presidential Cam-*

paign, 1976: Vol. 3, The Debates. Describes the debates within the context of the general election.

9. (1980) Bitzer, Lloyd, and Theodore Rueter. *Carter vs. Ford: The Counterfeit Debates of 1976.* A critical review of the debates, formats, forensics, and debate texts.

10. (1981) Kraus, Sidney, and Dennis Davis. "Political Debates," in Dan D. Nimmo and Keith Sanders (Eds.), *Handbook of Political Communication* (pp. 273–296). Reviews debates in terms of contemporary political theory and empirical effects.

11. (1981) Ritter, Kurt W., (Ed.). *The 1980 Presidential Debates.* Special issue of *Speaker and Gavel* (Vol. 18, No. 2). Articles on myths, issues and images, candidate preparations, arguments, formats, opinion, and effects of the Carter–Reagan debates.

12. (1982) Davis, Dennis K., and Sidney Kraus. "Public Communication and Televised Debates," in Michael Burgoon (Ed.), *Communication Yearbook 6* (pp. 289–303). Places debates in the context of public communication from the Greeks through the modern times.

13. (1983) Martel, Myles. *Political Campaign Debates: Images, Strategies, and Tactics.* One of Reagan's 1980 debate advisers discusses televised debates from the point of view of the candidate, formats, debate strategies and tactics.

14. (1984) Swerdlow, Joel L. *Beyond Debate: A Paper on Televised Presidential Debates.* The Twentieth Century Fund's second update of debates provides a brief historical account and suggests ways to improve debates.

15. (in press) Swerdlow, Joel L., (Ed.). *Presidential Debates: 1988 and Beyond.* A series of articles most of which are written by professionals.

The purpose of the present effort is to examine the various assessments considering the experience of television in presidential elections, reviewing what we have learned about televised debates, and evaluating that knowledge in the context of the election process, specifically, and the political process, generally. Also examined are the media and the role they occupy in presidential elections. Because critics often refer to the Lincoln–Douglas debates when reproaching presidential debates, comparisons of the two are made whenever appropriate. Throughout these discussions an emphasis is placed on the implications for public policy.

To suggest policy that will be accepted and adopted by politicians and the public is at best difficult. Proposals for changes in public policy based on experience, even when scientific data support those changes, must be subjected to an assessment of the *values* and *pre-dispositions* of the proponent. These values and predispositions, however, may not necessarily inhibit the proponent's *objectivity.*[9]

As a proponent of televised presidential debates, it may prove useful to relate the assumptions underlying these discussions:

1. Presidential debates further democratic goals.
2. They serve the majority of the electorate better than any other single campaign communication device that attempts to present both the candidates' personality and their positions on issues.
3. Future televised presidential debates will reach the largest single electoral audience (as they have in the past).
4. These debates, and the attention given to them by the electorate, have the potential to bring about changes that improve the presidential selection process and use of television in elections.

A review of the use of television in the presidential election process should provide the context for examining televised debates.

ENDNOTES

1. These "debates" have been variously called, *great, counterfeit, confrontations, press conferences, face-to-face,* and *contests.* The term *The Great Debates* was used by NBC President, Robert Sarnoff in a telegram to Speaker Sam Rayburn in 1960 when the House was considering passage of the Senate Resolution to allow the Kennedy–Nixon debates to be broadcast without providing equal time for other presidential candidates. Lee Atwater, in a 1984 Reagan campaign memo, called the debates "artificially contrived 'pressure cookers' which do not coincide with the actual pressures that confront a President," quoted in J. Germond and J. Witcover, *Wake Us When It's Over: Presidential Politics of 1984* (New York: Macmillan Publishing Company, 1985) p. 527. In this discussion, the term *debate* is used generically.

2. The first major political campaign debate in American history was for the senate seat in Illinois. Douglas won that election, but lost his bid for the presidency to Lincoln 2 years later.

3. The 1988 election may also include minor party candidates. Minor party candidates have had a great deal of difficulty in their attempts to be included in debates during the general elections since 1976. Their endeavors for debate recognition are detailed later.

4. "The 1976 presidential debates were broadcast in over 100 countries. An exact audience count was impossible, but it was estimated that over 150 million persons outside the United States saw each of the presidential debates. It is hoped that those who witnessed these historic events viewed them as a

demonstration of American democracy at its best." J. Karayn, "Presidential Debates: A Plan for the Future," in S. Kraus (ed.), *The Great Debates: Carter vs. Ford, 1976* (Bloomington: Indiana University Press, 1979) p. 219.

5. D. Sears and S. Chaffee, "Uses and Effects of the 1976 Debates: An Overview of Empirical Studies," in S. Kraus (ed.), *The Great Debates: Carter vs. Ford, 1976, op. cit.,* pp. 223–261.

6. Ibid., p. 248.

7. Ibid., p. 256.

8. A comprehensive bibliography of research and comment on televised presidential debates appears in the Bibliography.

9. This writer is guided by the statement, "It is not necessary for the scientist to sacrifice objectivity in the execution of a project. The place for nonobjectivity is in deciding what ultimate goals are to be implemented. Once this choice is made, the scholar proceeds with maximum objectivity and uses all available methods. H. Lasswell, "The Policy Orientation," in D. Lerner and H. Lasswell (eds.), *The Policy Sciences,* (Stanford: Stanford University Press, 1951) p. 11.

2

OVERVIEW:
TELEVISION AND THE
PRESIDENTIAL ELECTION

American politics and television are now so completely locked together that it is impossible to tell the story of one without the other.[1]

Campaigns for the presidency begin quite early these days. We now have a cadre of former presidential candidates and other politicians who have had televised debate experience. The League of Women Voters hopes to continue with their sponsorship of presidential debates.[2] Television networks began their 1988 plans by reviewing their coverage of 1984 immediately after that election. The majority of American citizens, however, do not concern themselves with such matters until the campaigns gain steam and election events dominate the newscasts. The hoopla that is created in a presidential campaign attracts the public's attention, although not enough to encourage voting among the approximately 50% of eligible citizens who have not voted in each of the recent presidential elections.

There has been an increase in voting on the basis of issues and candidate characteristics. This was accompanied, however, by a decrease in party affiliation, and a dissatisfaction with the political process. The most recent, thorough, scientific, and credible account of the American electorate comes from the University of Michigan's Survey Research Center. Examining a series of surveys conducted from 1952 to 1972, this landmark study essentially concluded that "Today [the American public] is more politically aroused, more detached

7

from political parties than at any time in the past forty years, and deeply dissatisfied with the political process."[3]

For most voters, presidential elections in America have become a dreary necessity filled with hoopla created not by the candidates themselves, but by an elite corps of campaign specialists trained in the use of television and public opinion polling to instill positive images of their client-candidates among the electorate.

Pretelevision political campaigns often were characterized by a presidential candidate speaking and waving to a small group of flag-waving supporters on the rear platform of a train at a whistle stop while a small band played patriotic tunes. Today, the characterization of a presidential political campaign often includes images of the relationship between the voter-viewer and television. This technological leap from the locomotive to radio and then to television, recently accompanied by computers and a host of electronic innovations, has altered the political process and the way campaigns are conducted.[4]

With each of these technological advances, both the sending and receiving of political information changed. Our *thinking* about political events changed. What constituted political reality for us was not the influence of a political event alone, but the interpretation (often, the alteration) of the event by the mass media, especially television.

Perhaps the first time that television influenced the conduct of a political event occurred during the Democratic convention in 1948 when a television pool director for *Life* and NBC coached southern delegates to remove their badges and hurl them in protest before the cameras. Gilbert Seldes, a well-known mass media critic, observed:

> The director that suggested the piece of business was not false to the meaning of the event, but he had illustrated the way in which the great instrument for conveying the simple truth can be subdued to uses of accepted faking.[5]

With the advent of the mass diffusion of television sets after the Second World War, it became apparent that the transmission of a political event brought about a "unique perspective" (something different than what was actually taking place) simply because it was televised. This was not evident when Franklin Roosevelt gave the first television address by an incumbent president during the 1939 World's Fair in New York; nor was it apparent when television was covering (for the first time) the party conventions in 1940.[6]

The "unique perspective" became evident when the first thorough investigation of television's rendition of a real world political event occurred about 2 weeks after President Harry S. Truman summarily dismissed General Douglas MacArthur for not following T policies during the Korean War. On April 26, 1951 (just 5 yea̲̲ ̲̲̲̲̲. television sets were introduced in America) Chicago celebrated the return of the General (a hero in World War II) with four events, all of which were televised. Kurt Lang and Gladys Engel Lang, then sociologists at the University of Chicago, compared the reactions of people who actually observed one of the events, a motorcade parade, with those who viewed the parade by watching television. They found that television modified (reinterpreted) the event; the reactions of those observers along the parade route was substantially different from those in front of the television set. The researchers questioned "whether public moods were being accurately conveyed by television."[7]

There is also a distinct difference between viewing a political event on television and listening to the radio broadcast of that event. Viewers of the first 1960 debate between Kennedy and Nixon rated Kennedy the victor, whereas radio listeners thought Nixon had the edge.[8] Television's "unique perspective" puzzled the political community that was to feel its impact in ways that changed the face of politics, and the power of the political parties.

TELEVISION AND POLITICAL PARTIES

Not only could television affect the public's perception of political events, but it changed the politics of campaigning and significantly altered the political process itself. Political parties found that candidates could go directly to the public via television and gain support. Thus, party conventions, for the most part, are now anticlimatic in the selection of the presidential nominee. A variety of explanations can be offered to account for the waning influence of political parties in the election process, but it would be difficult to avoid television as the antecedent condition.

The impact of television on the election process changed the relationships among political parties, candidates, and voters in three important ways. First, *television pre-empted the parties' role in the presidential selection process through its ability to command the attention of voters directly, allowing candidates to gain momentous exposure and support long before the nominating conventions took place.*

Americans have become accustomed to viewing television for news. As the audience grew from 1959 to the present, voters changed from relying on newspapers and radio to television for most of their information about political issues and events. Leo Bogart, executive vice-president and general manager of the Newspaper Advertising Bureau, and an authority on media consumption, reviewed several studies commissioned by the Television Information Office since 1959:

> In [1959] 57% [of the American public] said they usually got most of their news "about what's going on in the world today" from newspapers, while 51% named television and 34% radio. . . . By 1963 television and newspapers were evenly ranked, and in 1967 television had swung ahead. Since 1972 the fluctuations have been minor, and in 1978 television was named by 67%, newspapers by 49%.[9]

An analysis of voters' use of television news for information on campaign activities during the 1950s is also noteworthy:

> Television viewing soars from 1952 to 1960 and remains at that high level while reliance on the radio declines proportionately. . . . The growth of television as a source of campaign news comes at the same time as the growth in political interest. . . . [It] is likely that television has introduced a new dimension to campaign attentiveness.[10]

Hence, the decline in the influence of political parties came about along with the growth of television. Other perspectives (e.g., ideology, candidate identification through party affiliation, etc.) could have accounted for the declining influence of the parties in the selection process during the 20-year period, 1952–1972, but the data failed to confirm any of these as causes. "In each case, the data confirm a decline in the attachment of the citizenry to the political parties. Party affiliation, once the central thread connecting the citizen and the political process, is a thread that has certainly been frayed."[11]

The second explanation for the decline in party affiliation (partisanship) and the rise of television's impact on the election process can be found in the data on political socialization.[12] *As television was diffused in American society from 1948 on, it gradually replaced the influence of intergenerational party identification, and new voters came to rely on it for their political information.*[13] Parental transmission of their political party identification gave way to their offsprings' exposure to political events via television. This decline in partisanship "[prompted about half of] the new voters entering the electorate at the end of the 1960s . . . to become Independents, not to switch to the opposition party [of their parents]."[14]

Even parents who have held long-term commitments to a particular party have been affected by television. Television has "interfered" with the stability of political party preference among older voters. The broadcasting of political events so impressed the electorate in the 1960s (and today) that parties could no longer count on their long-time supporters:

> The data on recent changes make clear that some political events can interfere with the development through the life cycle of that long-term commitment. Such events seem to have been powerful in recent years because they have not only retarded the acquisition or development of a party preference, but they have also reduced the significance of party affiliation for those who remain identified with a party. Citizens who identified with a party are less guided by their affiliation in the seventies than they were in the fifties.[15]

The decline in voters' reliance on party as a determinant of their vote coincides with an increase in exposure to politics on television. This provides us with the third explanation of television's role in the political process. *Exposure to politics on television accounts for the voter's attitudes toward issues and candidates, and often helps determine his or her vote.* Data supporting this explanation (from 1952 on) are, at times, interpreted differently by researchers. Some argue that increased levels of education during that period prompted voters to consider issues rather than relying on the party for their vote decision. At best, this position is weakly supported by the data. Nie and his associates have concluded that, "It is exposure to politics, not attainment of higher levels of education and its accompanying cognitive capacity, that seems to lead to the greater coherence of citizen attitudes."[16]

Many students of mass communication altered their previous conception of television as having minimal or limited effects as a result of their examining the evidence of many studies that suggested otherwise.[17] Having come to that conclusion, some researchers and policymakers became concerned about television's influence in society.

Those concerned with political communication from either a research or commentary perspective began to investigate a variety of aspects about television in political campaigns. And, of course, the broadcasting industry responded to research findings and commentaries about television effects whenever they felt they had an invested interest to protect or advance. As a matter of fact, most broadcasters were concerned about changes in the election process because those changes affected their coverage of political events, especially in response to regulatory actions of the Federal Communication Commission (FCC) and to requests from political interest groups and candidates.

In a very real sense, then, television is today a powerful source of communication in the election process. Television, and the mass media generally, have dominated and influenced electoral politics since at least 1968. This type of campaigning has been termed, *The Permanent Campaign,*[18] displacing political parties in favor of a predominate corps of participants. "This is an electoral politics whose activities and motivations at the elite level are structured by the mass media, individual candidates, and their staffs of pollsters, media consultants, and image manipulators."[19]

TELEVISION AND PRESIDENTIAL CANDIDATES

Candidates for the presidency have long known the advantages of publicity. Name recognition among voters is an immediate goal of candidates seeking office, particularly if their exposure to the voter has been minimal. Face recognition is also of primary concern to candidates. This is somewhat curious because election ballots display names of candidates and not their faces. An experienced reporter covering presidential campaigns in the 1920s labeled this concern for recognition, *Name and Face Stuff:*

> there is no way for any one to match the Presidential publicity. . . . It is not a question so much of [candidates] getting their views and opinions on the issues before the people, though that is of course desirable, there being always a small minority interested in such things and capable of understanding. The big thing and the vital thing, however, is to get their names and their faces familiar to the voters. This is the primary purpose of all political publicity—the other purposes are all secondary. . . . But getting away from mere "name and face" stuff, vital as it is, there are so many kinds of political publicity . . . that it is impossible to catalogue them all.[20]

If publicity on radio and in newspapers was "impossible to catalogue" in the 1920s, the introduction of television in presidential campaigns 3 decades later offered the publicity hounds and the candidates numerous new and mysterious paths to the voter. Presidential candidates greeted the new medium of television with both awe and suspicion. Many thought it to be a challenge and an opportunity, whereas some were concerned about the costs involved and their ability to use it effectively. Others had concerns about being overexposed, underexposed, or closely monitored over time. Depending on their predispositions, presidential candidates were either enthusiastic or reserved when it came to using television.

General Eisenhower was a willing participant in appropriate tele-casts initiated by the Republican party, but "felt most at home and was most effective in very informal settings."[21] Other presidential candi-dates were attracted to television. Senator Estes Kefauver, for exam-ple, "had been made into a national figure overnight by television coverage of his crime [committee's] investigations. He and most of the other Democratic candidates for the nomination eagerly accepted at-tentions of television."[22] Overall, presidential candidates quickly came to recognize that television provided the opportunity for immediate, more engaging, exposure to voters than radio. With the addition of the visual dimension, this new medium was believed to be much more powerful than other communication media. To use it effectively, can-didates came to rely on media experts, pollsters, and "image mer-chants" (see discussion on Campaign Experts). The telegenic presi-dential candidate was "cast" in the leading role among those seeking the office.

In the early 1950s, during television's infancy, prospective presi-dential candidates were being assessed in terms of their personalities and their ability to use television effectively.

Personality of the candidate was thought to be responsible for much of his success in a campaign. After the first substantial television cam-paign experience in 1952, commentators debated about whether it was personality or television that was responsible for General "Ike" Eisenhower's victory at the polls. In an attempt to gauge Ike's political popularity, Hyman and Sheatsley analyzed public opinion data of 1947 and 1948. Although not resolving the effect of television, they concluded that Ike's personality, more than issues of Communism, the Korean conflict, and corruption was responsible for the result in 1952.[23]

Ability to *perform* on television became one of the most important among the criteria to assess potential successful candidacies: "We must choose able and personable candidates who can 'sell themselves' because TV has changed the course of campaigns."[24]

It is important to recognize that television cannot "sell" what is not "saleable." Although it has the potential for creating a "public figure" that voter-viewers could support, presidential aspirants who perform well on television may not necessarily gain the office. A case in point was the race between Stevenson and Kefauver in 1952. Kefauver, better known and more exposed to the voter through television than Stevenson, lost the Democratic presidential nomination:

> In spite of the television impressions and the television popularity, Kef-auver lost the nomination to a candidate relatively unknown to the

video audience. That occurrence appears to suggest a limitation on the possible role or influence of television.[25]

This early finding of television's lack of influence in a particular presidential election demonstrates the transactional nature of political personalities and preferences of voters who view them. If there is not a "goodness-of-fit" between the candidate's personality and the voter, television may not prove useful for even the best of political television performers. It is in the context of the political climate, voter preferences, and the structure of the candidate's personality that the effects of television exposure will be determined for candidates with television talents and those without.

Still, the "permanent campaign" prevails. "The first rule of such a campaign is that the candidate is reasonably telegenic and reasonably comfortable with the electronic media. As Mondale himself commented following his loss to Reagan, he is neither."[26] Although this state of contemporary electoral politics is an anathema to many who believe that strong political parties further democratic ideals, apparently it serves both candidates and voters.

TELEVISION AND VOTERS

One of the most researched aspects of the political process has been the attempt to understand what accounts for voting decisions among the electorate. For a long time, and well into the television era, it was presumed that voters' predispositions—their inclination to vote based on party affiliation, parental influence, income, religion, and other political socializing factors—were the primary determinants of their vote choice. These predispositions, it was argued, formed the voter's ideological resolution on issues and candidates. What the voters "brought" with them when they attended to political messages in the media were more persuasive in determining their votes than were the media messages they received. How was this conclusion arrived at?

During the 1940 presidential election campaign between Franklin Roosevelt and Wendell Willkie, Lazarsfeld, Berelson, and Gaudet, sociologists at Columbia University's Bureau of Applied Social Research, conducted the first panel study of voters (*repeated interviewing of the same people*) "to discover how and why people decided to vote as they did."[27] This now classic study, *The People's Choice*, conducted 8 years before television, found that the media *reinforced* voters' prior decisions: "For them, political communications served the important purpose of preserving prior decisions instead of initiating new decisions. . . . It had the effect of reinforcing the original vote decision."[28]

Reinforcement came about in a way that later appeared to some students of mass media and politics as being antithetical to one of the goals of democracy—citizens using a free press to gain information about candidates and issues, *culminating with an informed vote choice.* The effect of media reinforcement on prior (before the campaign) vote decisions came about because "predispositions lead people to select communications which [were] congenial, which support[ed] their previous position."[29] *Selectivity* of political messages was the operant voter condition. Voters somehow managed to be exposed to, pay attention to, and retain those mass media messages that conformed to their predispositions. They were not, generally, exposed to information that opposed their point of view. And when they inadvertently were exposed to opposing views, they did not retain the information.

Reflecting on these findings, it should be emphasized that during the period surrounding the 1940s voters were socialized into the political system with strong partisan beliefs and attitudes held by their parents. Parents affiliated with the Democratic party raised children who eventually became Democrats. Republican parents weaned future Republican voters. If this "political genes theory" seems implausible, another major finding of the Lazarsfeld et al. study may even convince biologists to look for those "genes." Over 50% of the panel members knew in May (before the party conventions nominated their candidates) for whom they would cast their vote, and voted that way in November. In other words, before the campaigns began the voter knew that he or she would vote for his or her party's candidate.

The mass media, therefore, were not deemed influential in the voting decision process. Mass communication (then radio and print) was thought to be just a number of different channels through which political information flowed to the voter. After receiving the information the voter either agreed, complied, disagreed, disregarded, altered, or ignored the message depending on his or her predispositions.

Despite the growing influence of television for 3 decades after the Lazarsfeld et al. study, their conclusions about media's impact on the electorate were essentially embraced by social scientists. Studies failed to seriously investigate the role of the media in electoral politics. Ideology, party influence, family conditioning, and the like commanded the attention of political scientists. In response to questions about the effects of television in presidential campaigns, many researchers deferred to Lazarsfeld et al. The operant condition of media effects on the electorate was described by one phrase—*reinforcement of voters' predispositions!*

To many lay observers this limited effect was in conflict with their perceptions of the media, particularly television, as powerful persuasive carriers. To some historical critics of the media, and to some social scientists, the assertion of a benign press (print or electronic) merely funneling information about candidates and their stands on issues without changing voters' preferences was preposterous.[30]

A thorough review of the major classical studies on voting revealed that in the 1940s and 1950s, questions about media's impact were not adequately constructed to find effects.[31] In Pool's discussion of the limitations of the classics he suggested that *The People's Choice* included "much fascinating material on the role of the mass media, but not on their effects." He also examined the second classical study, *Voting*,[32] conducted 8 years after the first, and concluded that "it adds little to the earlier volume in its treatment of the mass media." Pool claimed that *The People's Choice* "is much more sketchy in its treatment of the impact of the campaign messages."[33]

In 1952 the impending influence of television was evident when voters saw the first television commercials used in a presidential campaing (Eisenhower's), and the first televised conventions.[34] Some lay critics, however, were equivocal about these new incursions into the electoral process. One claimed that "though television does a good job in distilling the essentials of a political campaign to voters, it would never replace traditional forms of electioneering."[35] But, as early as 1956, an examination of television and the political process concluded: "It seems certain that television offers an unexampled resource for political communications and for the political education of the nation as one community."[36]

Yet, even through the 1960s, after the first televised presidential debates, and after the televising of 10 national party conventions, presidential election scholars were making predictions about television limitations in the campaign process that later would prove to be erroneous. For example, two well-respected observers of presidential elections, Nelson Polsby and Aaron Wildavsky, claimed in 1967:

> With television occupying an important place in American life, [candidates'] ability to make a good impression is not a trivial matter. There is little reason to believe, however, that we are headed for a society in which TV performers can run for public office and expect to win.[37]

By 1974, in a subsequent edition of their book, the second sentence about "TV performers" was eliminated from the text.[38]

Because voters' party affiliation was, according to the classical studies, *the* indicator of voting behavior it was difficult for many scholars in the television age to even question, let alone, abandon that view. Understandably, Polsby and Wildavsky insisted that, "By far, the majority of people vote according to their habitual party affiliation."[39] For the most part, that assessment remains valid today, but it must be amended to include the decline in partisanship and the rise in ideology and candidates' personalities as factors influencing vote choice. A reexamination of the presidential election data makes a strong case that from 1964 on voters have increasingly come to rely on the issue positions and personality characteristics of candidates when casting their ballots.[40]

These positions and characteristics are presented to the voters largely through television, not by mere transmission alone, but by a series of condensed statements about issues; by the camera closeups of a candidates, and their nonverbal cues that elicit emotional responses in voters;[41] and by the rehashing and reassessing of candidates' television performances by commentators.[42]

Many observers of television's impact on voters decry such projections that appear to be insignificant and trivial in the presidential selection process:

> To be sure, the campaign of 1984, like its predecessors in recent decades, suffered from the massive intrusion of television with its tendency to trivialize substantive differences and emphasize personality differences. Nevertheless, despite the electronic medium's shadowy presentations of reality, much like those in Plato's cave, the candidates still conveyed starkly different sets of political ideas and different visions of the nation's future.[43]

Certainly, television coverage of presidential campaigns could be much improved, but even in its present state voters find their political information in ways, sometimes astonishing, that allow them to gain impressions of candidates and their positions. For example, it came as a surprise to almost everyone in the broadcasting industry to find a major study of the 1972 presidential race (conducted by two political scientists) concluding that voters learned more about Richard Nixon and George McGovern from political spots than they did from the combined nightly newscasts of the networks![44]

In a somewhat similar finding, Mendelsohn and O'Keefe noted that voters who could not make up their minds about Nixon and McGovern "did not turn to the serious aspects of the media for help," but were captive to "guidance-giving information" from political advertising that was interspersed with their television entertainment viewing. These researchers also found that:

The less difficulty switchers had in shifting their votes, the more likely they were to be influenced by commercials. Similarly, the more use they made of the media (particularly television) for political news and information, the more apt their vote decisions were to have been influenced by political commercials.[45]

Although it is certainly desireable to have voters so interested in the presidential candidates—seeking out authoritative information, subscribing to critical journals, reading editorials and commentaries, and selecting radio and television public affairs programming that is politically informative—given the political interest level of most voters, that ideal state is not likely to come about without fundamental changes in our institutions.[46]

In addition to the candidates' commercials, their personalities and their television performances, the factors of party influence and ideology must be considered in determining voters' choices in a presidential campaign. Although party has declined and ideology has increased, party is still more of an influence on vote choice than is ideology. Pomper analyzed the results of 1984 election, comparing the influence of ideology and party and concluded that, "Compared to 1980, ideology has become more important—although still less of an influence than party."[47]

Ideology of the candidate is conveyed to the voter in several ways, but the most prominent and enduring is through television. Television does not reinforce party affiliation of candidates as much as ideology. Ideology and partisanship of voters, according to the classical literature on political socialization, have been the province of parental and familial influence. In elections before 1960, the ideological positions of the two major parties were well defined and the voter could easily discern the differences between them. Although moderates could be found in both parties, liberals dominated the Democratic party, and conservatives within the party did not, by and large, defect to the Republican party during presidential elections. Ideology and partisanship were flip sides of the same coin.

Today, a different coin has been minted. Ideology of the candidate is easier for the voter to identify with than is the ideological position of the party. As suggested earlier, voting on the basis of issues is increasing, whereas straight ticket (party) voting is on the decline. Television brings to voters the "credentials" of candidates that include their ideology, personalities, and their ability to convey their ideas through the medium. Young voters today have been raised with television, and they expect to see presidential candidates perform at least adequately on television. Arguments that candidates' television performances, like those exhibited in debates, do not present qualifying credentials for the presidency fail to deal with the relationship between television and the voter.

In such a parsimonious discussion about television and the voter it should be emphasized that election researchers and campaign experts usually hold one of three views about the medium's influence on voters. These relate to short- and long-term effects of television. Some students believe that television affects voters in the short run, for instance in an election campaign. Another group finds that television's greater impact is over time, spanning from one campaign to another, where the habitual use of the medium by voters has its most important effect. Still, others vacillate between the two views, or combine both. Each viewpoint can be supported depending on the variables that one chooses to examine. But it is difficult for this observer to conclude that political television has limited or no effects on voters.

TELEVISION CAMPAIGN EXPERTS, POLLSTERS, AND POLLING

The employment of experts to advise candidates, and to develop, use, and manage media activities existed in presidential campaigns before television. Candidates have relied on a variety of specialists in preparing speeches and radio appearances, and on a variety of sources in the assessment of public attitudes. President Franklin Roosevelt counted on playwright Robert Sherwood for help with many of his speeches,[48] and engaged Norman Corwin, a famous radio writer and producer, to create one of the most successful radio ads in the 1944 campaign.[49]

Harry Truman was the first president to use television in the White House, and the first to employ the services of a media adviser. "The adviser, Leonard Reinsch [who later served as chief adviser to Senator Kennedy during the 1960 televised debates] tried in vain to change Truman's flat Missouri accent and rapid delivery."[50] As television became a crucial element in presidential election campaigns, the need arose for individuals whose expertise, like Reinsch, included the ability to help a candidate sustain a positive visual impression among voters—a projection of the candidate that has come to be referred to as "a favorable *image*."

These experts were soon to be pejoratively called, *image manipulators*. The phrase has at least two implications: (a) somehow candidates were being presented to the public as something other than what they really were, and (b) a gullible, unsophisticated public can be induced to accept the projected "new image" of the candidate. Paraphrasing Lincoln, "These image manipulators create candidates able to fool most of the voters most of the time in most presidential campaigns." That is, of course, an oversimplification and somewhat of a misrepresentation of what these experts do.

Certainly, President Reagan had a cadre of image experts, yet it would be difficult to demonstrate that what we saw of him on television during the campaign was not what we got from him during his administration. If Reagan's image experts managed to "manipulate" the public into believing he was something other than what he really was, they also managed to maintain that image during his administration. It is not likely that political and promotional experts made out of Ronald Reagan's personality a different one that the public could accept. Similarly, the image makers in Walter Mondale's 1984 campaign could not, or at least, did not present to the voters a dynamic political television personality. Yet, image experts *did* exert their influence in the Reagan and Mondale campaigns.

The experts' preparation and coaching of the candidates for the two televised debates in 1984 is a case in point. Reagan's and Mondale's performance in the first debate was not as expected. Reagan faltered and Mondale seemed to be in command. In the second debate, however, the candidates were true to form; Reagan was his easygoing self, and Mondale was uncomfortable as he had been in most of his previous television appearances.

Germond and Witcover, claiming they almost fell asleep during the campaign, were struck by the debates:

> inexplicably to all those closest to the President and to millions who admired him from a distance, that [first] ninety-minute televised confrontation with Mondale revealed a *different Ronald Reagan*. The Great Communicator was strangely awkward, halting, even confused before the cameras that had been major instruments in his success, first as an actor, later as a politician . . . Mondale—seventeen years Reagan's junior—was a model of decorum, treating Reagan with cool deference while scoring debating points heavily against the older man . . . [which] triggered what the press at once labeled "the age issue." (italics added)[51]

Thinking that Mondale would come out scrapping in the first debate, Reagan's experts muffed coaching the candidate "through extensive rehearsals, armed with a detailed briefing book and assaulted by [the] tough, aggressive [debating] from the . . . Mondale stand-in, David Stockman. . ."[52] Debate coaches criticized Reagan's performance in rehearsals. That approach was altered in the preparations for the second debate by Senator Paul Laxalt, Reagan's friend and confidant.

Although the first debate raised the "age question," the second one dismissed it. Reagan's one-liners, often coached, appear to be responsible for subsequent good press. He resolved the "age question" with "I am not going to exploit, for political purposes, my opponent's youth and inexperience." In the 1980 debate with Carter, Reagan said, "There you go again!" and "Are you better off than you were 4 years ago?"

Mondale's only one-liner occurred earlier in the primaries on Super Tuesday, during the Atlanta debate. Gary Hart was discussing his economic proposals, and Mondale responded with: "Where's the beef?" That phrase, taken from the television spot for Wendy's hamburgers, was the brainchild of Mary Goehring, a friend of Bob Beckel, Mondale's campaign manager. It was discussed at length the day before and the day of the debate.[53]

The work of the image merchants was evident. The notion that voters could be duped into accepting candidates' personalities that were somehow fabricated by experts, rehearsed by candidates, and displayed in front of the cameras, is perhaps the quintessence of political campaign television. Despite the fact that some political analysts consider voters to be responsible,[54] socialization into television creates among voters a receptivity to the workings of image merchants. Actors and candidates often are so at ease in their execution of their roles, and audiences are so accustomed to accepting the "reality" of their performances, that the television entertainment environment and the television political campaign environment have become virtually identical.

Reagan, of course, enjoys the best of the "two environments"— entertainment and politics. The "Teflon" presidency came about precisely because of his ability to use television to convince a majority of Americans that despite his occasional misstatements and errors of judgment he is a strong and principled leader. Although he has the talent and experience to present himself to the public, he still relies on both image merchants and pollsters.

Using polling as a means of assessing the public's concern about issues is in keeping with democratic ideals associated with representative government. However, the use of polling by candidates and the media, and the instant computer analysis of polling results by the media, have been the subject of much criticism. Edwin Newman, a respected television journalist, would rather do without them:

> In the annals of television, the inventor of the exit poll may take his
> place with DeForest, Baird, Sarnoff, and Paley . . . it is a fact that this
> country is up to its ears in public opinion polls. . . . There is not the
> slightest reason to believe that American life would be poorer if there
> were no public opinion polling.[55]

Newman asserts that polling in elections "may be dangerous . . .
they must push politicians in the direction of telling people what they
think those people want to hear." He questions the role of the media
when conducting polls because he feels "they risk affecting the outcome of the vote."[56] That claim can be levied against editorials, political cartoons, and other aspects of campaign coverage. Certainly, the
coverage of presidential campaigns, and especially televised debates,
include "horse-race" assessments of who is winning at any given
time.[57] A more important question is: to what extent is the coverage
of the horse-race aspects of presidential campaigns diminishing the
coverage of issue positions of candidates? Given political television,
the real danger rests with getting rid of the baby (issue discussions)
with the bathwater (horse-race monitoring).

Cleansing television political news of undue voter influence often
requires fundamental changes in traditional institutions. Newman
and most other journalists do not want the government to interfere
with the press in their coverage of elections. Current discussions about
the influence of exit polling, and the influence of early predictions of
election results while most of the country's polls remain open,[58] have
come up with some rather unusual suggestions. Broadcasters have
indicated their willingness to curtail the use of exit polling and election predictions, and Congress is deliberating the idea of suspending
time zones, and establishing 24-hour polls, beginning and ending at
the same time.

These institutional changes are to be welcomed, but the use of
polling, pollsters, and image merchants will most likely remain a staple in election campaigns. Moreover, the new technology—computers, satellites, and the like—breeds a flock of experts who migrate
every 2 to 4 years from the marketing industry to political campaigns.
Among them, it will be difficult to expostulate candidate campaign
practices. For their adherence to change may well result in the elimination of the need for much of their services, if not the need for the
"image industry" itself—an industry that contributes heavily to the
increased costs of presidential politics.

Polling and other tactical campaign practices ultimately depend on
the public's acceptance of them. It would indeed be ironic if public
opinion outcry was for the elimination of political polling during pres-

idential campaigns; polling would become the pollsters undoing. But even Newman would admit that polls do create voter interest in presidential campaigns. More importantly, even the horse-race aspects of a presidential campaign can serve the electorate by motivating them to watch televised debates, a campaign element that voters want, need, and learn from.

Although not free from image merchants, the confrontations between presidential candidates, appearing together on television for 90 minutes has captured the interest of the American public in four elections. They are the most innovative, beneficial events in presidential campaign history. They appear to be institutionalized. Some observers would make them mandatory. They have been commended and criticized by voters, candidates, and the media.

The following chapter discusses the televised presidential debates, how they came about, and the most often criticized aspect of the confrontations, their formats.

ENDNOTES

1. Theodore H. White, *America in Search of Itself: The Making of the President, 1966–1980* (New York: Harper & Row, 1982) p. 165.

2. The League of Women Voters Education Fund has sponsored presidential debates since 1976. These women (and some men) have been involved with almost every aspect of mounting political debates in caravan-style in major cities through the country—negotiating with commanding candidates and their exacting staffs, and dealing with tough demanding editors, TV commentators, broadcast officials, local Leagues, and even scholars. They have been criticized, sued, complimented, and disparagingly called, "little old ladies." Although there are legitimate concerns about their procedures in one or another aspect of preparing for and conducting televised debates, by far their contribution to the presidential campaign process has been conscientious and commendable. A discussion of the many suggestions for future debate sponsors appears in chapter 6.

3. N. H. Nie, S. Verba, and J. R. Petrocik, *The Changing American Voter* (Cambridge: Harvard University Press, 1979) p. 1. This book, widely acclaimed by scholars and professionals, received the Woodrow Wilson Prize of the American Political Science Association.

4. For a thorough account of technological development and its impact on society and the media see B. H. Bagdikian, *The Information Machines: Their Impact on Men and the Media* (New York: Harper & Row, 1971).

5. G. Seldes, *The Great Audience* (New York: Viking Press, 1950) p. 207; also quoted in C. Thomson, *Television and Presidential Politics* (Washington, DC: The Brookings Institution, 1956) p. 5.

6. E. Barnouw, *The Golden Web: A History of Broadcasting in the United States, 1933–1953* (New York: Oxford University Press, 1968) p. 257.

7. See K. Lang and G. E. Lang, "The Unique Perspective of Television and its Effects: A Pilot Study." *American Sociological Review,* vol. 18 (February, 1953) pp. 3–12; see also, an expanded version in G. E. Lang and K. Lang, *Politics and Television Re-Viewed* (Beverly Hills: Sage Publications, 1985).

8. S. Kraus (Ed.), *The Great Debates* (Bloomington, IN: Indiana University Press, 1962).

9. L. Bogart, *Press and Public: Who Reads What, Where, When, and Why in American Newspapers* (Hillsdale, NJ: Lawrence Erlbaum Associates, 1981) pp. 181–182.

10. Nie et al., pp. 272–273. It should be noted that between the 1956 and 1960 elections "attention to the campaign in newspapers and magazines also rose" (p. 273).

11. Nie et al., p. 73.

12. For a review of this literature see, S. Kraus and D. Davis, *The Effects of Mass Communication on Political Behavior* (University Park: Pennsylvania University Press, 1976). See also, F. Greenstein, "Political Socialization," in *International Encyclopedia of the Social Sciences* (New York: Macmillan/Free Press, 1968); J. Dennis (Ed.), *Socialization to Politics: A Reader* (New York: Wiley, 1973); S. Chaffee, "Mass Communication in Political Socialization," in S. Renshon (Ed.), *Handbook of Political Socialization* (New York: Free Press, 1977); and C. Atkin, "Communication and Political Socialization," in D. Nimmo and K. Sanders, *Handbook of Political Communication* (Beverly Hills: Sage Publications, 1981).

13. One may ask why the introduction of radio did not supplant the influence of parents' party identification on their children. This writer could not find studies that offered explanations. Perhaps the visual dimension of television made the difference.

14. Nie et al., p. 73.

15. *Ibid.*

16. Nie et al., p. 155. In suggesting different interpretations "of the change in the structure of political attitudes" the researchers combine historical insight with their data. They suggest that citizen attitudes change as a result of issues facing them, and that, "The introduction of television or the spread of mass higher education would be the kind of explanatory factor consistent with the data" (pp. 174–175).

17. See, for example, Kraus and Davis, *op. cit.* and Nimmo and Sanders, *op. cit.*

18. S. Blumenthal, *The Permanent Campaign* (New York: Simon & Shuster, 1982).

19. W. Burnham, "The 1984 Election and the Future of American Politics," in E. Sandoz and C. Crabb, Jr. (Eds.), *Election '84: Landslide Without A Mandate?* (New York: Mentor, New American Library, 1985) p. 206.

20. F. Kent, *Political Behavior: The Heretofore Unwritten Laws, Customs and Principles of Politics as Practiced in the United States* (New York: William Morrow & Company, 1928) pp. 261–263.

21. C. Thomson, p. 11.

22. *Ibid.* For a concise account of television's coverage of congressional

hearings see N. Minow, J. Martin and L. Mitchell, *Presidential Television* (New York: Basic Books, 1973): ". . . 20 to 30, million people saw the hearings of the Senate Crime Investigating Committee chaired by Senator Estes Kefauver, who was catapulted into national prominence and almost overnight became leading contender for the presidency" (p. 107).

23. H. Hyman and P. Sheatsley, "The Political Appeal of President Eisenhower," *Public Opinion Quarterly* (Winter 1953–54), pp. 443–460.

24. Leonard Hall in a speech to the National Federation of Republican Women on March 1, 1955. Quoted in *Newsweek* (March 14, 1955), p. 28. This is probably not the first reference comparing a candidate to a commodity. The expenditure of money for a given product or service is, in many ways, different from voting for a particular candidate. Yet, many campaign experts, some of whom have come from advertising and public relations positions, frequently make this comparison.

25. Department of Marketing, Miami University, *The Influence of Television on the 1952 Elections* (1954) p. 22. Quoted in Thomson, p. 136.

26. Burnham, p. 208.

27. P. Lazarsfeld, B. Berelson, and H. Gaudet, *The People's Choice: How The Voter Makes Up His Mind In A Presidential Campaign* (New York: Columbia University Press, 1944).

28. *Ibid.,* p. 87.

29. *Ibid.,* p. 89.

30. "The president-press relationship . . . is highly important . . . because presidents have learned how to use the massive power of the media, particularly television, to influence the way people think . . ." J. Tebbel and S. Watts, *The Press and the Presidency From George Washington to Ronald Reagan* (New York: Oxford University Press, 1985) p. 318–319. For social science evidence providing a different view of mass communication effects in politics see, Kraus and Davis, *op. cit.*

31. Kraus and Davis, pp. 8–54.

32. B. Berelson, P. Lazarsfeld, and W. McPhee, *Voting: A Study of Opinion Formation in a Presidential Campaign* (Chicago: University of Chicago Press, 1954).

33. I. Pool, "TV: A New Dimension in Politics," in E. Burdick and A. Brodbeck (Eds.), *American Voting Behavior* (Glencoe, IL: Free Press, 1959) pp. 236–261. Also quoted in Kraus and Davis, pp. 52–53.

34. See C. Thomson, *op. cit.* See also, H. Simon and F. Stern, "The Effect of Television upon Voting Behavior in Iowa in the 1952 Presidential Election," *American Political Science Review,* 49(1955) pp. 470–478; J. Siebert, *The Influence of Television on the 1952 Elections* (Ohio: Department of Marketing, Miami University, 1954; and H. Craig, "Distinctive Features of Radio-TV in the 1952 Presidential Campaign, (unpublished master's thesis, State University of Iowa, 1954). For an interesting discussion of television's impact on presidential images (Eisenhower and Stevenson) see Pool, *op. cit.*

35. See, for example, "How Much Has Television Changed Campaigning?" *New York Times Magazine,* November 2, 1952, pp. 31 ff.

36. C. Thomson, p. 168.

37. N. Polsby and A. Wildavsky, *Presidential elections: Strategies of American*

Electoral Politics, 2nd edition (New York: Charles Scribner's Sons, 1968) p. 141.

38. *Ibid.,* 4th edition (1976) p. 177.

39. *Ibid.,* p. 3.

40. Nie et al., p. 175. These authors also cite the "spread of mass higher education." This writer would include candidate personality.

41. J. Lanzetta, D. Sullivan, R. Masters, and G. McHugo, "Emotional and Cognitive Responses To Televised Images Of Political Candidates," in S. Kraus and R. Perloff (Eds.), *Mass Media and Political Thought: An Information Processing Approach* (Beverly Hills: Sage Publications, 1985) pp. 85–116. "Reactions to political leaders and changes in support for candidates are in part a function of the emotions they elicit, and hence are not likely to be determined solely by party identification or issue evaluation. Although affective responses are themselves a function of prior attitudes, the nature of expressive displays is also critically important. Indeed, under certain conditions these non-verbal displays can exert an influence independent of prior attitude on the emotional reactions to and judgments of a political leader. Could these [Reagan] non-verbal cues be the 'Teflon' in the 'Teflon factor'?" (p. 113)

42. A random review of news magazines such as *Newsweek* and *Time* from January through October in 1976, 1980, and 1984 will demonstrate the attention given to candidates' ability to perform on television by political commentators and those reporters assigned to cover election events.

43. H. Plotkin, "Issues in the Campaign," in M. Pomper (Ed.), *The Election of 1984: Reports and Interpretations* (Chatham, NJ: Chatham House Publishers, 1985) p. 35.

44. T. Patterson and R. McClure, *The Unseeing Eye: The Myth Of Television Power In National Elections* (New York: G. P. Putnam's Sons, 1976).

45. H. Mendelsohn and G. O'Keefe, *The People Choose a President: Influences on Voter Decision Making* (New York: Praeger, 1976) p. 193.

46. With regard to political commercials, for example, over a decade ago, Murray Edelman, George Herbert Mead Professor of Political Science at the University of Wisconsin, advocated the "prohibition of spot announcements" in presidential campaigns. M. Edelman, "The Politics of Persuasion," in J. Barber (Ed.), *Choosing The President* (Englewood Cliffs, NJ: Prentice-Hall, 1972) p. 172. For a discussion of changes in the electoral process see the final chapter.

47. G. Pomper, "The Presidential Election," in M. Pomper (Ed.), *op. cit.,* p. 85.

48. M. Freedman, *Roosevelt and Frankfurter: Their Correspondence, 1928–1945* (Boston: Little, Brown, 1967) p. 651.

49. K. Jamieson, *Packaging the Presidency: A History and Criticism of Presidential Campaign Advertising* (New York: Oxford University Press, 1984) p. 26.

50. N. Minow, J. Martin, and L. Mitchell, *Presidential Television* (New York: Basic Books, 1973) p. 33.

51. Germond and Witcover, pp. 1–2.

52. *Ibid.,* p. 3.

53. *Ibid.*, pp. 187–188.

54. V. O. Key, *The Responsible Electorate* (Cambridge, MA: Harvard University Press, 1966).

55. E. Newman, *op. cit.*, p. 26.

56. *Ibid.*

57. See for example, S. Kraus, *The Great Debates* (Bloomington, IN: Indiana University Press, 1962); Kraus and Davis, *op. cit.;* and S. Kraus, *The Great Debates: Carter vs. Ford, 1976* (Bloomington, IN: Indiana University Press, 1979). See also chapter 4.

58. Apparently, predicting election results from early returns does not significantly affect the votes of those who intend to vote and have not done so. There is no underdog or bandwagon effect. Predictions may, however, affect voter turnout and may play a role in the outcome of local elections. See, for example, D. Fleitas, "The Underdog Effect: An Experimental Study of Voting Behavior in a Minimal Information Election." Unpublished doctoral dissertation, Florida State University, 1970; and H. Mendelsohn and I. Crespi, *Polls, Television and the New Politics,* (San Francisco: Chandler, 1970). For a brief, excellent discussion of predicting elections see, Polsby and Wildavsky, *op. cit.*, pp. 191–197. See also, P. Tannenbaum, "Policy Options in Early Election Projections," in J. Bryant and D. Zillmann (Eds.), *Perspectives On Media Effects,* (Hillsdale, NJ: Lawrence Erlbaum Associates, 1986) pp. 189–203.

3

DEBATE FORMATS:
A NEGOTIATION

[I]t all depends on what the candidates want. If the candidates wanted to have it in the middle of the Pacific Ocean on an aircraft carrier, with the Mormon Tabernacle Choir humming in the background, if they really wanted it, they were going to have it.[1]

The image merchants (more precisely, influential newspaper editors in the role of candidate advisers) were on the political scene when candidates for the U. S. Senate, Abraham Lincoln and Stephen A. Douglas, prepared for a series of debates in Illinois.[2] A major issue confronting the nation was slavery. The country was in severe inner turmoil. Information was slow to reach the public, and when it did it was usually altered somewhat and secondhand. The 1857 Supreme Court decision in *Dred Scott v. Sanford*[3] led Lincoln in the debates to believe that preventing slavery in the territories by any governmental action would be unconstitutional. Douglas responded that "the people have the lawful means to introduce it or exclude it as they please."[4] The Freeport exchange between Lincoln and Douglas, and the other six debates were witnessed by relatively few voters (about 15,000 at each site except the town of Jonesboro, in which the debate attracted only 1,500). Although they were not presidential debates, it was the first time in our history that opposing candidates went before the public to debate.

Lincoln suggested that they debate and Douglas accepted. They agreed on a set of ground rules: there would be seven 3-hour debates (between August 21 and October 15, 1858)[5]; each would take place in different Congressional districts; the speaking order was to be alternated, 1 hour for the opening speaker, 1½ hours for the opponent, and the opening speaker took the remaining 30 minutes to close the debate. Because Lincoln made the challenge, Douglas had the advantage by opening and closing four of the seven debates. These arrangements were agreed upon in an exchange of two simple letters between the Congressional candidates.

In today's negotiations for political debates, simple letters have been replaced by complex, extended conferences between candidates, their staffs of experts, and a third group, usually the sponsor of the proposed debates. Broadcasters are inevitably present, either in the negotiation meetings, or are consulted between the meetings.

The debates between Lincoln and Douglas were subsequently reported by the press with comments and editorials on the substance of the encounters, not on the ground rules. Debates in the television age have been subjected to investigations and discussions of issues, images, candidates' backgrounds and performances, staff personalities, sponsors' motives, electronic and press coverage, and more. Although the Lincoln–Douglas debates differed from the modern debates in several distinct aspects, including both the office sought and the method of presentation, they have been held up as the standard for comparison of subsequent debates.[6]

During the election campaigns of 1960, 1976, 1980, and 1984, Americans watched presidential candidates in joint appearances labeled "debates."[7] The formats of these appearances resembled those of classical debates, but in most features they were not debates at all. If the democratic process is to be well served in the future by such televised meetings of presidential candidates, it behooves us to understand what forces are at work in organizing them and for what benefits. Two facts are fundamental to this understanding.

The first fact is that the candidates are not interested in educating the public or in arriving at truth, but in *winning* the election. The second is that the candidates want to, and ultimately do, *control* most of what they do in campaigns. The various aspects of a political campaign, its strategies and tactics, are designed to gain the office sought. The rationale is simple: More control over events increases the probabilities of impressing the electorate, gaining advantages over the opponent, and winning the election.

Candidates accept debate invitations when they perceive it is to their advantage to do so. Once involved, candidates, through their representatives, seek control of the *format*—the ground rules by which the appearances are conducted. In the process of determining format elements candidates have had ultimate control. The television networks or the sponsoring organizations may set up the rules, but the candidates may veto any of them by refusing to appear. It is the format that determines how well the candidates can protect their weaknesses and exploit their strengths.

Although most of the published studies of televised debates have concluded that, on the whole, the debates were helpful to American voters, several criticisms have been advanced.[8] Political pundits, scholars, and other critics have argued that format (in the broadest sense), more than any other element was responsible for the damaging aspects of the telecasts to one or other of the candidates. Kennedy looked better than Nixon in the 1960 debates. It was suggested then that the format, in part, allowed the *appearance* of the candidate to become more important than the *substance* of his statements. Ford's Eastern European gaffe (1976)[9] and Carter's revelation that he consulted with Amy (1980) are two more results of faulty format design. Even the most cursory examination of postdebate media reports in the 4 campaign years displays a variety of criticism on how the debates were presented (see chap. 4).

Modern debating practice can be traced back to early Greek notions about public communication. Greek philosophers maintained that public argumentation required a structure to make it useful to society. The debate format was one structure that emerged. A fundamental assumption behind debates is that true arguments can always be presented more persuasively than false arguments if the situation in which the arguments are presented is arranged so that all participants have equal opportunity. Therefore, if two equally matched speakers are given equal amounts of time to present opposing arguments on an issue, an audience should be able to separate truth from falsehood and to reach a correct conclusion about the issue. It was believed by the Athenians that debates and the formats that contain them could provide an important tool for decision making by the public.

Persistent among the several criticisms of the presidential "debates" has been the lack of adherence to classical debate format, although some critics were willing to accept modern adaptations. One important critic, J. J. Auer, isolated elements of a specifically American debate tradition. He suggested that "a debate is (1) a confrontation, (2) in equal and adequate time, (3) of matched contestants, (4) on a stated proposition, (5) to gain an audience decision."[10] Applying these criteria to the 1960 telecasts, Auer found that only one fit, that of matched contestants. He labeled the Kennedy–Nixon encounters "The Counterfeit Debates" because they failed to satisfy genuine debate criteria—a criticism that also applies to the subsequent meetings between Carter–Ford, Carter–Reagan, Anderson–Reagan, and Mondale–Reagan.

Underlying criticism such as Auer's is the sincere belief that only "genuine" debate advances ideals inherent in democratic theory, that the electorate is best served by clear, concise, and thoughtful discussions of issues, and that the political process of choosing our leaders is enhanced by the traditional debate structure.

Most critics are realistic about the presidential debate process and its format. In analyzing the panelists' questions and the responses to them by Carter and Ford in the 1976 encounters, another critic, Louis Milic,[11] suggested that it is "naive today to suppose that there is any chance of returning to the rhetorical tradition of the nineteenth century." He argued for minor changes and concluded that "the disappointment with the format, the tinkering with the form, length, and subject matter of the questions, are all in a sense irrelevant . . . [since politicians have learned] to answer any form of question with any degree of accuracy." A political scientist, Nelson Polsby, assessed the 1960 and 1976 debates as "notable for their intellectual bareness" and said that they "suggest the possibility that debates are most likely to occur when there is the least to debate about."[12]

Despite these criticisms and appeals for change in format, the basic design has varied only slightly among the 4 debate years. Even after Bitzer and Rueter recounted the flaws of the Carter–Ford format, they included among four suggested formats, only one (a Lincoln–Douglas type) that closely fits the American debate tradition.[13]

Auer[14] continued to be irked by how presidential debates are conducted: "the so-called *great debates* are in fact based upon *great myths*." His "myths" are that presidential debates are great debates; candidates debate in order to inform the electorate; debates affect voters' decisions; and candidates will regularly volunteer to debate. Auer concluded that "it is difficult to find an objective assessment of debate impact upon voting behavior." Yet, the academic literature is filled with scientific studies on the impact of debates on voting decisions.[15] He argued that "voters . . . tend to judge by seeing how well their prior opinions held up, and thus their innate resistance to change is a filtering factor." Although not specifically stated, one assumes that part of the rationale underpinning Auer's criticisms of presidential debates includes the assumption that the traditional debate format *would* affect voting behavior. This would be in keeping with his final essential debate element—"to gain an audience decision." Because we have not seen the traditional debate format in presidential debates, that assumption remains untested.

Upon the advice of their staffs, candidates have been unwilling to participate in a debate with a traditional format. Myles Martel, a member of Reagan's 1980 Debate Task Force, summed up the position held by debate advisers:

> It would be no exaggeration to compare the 1980 presidential debate process with an advanced game of chess. Nearly every move regarding the decisions to debate, formats, strategies and tactics, and the execution of the debate themselves, was fraught with political implications. *One mismove—one untoward statement or look—and the election could have been lost.*
>
> As a fervent advocate of political debates, I left this experience more convinced than ever that the candidates should retain control of the process, particularly the decision to debate, scheduling and format design. To make presidential debates mandatory and to make a neutral third party mainly responsible for their preparation raises to great a risk that, intentionally or not, one candidate could become favored over the other. (italics added)[16]

The unsatisfactory form of the debates is due to candidates and their staffs, who ultimately decide on the format and, along with the representatives from television networks and sponsoring organizations, bring about what may be termed *a negotiated format.*

THE NEGOTIATION PROCESS

Because presidential candidates are not required to debate, their acceptance of and subsequent participation in televised debates are matters for negotiation. The question whether to debate depends on the candidates' perception of their self-interest, that is, getting an advantage over the opponent. Candidates want to get elected. Protestations to the contrary notwithstanding, they are interested in obtaining votes, not in educating the electorate. If a potential course of action is perceived as advantageous, it may be accepted. The test is always "Will this help us win?". It is this concern that dominates all discussions of alternative strategies and action.

Because the format is always a result of political decision making, it is difficult to conceive of a genuine debate replacing the innocuous question-and-answer programs. Politicians are more accustomed to the press conference format. Candidates are fearful about their ability to perform in a traditional debate, and they prefer to depend on familiar format with predictable audience response rather than risk anything unknown. A review of the negotiations for the 4 debate

TABLE 1

Negotiated Formats for Televised Presidential Debates in the General Elections of 1960, 1976, 1980, and 1984

Location and Time	Candidates	Moderator* and Panelists	Format
Sept. 26, 1960 WBBM–TV, CBS Chicago, IL 9:30–10:30 p.m. EDST	John F. Kennedy Richard M. Nixon	Howard K. Smith*, CBS Stuart Novins, CBS Sander Vanocur, NBC Charles Warren, MBS Robert Fleming, ABC	Opening statements (8 min.) Alternating questions to candidates on domestic issues Answers from candidates followed by rebuttal comments Closing statements (3 min.)
Oct. 7, 1960 WRC–TV, NBC Washington, DC 7:30–8:30 p.m. EDST	John F. Kennedy Richard M. Nixon	Frank McGee*, NBC Paul Niven, CBS Alvin Spivak, UPI Hal Levy, *Newsday* Edward P. Morgan, ABC	No opening or closing statements, end determined by clock Alternating questions to candidates on any subject Answers from candidates (2½ min.) Rebuttal comments from opponent (1½ min.)
Oct. 13, 1960 Split-Screen Telecast ABC, Los Angeles (Nixon) ABC, Los Angeles (Panel) ABC, New York (Kennedy) 7:30–8:30 p.m. EDST	John F. Kennedy Richard M. Nixon	William Shadel*, ABC Douglass Cater, *The Reporter* Frank McGee, NBC Charles Von Fremd, CBS Roscoe Drummond, *New York Herald Tribune*	No opening or closing statements, end determined by clock Alternating questions to candidates on any subject Answers from candidates (2½ min.) Rebuttal comments from opponent (1½ min.)
Oct. 21, 1960 ABC, New York 10:00–11:00 p.m.	John F. Kennedy Richard M. Nixon	Quincy Howe*, ABC Walter Cronkite, CBS Frank Singiser, MBS John Chancellor, NBC John Edwards, ABC	Opening statements (8 min.); closing statements (4½ min.) Alternating questions to candidates on any subject Answers from candidates (2½ min.)

Date / Location	Candidates	Panelists	Format
Sept. 23, 1976 Walnut St. Theater Philadelphia, PA 9:30–11:00 p.m. EDT	Jimmy Carter Gerald R. Ford	Edwin Newman*, NBC Frank Reynolds, ABC Elizabeth Drew, *New Yorker* James Gannon, *Wall Street Journal*	Rebuttal comments from opponent (1½ min.) No opening statements; closing statements (3 min.) Alternating questions to candidates on domestic issues Answers from candidates (3 min.) Optional follow-up questions permitted; answers (2 min.) Rebuttal comments from opponent (2 min.)
Oct. 6, 1976 Palace of Fine Arts San Francisco, CA 9:30–11:00 p.m. EDT	Jimmy Carter Gerald R. Ford	Pauline Frederick*, NPR Richard Valeriani, NBC Henry Trewhitt, *Baltimore Sun* Max Frankel, *New York Times*	No opening statements; closing statements (3 min.) Alternating questions to candidates on foreign affairs Answers from candidates (3 min.) Optional follow-up questions permitted; answers (2 min.) Rebuttal comments from opponent (2 min.)
Oct. 13, 1976 Alley Theatre Houston, TX 9:30–10:45 p.m. EDT	Robert Dole Walter F. Mondale	Jim Hoge*, *Chicago Sun-Times* Marilyn Berger, NBC Hal Bruno, *Newsweek* Walter Mears, AP	Opening statements (2 min.); closing statements (3 min.) Alternating questions (⅓ domestic, ⅓ foreign, ⅓ open) Both candidates answer the same questions (2½ min.) First candidate to answer a question has a rebuttal (1 min)

(continued)

TABLE 1
(Continued)

Location and Time	Candidates	Moderator* and Panelists	Format
Oct. 22, 1976 Phi Beta Kappa Hall Williamsburg, VA 9:30–11:00 p.m. EDT	Jimmy Carter Gerald R. Ford	Barbara Walters*, ABC Joseph Kraft, columnist Jack Nelson *Los Angeles Times* Robert Maynard, *Washington Post*	No opening statements; closing statements (4 min.) Alternating questions to candidates on any subject Answers from candidates (2½ min.) Follow-up questions permitted; answers (2 min.) Rebuttal comments (2 min.)
Sept. 21, 1980 Convention Center Baltimore, MD 10:00–11:00 p.m. EDT	John B. Anderson Ronald Reagan	Bill Moyers*, PBS Charles Corddry, *Baltimore Sun* Stephen Golden, *New York Times* Daniel Greenberg, columnist C. Loomis, *Fortune* Lee May, *Los Angeles Times* Jane Bryant Quinn, *Newsweek*	No opening statements; closing statements (3 min.) Alternating questions to candidates on any subject Answers from candidates (2½ min.) Rebuttal comments from both candidates (75 sec.)
Oct. 28, 1980 Public Music Hall Cleveland, OH 9:30–11:00 p.m. EDT	Jimmy Carter Ronald Reagan	Howard K. Smith*, ABC Harry Ellis, *Christian Science Monitor* William Hilliard, *Portland Oregonian* Marvin Stone, *U.S. News & World Report* Barbara Walters, ABC	No opening statements; closing statements (3 min.) Alternating questions on domestic and foreign policy (1st Half) Same questions to both; follow-up questions Answers from candidates; rebuttals (1 min.) (2nd Half) Answers from candidates to same questions

			Two opportunities for rebuttal comments
Oct. 7, 1984 Center for the Performing Arts Louisville, KY 9:00–10:30 p.m. EDT	Walter F. Mondale Ronald Reagan	Barbara Walters*, ABC Diane Sawyer, CBS Fred Barnes *Baltimore Sun* James Wilghart, Scripps-Howard	No opening statements; closing statements (4 min.) Alternating questions to candidates on economic policy and domestic issues Follow-up questions permitted; answers (1 min.) Rebuttal comments from opponent (1 min.)
Oct. 11, 1984 Pennsylvania Hall Civic Center Philadelphia, PA 9:00–10:30 p.m. EDT	George Bush Geraldine Ferraro	Sander Vanocur*, ABC Robert Boyd, *Philadelphia Inquirer* Jack White, *Time* John Mashek, *U.S. News & World Report* Norma Charles, NBC	No opening statements; closing statements (4 min.) Alternating questions to candidates on any subject Answers from candidates (2½ min.) Follow-up questions permitted; answers (1 min.)
Oct. 21, 1984 Music Hall, Municipal Auditorium Kansas City, KA 8:00–9:30 p.m. EDT	Walter F. Mondale Ronald Reagan	Edwin Newman*, PBS, King Features Morton Kondracke, *New Republic* Georgie Ann Geyer, *Universal Press Syndicate* Henry Trewhitt, *Baltimore Sun* Marvin Kalb, NBC	No opening statements; closing statements (4 min.) Alternating questions to candidates on foreign policy and defense Answers from candidates (2½ min.) Follow-up questions permitted; answers (1 min.) Rebuttal comments from opponent (1 min.)

campaign years reveals how each format (displayed in Table 1) came about.

The 1960 Debates

In 1960 the television networks wanted to mount the first presidential televised debate in imitation of the Oregon presidential primary debate between Thomas Dewey and Harold Stassen in 1948. In that year, the candidates agreed to debate one issue—outlawing Communists as school teachers. That format provided for 20-minute opening statements by each candidate followed by rebuttals of 8½ minutes. Both Kennedy and Nixon rejected that format. They feared it would attract little audience interest. They also believed that no single issue facing the nation was so important as to exclude all others. The head-to-head confrontation (especially, the rebuttals) might prompt one or the other to make a casual remark that would endanger our foreign relations.

Negotiations for the debates were conducted in a series of 12 meetings between the candidates' representatives and the networks. Although the networks wanted a more direct confrontation than that in the format insisted on by the candidates, their main objective was to have the presidential candidates agree so that televised "debates" could be aired. NBC head, Robert Sarnoff, conceded that the format "may not fulfill the traditional conception of a debate. Yet I believe it is serving the public more effectively than the classical debating format might have done."[17] His competitor at CBS, Dr. Frank Stanton, likewise supported their compromise with the candidates:

> The interposition of the panel was at the firm insistence of the candidates and represented a compromise with which the networks were not too happy. The networks preferred the more traditional format in which each candidate would question the other. But we were eager to get on with the face-to-face broadcasts. . . . Nevertheless, the format was fundamentally the same question-and-answer dialogue and commentary, that from Socrates' time, has been a favored means of throwing light on the characters and minds of men.[18]

The networks and the candidates settled on a format (see Table 1) that included a moderator and panelists, which in effect, set the precedent for candidate control of format. These debates were variously termed *The Great Debates, joint appearances, discussions,* and *Face-To-Face* encounters; but the term *debate* stuck.

Political campaigning habits and expectations about the effects of television dominated all other considerations, and candidate self-interest governed the negotiations. The traditional debate format, then, was to remain safely in history books, where it could be invoked to give sanction to the current proceedings.

The 1976 Debates

Although 16 years (three presidential elections) passed without debates, it was immediately apparent that candidates would once again take control of the televised encounters. On August 19, 1976 in accepting the Republican nomination, President Gerald Ford challenged his opponent: "I am ready, I am eager to go before the American people and debate the real issues face-to-face with Jimmy Carter."[19]

Five days later Ford met with reporters in Vail, Colorado and detailed elements of his format for the debates:

> It is my very strong conviction that the American people have a right to know where I stand on the issues and where my opponent stands on the issues. I challenged my opponent to a series of debates. I feel very strongly that the first debate should come a day or two after Labor Day, and I suggest perhaps September 8, September 9, and September 10.
>
> I think there should be four debates, and each debate should involve no less than 90 minutes on each occasion. The subject matters, of course, are those issues that the American people will want to know where my opponent stands, where I stand. They have a right to know.
>
> I feel, for example, the first debate ought to involve national defense. The other three issues would be domestic policy, foreign policy, economic policy.
>
> With the overall format and with the debates starting as quickly as possible, I think we will get this campaign off on the right track. I look forward to the first one and each of the next three, and the sooner we get started, the better.[20]

Following his remarks several reporters asked Ford about debate details:

Q.: Have you passed this word on to Carter yet on the debates?

Ford: I am depending on all of you to transmit this information.

Q.: Mr. President, are these debates designed to help you pull up in the polls?

Ford: No, the debates are designed specifically to give the American people the right to know that I stand here on a particular issue, and Mr. Carter stands differently. The American people, I think, will benefit from an in-depth discussion of the four issues—defense, economic policy, domestic policy, and national defense.

Q.: Will this be one-on-one, or—

Ford: Those details are going to be worked out by one or more people representing me and whoever Mr. Carter decides on his behalf.

Q.: Can you tell us who those people will be?

Ford: We will make an announcement on that in the next day or so.

Q.: Have the Carter people agreed to these plans?

Ford: Those are the negotiations that I think will have to be worked out by those representing me and those representing Mr. Carter.[21]

According to one of Ford's representatives, negotiations and preparations included an examination of the research on the 1960 Kennedy–Nixon debates:

You may be interested to know that your 1962 book was of enormous help as we negotiated this year's debates and the prepared materials for the President. In fact, I had an opportunity to discuss portions of your book directly with the President in the days preceding the first debate.[22]

Although the candidates' motives and the format in 1976 were similar to those in 1960, a new group of participants, representatives from the League of Women Voters Education Fund (the League), joined the negotiation process.[23] In 1960 a Joint Resolution of Congress had temporarily suspended the "equal time" provision (Section 315 of the Communications Act of 1934) in order to allow the networks to broadcast the debates on radio and on television, without providing the same opportunity for the more than 100 fringe party candidates. In 1976 Congress was unwilling to use that device. Instead, a series of legal moves allowed the networks to cover the debates as "bona fide news events" under the sponsorship of the League (or ostensively, for any other sponsor). Throughout the 1976 negotiations, that legal decision influenced the various discussions about the inclusion of minor party candidates, the selection of panelists, the role of the networks, and the actions of the sponsors.

Whereas in 1960 the path was cleared by Congress, in 1976 the legal situation was obscure and led a number of minor party candidates to file suits pleading for their inclusion in the debates. These suits, as well as the League's careful attention to operating within the law, prompted its debate negotiators to move in a more "legalistic" manner than they most likely would have preferred. Moreover, the networks were conscious that they had been included among the defendants in the suits.

Only the participating candidates were relatively free from "legalistic" constraint. A few examples illustrate some of the problems that resulted from legal considerations during the negotiations.

James Karayn, debate project director for the League, believed that the evasion of Section 315 had placed the League and the networks in an adversarial situation:

> the networks won't stand still, the commercial networks, if we get debates in the Fall. How can we do this so . . . we don't end up in Court, or [with] somebody invalidating our efforts because we did either a naive or just an outright stupid thing, and somebody would say there was collusion. [Eugene] McCarthy, as you know, claimed there was collusion between the League and the networks.[24]

McCarthy's "collusion" accusation was dramatically heightened by the 27-minute "audio gap" in Philadelphia's Walnut Street Theater during the first debate. The networks, preoccupied with legal considerations, had refused to supply the League with an on-air feed forcing them to install their own audio system for guests in the theater. During the candidates audio check on the afternoon of the debate, Elliot Bernstein (senior special events producer for ABC, and the networks' pool producer) determined that the candidates would not be able to hear the panelists' questions because the two audio amplification systems (on-air and house) caused "feedback," distorting the sound. The League's system was disconnected and the networks' audio feed provided the theater with sound. McCarthy and others claimed that if the debate was in fact a bona fide news event it should have continued even when the network's sound failed. The culprit that failed was a foil-wrapped 25¢ capacitor.

For the networks (especially CBS, but also ABC, which served as pool for all networks), three issues predominated, all related to journalistic prerogatives under the First Amendment's guarantee of freedom of the press. These issues were the placement and use of unilateral cameras, the showing of audience reaction shots, and the selection of panelists. All three are actually aspects of format. Although some critics make a distinction between *format* (meaning the ground rules for the participants) and *televised debate* (meaning the production details), in reality these two terms are not mutually exclusive.

The right to use their own (unilateral) in addition to the shared (pool) cameras was requested by CBS and rejected by the League, because, Karayn said, many independent stations in Philadelphia had requested unilaterals and they could not grant some without granting all.[25] No unilaterals were allowed inside the Walnut Street Theater proper, although they were permitted in the lobby and in the balcony. Use of unilaterals would, of course, have permitted each network to telecast a different view of the debates.[26]

Audience reaction shots—showing a member of the audience on the television screen either while someone is speaking or immediately after—were requested by the networks. In negotiations between the candidates and the League representatives it was decided that there would be no audience reaction shots. Michael Raoul-Duval, President Ford's special counsel, vetoed the plan because "[President Ford] felt strongly about [the] real need to move the debate into a more issue-oriented mode . . . [It] was politically to his advantage, in his judgment, and that's why we made that decision."[27] Obviously, audience reactions to the debate as it was going on would add another dimension to the format, but it would also have permitted editorializing through the selection of audience shots (such as a snicker or a solemnly respectful expression).

Selection of panelists—questioners—caused considerable difficulty for the League (and would haunt them in subsequent debate years, especially in 1984). Karayn, who spent the summer of 1976 developing a plan for the debate procedures, suggested that candidates question each other. After a preliminary meeting with candidates' representatives in late August, Karayn realized that the head-to-head format suggestion might not be acceptable. He held meetings separately with candidates' representatives, but to no avail: The candidates did not want to question each other. The risk of being perceived as badgering the opponent, and the impression that the President was being attacked, were two of the reasons offered for not debating head-to-head.

Karayn asked the League's debate steering committee to develop a list of potential questioners, to select from among the list those the committee felt would be acceptable to the candidates, and to announce the selection to the candidates' representatives. The candidates' negotiators countered with a proposal that they be permitted to suggest panelists. Eventually, the League agreed to allow the representatives to submit a list of no more than 15 names in each category of print, broadcast, magazine, and wire services. The same procedure would follow in later debates. The candidates' lists were combined with the League's and selections were made. Although the League insists that it alone made the final selection, the process raised both legalistic and journalistic issues of collusion.[28]

In debriefing sessions which followed the debates and in interviews with representatives of the League, candidates, and the networks, it became clear that the most notable aspect of the negotiations was control of the process by the candidates. The effect on the 1976 format cannot be overstated.

There can be no question about who has the veto over major format elements. It is the candidates. During the discussion between Ruth Clusen (president of the League); Bernstein; and Raoul-Duval, President Ford's representative, it was asked whether the candidates could veto the panel's decision. Raoul-Duval's answer was "yes," because "ultimately we could pick up the marbles and walk out." For all practical purposes, candidates had final control over whether or not there was to be a debate. On the other hand, it would have been very difficult, if not impossible, for the networks to exercise a "veto" on a debate; once the candidates had agreed to debate, it would have been very difficult for the networks not to televise them.[29]

The message is clear: *Power over format ultimately resides in the candidates' camps.*

Unlike the debates of 1960, those in 1976 had both a sponsor, other than the networks, and a live audience. Also, because the event was to occur under one of the exemptions of Section 315 of the Federal Communication Act of 1934, and because the audience in attendance was in fact part of the event, questions of audience coverage, the networks believed, were theirs to decide, not those of the participants in the event.

Ford's debate advisers did not want an audience. They thought it might interfere with the President's concentration and distract him from looking directly at the cameras and the panelists. Ford's legal advisers, however, thought that the audience would make the status of the "bona fide news event" believable. The League and the candidates agreed, however, that no audience reaction shots would be allowed. The networks, of course, were quite disturbed by that decision.

Bernstein; Barry Jagoda, Carter's adviser for the debates; Robert Chandler, vice president of CBS News; and Raoul-Duval revealed their positions during the debriefing conference:

Bernstein: It was . . . a very important matter of principle for us. . . . As special events producer in the last 13 years, I have never been in a situation where we were told, once we were given the permission to cover something . . . where we can point a camera and where we can't. . . . This is something that lots of people would like to tell us to do.

Jagoda: [Our goal was to get] an opportunity to have substantive agreements and disagreements between the two candidates expressed to the American people. . . . The question of the audience was just a technical detail. There was no principle involved for us.

Chandler: We were put in a position that was intolerable for us. Had we gone to Russia and shot some sort of event there, and had the Russians said . . . you will not shoot in this direction, . . . everybody would have been horrified. And yet, here we are in the same kind of position, whether we want to take pictures of the audience or not, we've been invited to cover a news event and suddenly we're told that we cannot cover part of the event. Now, that is a matter of principle and it is quite important to us, and it was an intolerable situation. . . . As a matter of fact, we suggested, rather than put us in this position, why don't you drop the audience. [The League] said no, we have a tradition of audiences and we don't want to drop the audience.

Raoul-Duval: . . . That audience was a fiction, in my judgment. We did not want the audience. We wanted to negotiate away from it, and we accepted the audience not because it was the League's tradition. . . . We said yes to the audience only because of the position of the lawyer. . . . So that audience was, in essence, there as a legal fiction.[30]

Other than wide-angle shots of the audience before and after the debates, there were no audience reaction shots in 1976. Questions of format are affected by the presence of the audience, if only because it introduces another element in the negotiation process—another consideration for candidates, sponsors and networks to work out.

Audience reaction shots, which have long been part of the television journalists' craft, was also part of the message. Power over format and aspects of television presentation ultimately resides in the candidates' camps.

As Raoul-Duval pointed out, the only factor that could alter candidates' decisions was public opinion. Public opinion, however, exercises more influence on candidates' decisions whether to debate than on their views about format. Pollsters, columnists, and the news media generally, conduct and report poll and survey findings about the presidential race. Press access to information on the campaign trails is abundant. Whether debates will be held is a constant topic in media reports. Candidates are regularly asked about their intentions. Candidates and their advisers must respond because public opinion usually mounts in favor of presidential debates. That was and remains a significant factor.[31]

The moment debates are announced, negotiations are enveloped in secrecy. One who attempts to gain information about the negotiations as it proceeds gets the impression that what "gags" the negotiators is nothing less than the threat of punishment under a "Debate Secrets Act." Agreements are made about what can and cannot be released, either officially or off the record. Inevitably, there are leaks, but no one wants to upset the debate negotiating process. Sponsors fear debate cancellation; broadcasters fear some sort of retribution; and candidates' representatives fear, paraphrasing Martel, "One mismove and the election is lost." Public opinion, certainly in the short term, could hardly influence the determination of format, because little is publicly revealed about it until the negotiations are completed. Both from the candidates' point of view and from the League's, it would be bad publicity to let the public know that candidates have control over negotiations, and furthermore that they are even able to keep the fact of that control a secret. The following transcription from a debriefing session after the 1976 debates makes clear that all parties had agreed to withhold certain aspects of the negotiations from the public.

Raoul-Duval: Well, do we have an agreement and our agreement is no longer binding? (Laughter) . . .

Peggy Lampl (League executive director): We had an agreement about the negotiation—

Clusen: That we would not talk about it and we didn't.

Sidney Kraus (Professor; chairperson, debriefing conference): This is a debriefing session and everything is on the record. The language can be changed but everything is on the record. I hope that we're not going to keep secrets, or any other agreements here . . .

Raoul-Duval: I want to bring that out. It obviously is not for you or any other single person around this table to abrogate an agreement which three parties, the League, representatives from Mr. Carter and representatives from Mr. Ford agreed to, but we did have an agreement . . . and that is, we would not characterize the process of selecting the panel. I assume it is in everybody's interest that that is over with now.[32]

Clearly, the 1976 experience reveals how difficult it would be to persuade candidates to participate in traditional, genuine debate. Even if the force of public opinion were on the side of genuine debate it is doubtful that such would occur. Anticipating the possibility of debates in 1980, George Will in a broadcast made sense for "real" debates:

In 1976, in the first debate between Ford and Carter, the audio system failed, and both men stood there like stumps for 27 minutes, not exchanging a word. Some people considered that silent stretch the intellectual high point of the campaign—for 27 minutes, neither man was misleading the nation.

Will cited the recommendations in a Twentieth Century Fund report[33] that in the 1980 debates candidates should address arguments and questions to one another. He continued:

> True debates are rare. What goes on in Congress is usually mere declaiming, not debating—not the cut and thrust of people developing and defending arguments. And the 1976 "debates" were not real debates: They were more like joint appearances on "Meet the Press," or like parallel, simultaneous press conferences. We have enough press conferences during campaigns. We need what true debates can provide—a sense of how candidates can think on their feet, how—or if— their minds work when they are not programmed for a controlled situation. The debates should minimize the role of journalists as interrogators. Candidates should argue back and forth, with only minimal control. Increasingly, campaigns consist of 30-second commercials and other prepackaged episodes. Real debates would force candidates to think in public, to think without scripts. Such debates might be a dismaying spectacle, but it is better to be dismayed about politicians before rather than after the election.[34]

Will, Auer, and other advocates of genuine debate were not to be satisfied in 1980, another debate year in which candidates' self-interest and political posturing characterized format negotiations.

The 1980 Debates[35]

The election of 1980 has been described as volatile. Throughout the primary period, public opinion polls depicted a vacillating electorate. Shifts in voter intention were of such magnitude that, for example, Bush climbed from some 8 percentage points (Reagan had 50) in September 1979, to 45 points in January 1980. He moved ahead of Reagan, who dipped down to 36; in those 4 months, Bush gained 37 points, whereas Reagan lost 14. Between Bush's victory in the Iowa caucuses and the time just after the first debate in New Hampshire (less than a month) Reagan regained the lead, and moved ahead significantly to win.[36]

In the Democratic primary, Carter and Kennedy had similarly been engaged in campaigns that alternately faltered and plunged ahead. The electoral outcomes were generally unpredictable from primary to primary. Kennedy, behind in the polls, challenged Carter to several debates. The President, well ahead, refused each challenge. Inflation and unemployment were on the rise, however, and when the polls reflected an impatient electorate, Carter reconsidered and accepted a

debate with Kennedy during the Iowa primary. When the American hostages were taken in Iran and public opinion moved quickly to support the presidency (as it usually does when our country faces a foreign crisis[37]), Carter moved quickly to postpone (cancel) the debate with Kennedy.

Once Carter and Reagan became the nominees of their parties, the call for debates quickly arose among a variety of potential sponsors. The League, sponsors of several primary debates,[38] took the inside track with an early invitation to both candidates.

If the 1980 primary period was volatile, the candidates' jockeying for exposure and advantage, and the League's attempts to mediate problems, made the efforts to mount debates precarious, but kept them in the public's eye.[39]

The Baltimore Debate. The three-way race to the presidency in the general election made more complex what was already a campaign filled with critical events. John Anderson's candidacy—good for Reagan, bad for Carter—made difficulties for the League, which, once again, sought to sponsor debates. Anderson, running as a Republican in the primary, switched to an Independent candidacy for the general election. The League was prepared to extend debate invitations only to Carter and Reagan, but had to consider rising public support for Anderson's inclusion. They decided to rely on his standing in forthcoming polls as an indication of his qualification for participation (see chap. 5).

On September 9, the League announced that Anderson's standing in the polls demonstrated "significant voter interest" and that they had invited the candidates to a three-way debate. Reagan and Anderson accepted, Carter declined.

Thus, the candidates' strategies toward the debates crystallized, as did the League's own position. Reagan and Carter both knew (from their survey reports) who would benefit from Anderson's participation in the proposed debate. Reagan felt he had much to gain, and Anderson, of course, had nothing to lose. Carter, slipping in the polls as the economy lagged, and with the Iranians recalcitrant as ever, wanted to debate Reagan first. He would then consent to a three-way debate. Reagan refused to debate without Anderson, saying that it was not his place to "uninvite" a participant.

The League's position was forced—it could not alter the invitation. Other potential sponsors (e.g., the National Press Club) emerged, suggesting Reagan–Carter debates in a variety of formats. Carter was determined in his refusal to participate in a three-way debate. The League made plans to hold the debate and include an empty chair, a

ploy that threatened to reveal Carter's "cowardice."[40] With considerable pressure from the local Leagues throughout the country and from Democratic Party officials, the League withdrew the empty chair 4 days before the Baltimore debate. Ruth Hinerfeld, League President, said that the League had been "advised by legal counsel that the legal questions [of] having an empty 'chair' are sufficiently serious that we should not do so."[41] The debate program given to members of the audience, however, included Carter among the "invited candidates."

Earlier (September 15) Reagan and Anderson representatives met with the League for 2½ hours to make arrangements for the Baltimore debate. Among other elements of the format (see Table 1), it was agreed that each candidate would be allowed to question the other;[42] responses would be limited to one and one-quarter minutes. In last-minute negotiations, however, candidate-to-candidate questioning was eliminated from the format. It was this kind of flip–flop control by candidates that infuriated Lee Hanna, who, along with his brother Ed, were the League's 1980 debate producers. After the election Lee Hanna detailed his frustration with the negotiations:[43] "the candidates' representatives were pathetic in their desire to protect what they saw as their candidate's interests. The negotiations were exercises in frustration and hilarity." Hanna offered a solution that, had it been part of the League's debate invitations, most likely would have eliminated the Hannas' jobs: "[The League] will be solely responsible for the format, length, number, and subject matter of the debates . . . these are not matters to be bartered and brokered with the candidates."

In this debate negotiation, broadcasters were determined that candidates should not dictate the kind of shots the cameras could and could not take, and they out-maneuvered both the candidates' representatives and the League on this issue. As did Bernstein in 1976, Charles Frey, producer, special events and the ABC pool producer, pressed hard for reaction shots.

At the first meeting between the networks and the League, Frey stated that the pool would take reactions shots if they (the pool) deemed it appropriate. The League supported the candidates' position that there be no reaction shots. Subsequently there were several meetings about the issue with candidates' representatives refusing to budge, the networks insisting on maintaining their journalistic prerogatives, and the League, besieged with last-minute hassles,[44] in the middle, but officially with the candidates.

William Small and William Leonard, presidents of NBC News and CBS News, respectively, sent telegrams to the League and candidates' representatives detailing their networks' position on reaction shots

and cutaways. They wanted to be able to cut away from the candidates and panelists with reaction shots whenever they felt such would reflect an important part of the proceedings. Their unilaterals were not allowed in the hall. Outside the hall, the networks chose positions for these cameras that would allow access to, and interviewing of, dignitaries and audience members as they entered and left the debates. Essentially, the networks (as distinguished from the pool) wanted to cover the debates as news events, switching from the stage to the audience as they would in any other event.

During the evening of September 18, Frey, and Ed and Lee Hanna discussed the issue over dinner. The Hannas reported back to the League and to the candidates' representatives that the pool intended to honor shots requested by the networks' directors.[45]

On the 20th, the day before the debate, Hinerfeld outlined again the League's position on reaction shots in a letter to Frey and telegrams to Small and Leonard. With the pool insisting that they use their own discretion with reaction shots, Dick Wald, senior vice president for ABC News, called Frey at 11:30 on the morning of the debate and requested that Frey in his capacity as pool producer release the letter and telegram sent by the League. Carol Ann Rambo of pool public relations shortened the original version and released it. Not since 1960 had the networks been able to reaffirm their journalistic prerogatives in debate coverage as they had done on that day.

Once again, the League generated a long list of potential panelists, and again, the selected panel was composed of journalists. In 1976 and 1980, they toyed with the idea of including nonjournalists—experts in various fields—as panelists. Raoul-Duval thought that lawyers and professors were sometimes naive about politics, debating, and the political process. Harriet Hentges, who replaced Peggy Lampl as executive director and was a member of the League's 1980 debate negotiating committee, provided a significant criterion for selecting journalists, instead of experts, for the Baltimore debate. She insisted, "You have to have some feeling for . . . the person's knowledge and ability to *act in that sort of performance*" (italics added). It was not an accident that Barbara Walters appeared in three debates—as moderator (1976, 1984) and panelist (1980), that Sander Vanocur was a panelist in 1960 and a moderator in 1984, and that Howard K. Smith was the moderator for two debates, 1960 and 1980. Smith was also moderator for the several League-sponsored debates in the 1980 presidential primaries.

Broadcasters dominated the panels in 1960. In 1976, Karayn and the League included more print journalists. Among the 52 moderators and questioners in the presidential (and two vice-presidential

debates) 32 of them (62%) have been broadcast journalists. The rest
were print journalists; Table 1 shows the significant increase of print
journalists as panelists in the debates of 1980 and 1984.

If we must have panels of questioners, why must they be exclusively
journalists and television personalities? Journalists are trained to ask
questions, but they are not the only ones able to construct them.
Television personalities are able to perform effectively in front of a
camera, but they are not the only ones who appear before the lens. It
would be a novel innovation for journalists to cover debates without
journalists in them. Nonjournalists may bring a new and useful dimension to televised debates. Some historians, poets, novelists, and
professors may add questions with perspectives more germane to the
qualities of presidential leadership than some we have had in past
debates.

The Cleveland Debate. During the period after the Baltimore and
before the Cleveland debate, polls reported a slight lead for Reagan,
with some experts anticipating a very close outcome. Just a few days
before the Baltimore contest, the League, hoping to entice Carter to
enter that debate, invited Carter and Reagan to debate in Cleveland
without Anderson. A previously scheduled debate in Louisville was
cancelled (that city would have to wait until 1984 for its national
publicity); four had been planned originally.

The League had two teams, one in Washington, the other in Cleveland, diligently trying to salvage an already disappointing debate
schedule. Carter, midway in the period, accepted the debate invitation.

Ed Hanna, busy with the League's preparations in anticipation of
the Cleveland debate, was asked[46] if he thought that the League could
bring about a format similar to that in the Chicago and Houston
Republican primary debates, both of which had been wide-open, free-
wheeling debates, with candidates asking questions of each other. He
did not "feel that the candidates would buy it. Certainly Reagan
won't." Moreover, Hanna was ambivalent about the debate being
held:

> I'm sure that right now, maybe even as we speak, Reagan's people,
> weighing the present time limits, [are] trying to measure what is in
> effect a calculated risk. As we have known for quite some time, there are
> two camps within Reagan's people—one wanting to debate, the other
> camp saying, "No, don't do it. We did great in Baltimore. Don't push it.
> You're ahead so don't press your luck." But [Reagan's] no longer ahead.
> Well, looking at it from his point of view, if I were one of his advisers,

I've no doubt that I would have given him the same advice. But now I
don't know what I would advise him. Because it is really a toss of a coin,
and it may be a "heads you win, tails I lose here [in Cleveland]"
situation.

The League's Washington team worked behind the scenes trying to
induce Reagan's representatives to accept the debate invitation. Earlier, there was a dispute between Reagan's advisers, Ed Meese and Jim
Baker, about accepting the invitation. Baker was convinced that Reagan's acting ability and his personal manner would give him an advantage in a televised debate. Reagan accepted the Cleveland debate
invitation.

It was once again apparent that the format would follow precedent.
In this case, Reagan's advisers were against direct questioning by candidates because they did not want the voter-viewer to feel that their
candidate was badgering the President of the United States. Baker's
advice to Reagan on the night of the debate was couched in one word;
as *Newsweek* reported it, "Baker handed Reagan a 3-by-5 card with one
word on it: 'Chuckle.' When Carter began criticizing him, Reagan
chuckled, adding, 'There you go again.' The reply defused Carter's
attack."[47]

Posturing and role playing are inevitably part of the debate preparations that candidates and their advisers ritually perform. Both Carter and Reagan *rehearsed* aspects of their debate performance. Each
anticipated the other's reactions and possible tactics during these
rehearsals.

Format negotiations were based on strategies designed to win the
election. Although the League pressed for elements of genuine debate, the candidates would have none of that. Finally, in the long
negotiations, the League came up with 22 names for panelists. Again,
the candidates had a veto over those they opposed. Essentially, the
negotiations created a format modeled after the 1976 debates. Although some of Carter's public statements seemed to suggest a free-
wheeling debate with candidates questioning each other, neither his
nor Reagan's representatives would accept such a format during the
October 20 negotiating meeting in the League's Washington office.

The Cleveland debate was a culmination of a series of critical and
sometimes unforeseen events, some of them created by the campaigns, others, such as negotiations for the hostages in Iran, arising
independent of the campaigns. Accompanying the Cleveland debate
was the Anderson "debate" on Cable News Network fed to PBS stations. He debated an empty chair. One person "debates" are at best
political statements and at worst make a mockery of political debating.

Carter's and Reagan's debate performances were measured in terms of "who won" in the media reports and academic studies which followed. All political debates have been ultimately measured that way (see chap. 4). This simple explanation stands in the way of those who would like to move in the direction of genuine debate. Presidential candidates shun such suggestions as though they could cause a serious illness—a dreaded "political disease" that could kill their candidacies.

Extending the analogy, candidates' representatives behave like physicians embarking on a preventative care plan for their patients, guarding the political health of candidates. So intense is this protectionism that political staff members become interns and residents trained in a school of political medicine whose prescriptions occasionally have serious side effects, or cause fatalities: The Watergate break in and much of the subsequent cover-up were results of prescriptions by ideologues and zealots associated with the Republican National Committee and Nixon's staff of 1972.

The avoidance of genuine debate formats is in keeping with strategies designed to avoid perceived pitfalls. In developing these strategies, campaign staffs, consultants, and political elites seek advantages for their candidates, sometimes in most extraordinary ways.

Three such incidents were associated with the 1980 debates. In mid-1983 it was discovered that somehow President Carter's 1980 debate briefing book was in the hands of Reagan's advisers just before the Cleveland debate.[48] Closely following that bombshell it was revealed that George Will, a most respected conservative columnist and political analyst, was one of Reagan's Cleveland debate coaches. Immediately after the debate, Will, on ABC's *Nightline*, acclaimed Reagan's appearance as a "thoroughbred performance." He failed to inform the audience that he had coached the candidate. And, at the Baltimore Debate, a Carter staffer, Linda Peek (Jody Powell's assistant), allegedly attended the Anderson–Reagan debate in Baltimore masquerading as a guest and disguised with a wig.[49]

Evidently, the risks taken in these instances are not as potentially damaging to the candidate as risks associated with a genuine debate format. The logic of political campaigning is sometimes peculiar.

The 1984 Debates

As did Ronald Reagan in the 1980 Republican primaries, Walter Mondale in 1984 had to compete with several candidates for the Democratic nomination. Unlike Reagan, however, Mondale was unsure of his effectiveness on television. The day after he lost the election, Mondale claimed that his major liability was his ineffectual use of television.

This is indeed curious because the evidence suggests that Mondale was not a television neophyte. Mondale demonstrated his ability to use television on several important occasions. In his 1976 debate encounter with Senator Robert Dole, Mondale's television performance was effective. Reviewing studies of the impact of that debate, Sears and Chaffee found that:

> There was [a] significant attitude change as a consequence of the vice-presidential debate, where Mondale scored a personal triumph. His popularity, competence, and trait evaluation all improved following the debate, and more so among [debate] viewers than nonviewers.[50]

In the nine televised democratic primary debates of 1984 Mondale fared quite well, parrying and thrusting with whomever he faced. His "Where's the beef?" retort to Gary Hart was certainly as good a one-liner as Reagan's "There you go again!"

His acceptance speech at the San Francisco Democratic Convention revealed that Mondale had no qualms about debating Reagan on television. Mondale's performance in the first debate (Louisville) was certainly more impressive than Reagan's, although his debating posture in Kansas City (the second presidential debate) lacked his earlier vibrant showing.[51] As Pomper aptly asserted, "Mondale could claim credit for [Democrats' gains] because of his performance in the debates and his vigorous closing efforts. The election was a victory for Reagan, but not a personal defeat for Mondale."[52]

Reagan's victory can be seen as a triumph of the use of political television. The polls continually showed that Reagan was far ahead of Mondale. The President's popularity ratings hovered over the Mondale campaign like vultures about to devour a corpse. Reagan's ability to use television, beyond that of presidential access, weighed heavily in deciding the Mondale campaign strategy. Mondale's advisers were concerned over the voter-viewer's comparison between their candidate and Reagan. From the outset, Mondale found it difficult to mount a strategy based on issues. The polls and the continual pressure of women's organizations (most notably the National Organization of Women) to include a woman as vice president on the Democratic ticket[53] combined to influence the direction of the Mondale campaign. Under these circumstances it was reasonable to react with "political attractions" that might counter the popularity of the President and provide momentum for the campaign. These "attractions"—the selection of a woman as the vice presidential candidate and the televised debates—were two of the three highlights of the 1984 presidential election that deserve our attention.[54] Another aspect worthy of discussion is incumbency and debating.

There has been much discussion about the disadvantages for an incumbent president to debate, especially when he is ahead in the polls.[55] The 1984 election provides a unique opportunity to examine that thesis. And the conclusion is obvious: if ever an election set a precedent for the institutionalization of televised presidential debates this was the one.

The Debate Challenge. It was quite apparent in 1984 that Mondale's strategy placed great store on televised debates with Reagan. Using the Democratic National Convention in San Francisco as the springboard, the Mondale campaign orchestrated the formal debate challenge with statements made in the early parts of both Senator Edward Kennedy's speech introducing the nominee and Mondale's acceptance speech.

Senator Kennedy exclaimed that "In 1960, before the debates, they called Richard Nixon 'the great debater'—and in 1984, they call Ronald Reagan 'the great communicator.' But we remember who won the debates and the election: John Kennedy did—and so will Walter Mondale—and so will Geraldine Ferraro."[56] Mondale's summons: "I challenge Mr. Reagan to put his plan [for reducing the deficit] on the table next to mine—and debate it with me on national television."[57]

President Ronald Reagan—enjoying one of the highest popularity ratings of any president; unfettered by a primary; his campaign coffers filled; ahead in his re-election bid; and facing a challenger with several electoral problems—agreed to debate Democrat Walter Mondale. Just a few days before the first debate ABC News/*Washington Post* Poll reported President Reagan was leading Mondale by 18 percentage points, 55% to 37%. Given his enormous popularity and the incumbency, Reagan had little to gain and much to lose debating Mondale. Why, then, did President Reagan accept Mondale's challenge?

Apparently, the decision to debate had more to do with ego than with election savvy. His aides cautioned against participating in debates, citing his enormous lead and his ability, as President, to command attention of the mass media. Evidently, President Reagan was not willing to let Mondale garner campaign issues. Certainly, he was not prepared to concede that in a nationally televised debate he, the actor turned politician,[58] would be "damaged" by a challenger without such credentials. After all, he had clobbered Carter in the 1980 debate, and was indeed "the great communicator."[59]

In mid-September, then, Mondale was informed that Reagan would debate him, although not as often and as long as Mondale's negotiators had hoped for. The Mondale campaign strategy included a call for nine, 2-hour televised debates (three of which were to be vice presidential debates) on a wide range of issues. Reagan's negotiators would have none of that. They offered one, 1-hour, one issue debate. Both camps settled for two, 90-minute, presidential debates—one on foreign, the other on domestic and economic issues—and one, 90-minute vice presidential debate on both foreign and domestic issues.

An examination of the negotiations and preparations for the 1984 debates (held in Louisville, Philadelphia, and Kansas City) offers further evidence of candidate control, introduces additional questions about format and the selection of panelists, and raises doubts about the League's sponsorship of presidential debates.

The League Sponsorship. For the third presidential election in a row, the League of Women Voters Education Fund became the sponsor of the 1984 presidential debates. The League's administration of debates in 1976 and 1980 sometimes was met with criticism, but their handling of the 1984 negotiations and accommodations of candidate demands, particularly the procedures for selecting the panel of questioners, came under fire from several quarters. The issues raised can be traced back to 1976, but it is sufficient to begin with the formal announcement for 1984 debates.

In the September 17 announcement of plans for the debates, Dorothy S. Ridings, President, League of Women Voters, said the following:

> Arriving at this package has been a long and productive process. The League has been talking to the campaigns for more than a year about a debate this fall. In June we submitted a debates proposal to both campaigns as a starting point for discussions. *We knew from experience that the negotiating process would be a long one involving many strategic considerations on the part of both campaigns.* (italics added)[60]

If debates are to be institutionalized certainly the League feels that they should come along as sponsors. Although (as we see later) the League came under a good deal of criticism, they have by this time become debate experts. No other single group has had the amount of debate sponsorship experience (in both primaries and general elections) that the League has had. Indeed, despite a clamoring from many groups to sponsor presidential debates in the general elections since 1976 only the League has done so. As a result of these League-sponsored quadrennial debates, its leadership has taken on a different, more prominent, public presence.

For almost 2 decades now, the League's national presidents have had significant mass media exposure as spokespersons for the ensuing debates in presidential elections. There is little question among rank

and file Leaguers that one significant unofficial qualification for election as president of the League has become the ability to work with
politicians, campaign advisers, mass media personnel, and presidential candidates—in short, the ability to bring about and coordinate all
of the elements and personnel associated with televised presidential
debates. League presidents, like American presidents, must be able to
project a positive *image* as well as understand political *issues*. Although
the latter attribute has been part of the League's experience from its
beginnings, the former is largely a result of debate activities com-
mencing with the preparations for the 1976 presidential election.

In its attempt at planning from election to election, and then from
debate to debate, the national League has worked closely with its locals
to establish a modicum of continuity, sharing some administrative
debate experience, and "prepping" future local leaders. In 1980, for
example, anticipating that a debate would be held in their city, local
leaders from the Louisville League monitored preparations in Baltimore. Political maneuvering among local League leaders gave the
second presidential debate site to Cleveland.[61] Louisville would have
to wait 4 more years.

Still, all the debate planning in the world will be for naught if the
concepts and procedures under which they are to be held are basically
flawed, as was evidenced in Louisville.

The Louisville Debate. Much of the negotiations for the first 1984
presidential debate could have been anticipated beforehand. There
was the usual jockeying among candidate advisers to gain the best
conditions for their candidates. Among other minutia, placement of
podiums, lights, and even the backdrop were of concern to the negotiators. Mondale's camp wanted a black backdrop; Reagan's associates
insisted upon blue. But these were minor disagreements compared to
those in the panel selection process. That task brought the League,
the candidates representatives and members of the press into ha-
ranguing in public.

On October 6, the day before the debate, Ridings called a press
conference and began a tirade against the candidates' representatives'
behavior in negotiations to set the panel of questioners. Because this
was the first time that "secret" negotiations were publicly revealed in
such a manner, and because its relevance for format considerations is
paramount, it may prove instructive to examine Ridings remarks:

> [Ridings names three panelists for the Louisville debate and two for the
> Philadelphia vice presidential debate.] We regret that this announce-
> ment is late in coming. The selection process this year has been slow. We

declined up to now to comment on the reasons for this slowness because *we did not want the selection process to interfere with the seriousness and the purpose of the debates themselves. This year, however, the process has been abused.*

In our negotiations with the campaigns *the League agreed to submit lists of journalists for each debate, and we did this.* We submitted names of highly qualified journalists, 12 for each debate, grouped by their known expertise in the issue areas of each debate. They also are individuals we knew would ask incisive questions that would elicit substantive answers. In addition, we sought professional diversity; panelists would represent broadcast and print journalism. We also were looking for women and men and for minorities. Every person on our list was unquestionably qualified. They're all first rate journalists and superb questioners. So you can imagine our great dismay and disappointment to learn that most names were being vetoed by both campaigns. *This process was the same one we used in 1976, and not one name was struck that year. In 1980 a similar process was used, and while some names were struck, the panel was selected from the League's original list.* Ironically, we agreed to a panel reluctantly this year because we prefer a format using a single moderator. And now the selection process that we agreed to in good faith has been abused. After exhausting our initial lists we ended up submitting close to 100 names—again, all journalists with impeccable credentials—to both campaigns.

At this point only the three persons I have named are acceptable to both campaigns. We will have a debate tomorrow. But whether it is only with a panel of three, or if we are able to resolve this conflict today, I can only speculate at this moment.

The League remains committed to the concept of face-to-face debate among candidates for the highest office in the United States. There is a future for debates. Indeed, presidential debates are an expected and anticipated part of the campaigns. Similarly, *journalists as panelists, have become an integral part of the debate.* With massive problems and confusion resulting this year from the panelists selection process we'll require some soul-searching after this series is concluded. Thank you and I will be happy to answer your questions. (italics added)[62]

In the subsequent question-and-answer period, Ridings revealed that all parties had agreed to a panel with a moderator and four journalists, but "unfortunately our fourth panelist that we had agreement on and whom I asked to serve as panelist, Charlie McDowell of the *Richmond Times-Dispatch*, withdrew . . . because of his belief, which is similar to ours, that the debate format should use a moderator only and no panelists."

The League now assumed a firm stance: No more lists; either the candidates' negotiators agree on a journalist from the lists already provided, or the debate will include only three panelists.

   This press conference finally revealed the negative effects of the panel selection process essentially used by the League since 1976. In that year Richard Salant, former president, CBS News, then vice chairman of the Board, NBC, got into a brouhaha with League representatives about the method of selecting journalists. Salant's position, which is generally upheld by the press fraternity, was that neither the interviewee nor their representatives should have a voice in determining who the interviewers should be. The League's position was that some input from the candidates was necessary so that the (interviewers) panelists would be perceived as being "fair."[63]

   Ridings admitted that the selection process should be reexamined, and allowed that the "procedures required soul searching." She referred to the well-publicized incident in 1980 when George Will, the columnist, and political analyst for ABC, breifed Reagan prior to his debate with President Carter; he then "participated as a journalist in commentary after the debate."

   The panel selection process has been fraught with problems, causing continual disputes, raising format criticisms, and even nagging at the credibility of the debates. Now, during this remarkable League press conference, the issue was put succinctly when a reporter asked, "As you explained, the process involved the campaigns being able to say yes or no on these [journalists] people, right? [Ridings agrees] So how is the process abused if that's what they did? Are you saying that they were just too picky?" Ridings replied:

> Naturally we assumed that any strikes [sic] would be made for . . . a reason that would be considered partly political, partly campaign-strategy-oriented. We would not want a panelist with whom one candidate felt very uncomfortable, or whom they felt was biased towards their campaign, which was the reason we agreed to this process in the beginning. We feel that the process was abused and that many superfluous and unnecessary reasons were used to strike . . . There is no way . . . we could have given them 100 names of highly qualified journalists and end up with three. No way!

   But the way led to only three panelists, despite the League's desperate attempt to enlist Barbara Walters as both panelist and moderator. Walters refused in a symbolic protest against the process, but not the League. What occurred the following evening in the Robert S. Whitney Hall of the Kentucky Center for the Arts was, in effect, a "public demonstration" of *who* controls *how* presidential debates shall be conducted. It was also the first international display[64] of the League's inability, or refusal, to override the candidates vetoes, overcoming the final authority of the candidates.

Journalists responded with sharp, formidable criticisms against the selection process and the League's handling of it. Alfred R. Hunt, Chief of the Washington Bureau of the *Wall Street Journal,* among others, attacked the process: "only three journalists could be found who weren't blackballed by one of the campaigns and were willing to abide by this abysmal process."[65] Daniel Schorr, CNN news commentator, said the League had been "roundheeled . . . It should be their debate and they shouldn't let anyone dictate to them."[66]

Other critics lambasted the League and called for its dismissal from presidential debates sponsorship. *Broadcasting,* the leading industry publication interviewed two broadcasters who were negotiators in the Kennedy–Nixon debates. Frank Stanton, President Emeritus of CBS Inc. said, "I don't see any need for the League. We didn't have it in 1960." Leonard Reinsch, who was John Kennedy's chief debate adviser, joined Stanton in insisting that, "The purpose of presidential debates would be better served if the League of Women Voters were not involved."[67] And even one of the League's long time advisers, Newton N. Minow (former FCC chairman), suggested after the debates that the two major political parties should sponsor (run) the debates. Losing a panelist, however, evidently did not disturb the candidates' negotiators.

Both campaigns conducted mock debates in advance, with no-holds-barred questions posed by stand-ins for Mondale and Reagan.[68] The usual briefing books were prepared and studied. Strategies were argued and decided upon. Issues were examined in detail. Image considerations—ways of projecting a certain demeanor—were rehearsed. So intense were these preparations for the first debate that other aspects of the campaigns were brought to a virtual halt. The growing body of televised debate research and the experience of previous campaigns combined to form an immense resource commanding the attention of both advisers and candidates. It was evident that even the candidates' preparations for debate had been "institutionalized."

As the Louisville debate progressed, an extremely interesting reaction was developing among the audience in the hall. President Reagan was being perceived as losing control of the debate; Mondale appeared to be in command. The astonishment among members of the press and other guests invited to watch the debates in Whitney Hall was evident: Mondale, "the erstwhile wimp,"[69] bettered Reagan, the "great communicator."[70]

Reagan's advisers were concerned and adjustments were made for the second debate in Kansas City. Meanwhile, however, of immediate concern was the preparations for the vice presidential debate in Philadelphia. Two major considerations emerged from the initial debate: (a) the marred panelist selection process and the League were now under close scrutiny by the press and politicians; and (b) both candidates' performances in Louisville raised questions about the effect the interim debate between Vice President George Bush and Congresswoman Geraldine A. Ferraro would have on the campaigns.

The Philadelphia Vice Presidential Debate. There was a sense of excitement as well as a seriousness of purpose with the approaching of the vice presidential debate. Anticipating the first time that a woman debated in such a setting gave the press a reason to continue with one of the most covered events/issues in a presidential election (see chap. 4). The public's response to Mondale's success in the first debate gave the Mondale–Ferraro campaign a much needed boost: Using conservative figures, the gap was reduced by 6 points, from 18 to 12, providing some justification to the "horse race" press coverage that is associated with debates (see chaps. 4 and 5).

Hidden behind the seriousness of the event were some rather picayune concerns about technical details that ostensibly affect a candidate's television *image* and, presumably, *votes*. These details appear in negotiations from debate to debate. It will be recalled that in 1976 Carter and Ford were measured from their belt buckles to the floor so that the height of their podiums could be adjusted providing equal torso framing on the television screen. This year Ferraro needed some height adjustment:

> Nothing was overlooked by the two campaigns, down to the tiniest detail. *My height* compared to Bush's *was going to be a disadvantage for me.* He's over six feet. I'm five feet four inches. The Democrats didn't want him to be looking down at me or, more important, me looking up at him. Over Republican objections, we had a gently inclining ramp built out of the same material as the floor covering so that as I took my place behind the podium I would be closer to the same height as Bush without having to step up on anything. (italics added)[71]

Evidently, the candidate with the taller torso on American households' television sets better vends his or her candidacy to voters than the unfortunate candidate with the smaller torso. Lacking specific scientific evidence, debate television consultants insist on making such adjustments.[72]

In negotiations, the Democrats wanted face-to-face debates, but the Republicans vetoed that in favor of the usual press panel. This time the direct approach was nixed because of public perceptions about a spirited woman debating a decorous vice president. Before the debate Ferraro told two columnists that "she could hit him as hard as she liked, and he would not be able to return her fire in kind for fear as being cast as a bully."[73]

But Ferraro, the feisty campaigner, would be handicapped by the format, "unable" to confront Bush directly. Only one time during the debate had she found a way to circumvent the questioner and get to Bush directly. In response to Bush's statement, "Let me help you with the difference, Mrs. Ferraro, between Iran and the Embassy in Lebanon," she asserted, "Let me just say, first of all, that I almost resent, Vice President Bush, your patronizing attitude that you have to teach me about foreign policy." Curiously, however, the questioners avoided one of the most publicized issues in the campaign.

The most unique part of the general election was Ferraro's candidacy that ultimately found her in a quagmire of questions about her family's alleged association with organized crime figures. Despite increased media reports on this issue during September and early October, none of these questions were raised during the debate. Nor, had they appeared to disturb her debate preparations.

Robert Barnett, a Washington-based lawyer who had been involved in preparations for Mondale's 1976 vice presidential debate, acted as coordinator of a special debate staff for Ferraro. This staff came up with an 8 pound briefing book[74] that Ferraro studied nightly, for 2 weeks prior to the debate.

Additional preparations included the now-common practice of rehearsing the debate. Ferraro was questioned by "panelists" on several occasions, and just days before the debate went into a New York television studio where Barnett played Bush. The studio included a complete mock-up of the actual stage setting in Philadelphia. For 2 days these rehearsals were taped, studied, and criticized.

After the campaign, Ferraro described the contrived rehearsals:

> All the candidates were doing it, of course. Mondale. Reagan. Bush. But that's what always made these debates so phony. You get to say so little, and what you say is so well rehearsed that I'm not sure the public has any more idea of what the candidates really stand for than it did before the debate. And besides, that's not what a real debate is all about. A real debate involves a direct exchange between the opponents, a point-counterpoint. But the formats for these political debates have dictated that the results are contrived—more like theater than an intellectual contest.[75]

Somehow each time some one proposes some form of a classical debate format somebody, usually with the "upperhand" in negotiations, squelches the suggestion. It appears that we will have to wait for the "right" conditions, whatever they may be, for such debates. Those conditions, evidently, were not present for the final 1984 debate.

The Kansas City Debate. The net assessment of the Bush–Ferraro debate had been essentially a "draw" although the polls placed Bush slightly ahead (see chap. 4). In essence, the vice presidential debate, interesting for its historical import, did nothing significant to the momentum of the campaigns. Anticipation of the second presidential debate stemmed from how the two candidates dispatched themselves in Louisville.

Reagan's poor showing in the first debate astonished many political pundits. He appeared to be confused and distracted.[76] Reagan's unexpected performance raised questions about his age and his competence. Similarly, Mondale's unanticipated forceful performance prompted the media to reflect on their earlier appraisal of him as a "wimp" campaigner (see chap. 4). Certainly, the media expected the President's demeanor in this debate to either dispel the age issue or to exacerbate it further. Consequently, both the press and the campaigns looked to the Kansas City debate as a deciding factor in the last stages of the election. Both camps' preparations, therefore, considered the public perceptions of the contenders' performances in the Louisville debate.

This time the President's campaign advisers were not allowed to rehearse him with the kind of detail and rigorous questioning that had gone on in preparations for Louisville with David Stockman as Mondale's stand-in. Senator Paul Laxalt, the President's friend and confidant, attributed Reagan's lackluster display in Louisville to an arduous, artificial, preparation process that "brutalized" the President.[77] For the first debate, the rehearsals did not help Reagan to be himself—at ease and in control. Germond and Witcover, two of the most experienced presidential campaign watchers among members of the press, suggested that:

> [To insure that Reagan would be] relaxed and confident . . . his debate coaches decided . . . to employ a tactic most surprising in dealing with a professional actor of long experience. Their repeated criticisms of the President's answers in the rehearsals for the first debate had seemed to discourage him, so the second time around they intentionally applied an old-fashioned ego massage from time to time to keep his spirits up. . . . [T]he President of the United States, like any uncertain schoolboy, was given encouraging words when he came up with the right answers.[78]

Mondale, buoyed by besting Reagan in Louisville, and encouraged by the subsequent media reports, went all out for this last debate. He bypassed the Al Smith dinner in New York and intensified his preparations for the Kansas City encounter.

On the night of the debate, journalists in the press room were readying the tools of the trade, anticipating that the age issue would be of prime importance. Germond and Witcover noted media's attention to the age issue:

> The agreed-upon subject on this cool late October night in Kansas City was foreign policy. But the age issue was on the minds of all those crowded into the classic old theater. . . . In the 2 weeks since the first debate, . . . the question of Reagan's competence fueled a continuing stream of newspaper and television commentary.[79]

Many journalists came armed with potential "sidebars" and "shooting scripts" relating to Reagan's age and Mondale's new found television acumen. It was indeed curious that the last debate, a discussion of foreign policy some 2 weeks before voters would elect the next President of the United States, many members of the credentialed press corps were hunting around for stories on the effects of old age.[80]

The hunt, however, was short-lived. The age issue emerged early in the debate and was summarily dismissed with "One Hell of a One-Liner."[81]

Panelist Henry Trewitt of *The Baltimore Sun* raised the age issue: "You already are the oldest President in history. . . . I recall . . . that President Kennedy . . . had to go for days on end with very little sleep during the Cuban missile crisis. Is there any doubt in your mind that you would be able to function in such circumstances?"

Reagan replied, "Not at all Mr. Trewitt. And I want you to know that also I will not make age an issue in this campaign. I am not going to exploit, for political purposes, my opponent's youth and inexperience."

That exchange gave the audience in the theater, including the press corps invited to observe the debate from the balcony, a good minute's worth of hilarity. Germond and Witcover observed that reporters in the press room "nodded knowingly to each other; . . . for all practical purposes, the presidential election of 1984 was over."[82]

What had just begun, however, was a public examination of the way in which debates should be administered, an examination that was unlike others that had been undertaken in the past.[83]

Concluding Remarks

Any serious review of how debates come about will show that the candidates control the negotiation process, largely with the threat of nonparticipation, or with the ability to publicly embarrass sponsors and broadcasters.

Candidates' agents—campaign and television experts—insist upon control of factors relating to their expertise and or responsibility. These candidate surrogates jockey among themselves, seeking to gain one or another advantage for the campaign and the candidate. They want to have their way. Having their way on even the most insignificant detail reinforces their perception of controlling factors that they believe will help their candidate to come out of the debate ahead of the opposition. Hence, their concern over details is directly related to their perceived control of the negotiations. Each campaign's debate demands are constrained primarily, if not only, by the opposing campaign's counter demands.

Simply, then, debate negotiators insist on control because they want to move debate elements in favor of their candidate. Their reasoning runs from controlling negotiations to winning the election:

1. Controlling the negotiations increases favorable formats for candidate.
2. Favorable formats increases likelihood of achieving favorable exposure for candidate.
3. Favorable exposure increases likelihood of winning the debate.
4. Winning the debate increases probability of winning the election.

Advisers are not fools. They know that who wins the debate is of vital interest to the media. They know that the media, along with the public polls, play a significant role in determining who won a given debate. An investigation into media's role in covering televised debates (chap. 4) reveals a peculiarly interesting symbiotic relationship between debate negotiators and journalists.

ENDNOTES

1. Remarks by Jack Kelly CBS pool producer for the 1976 San Francisco debate in, Sidney Kraus (Ed.), "Presidential Debates De-Briefing," Crystal City Marriott, Arlington, Virginia, November 30, 1976, unpublished transcription, p. 123.

2. Newspapers and editors were powerful influencers of presidential campaigns. Horace Greely, Joseph Medill, Dr. Charles H. Ray, among others, were newspapermen who coached and advised Lincoln. In preparing for his Cooper Union speech, Lincoln consulted with Medill and Ray, both of whom offered several suggestions. Lincoln thanked them, but did not alter any part of the speech based on Medill's and Ray's suggestions. "Greely was a master showman, an amiable medicine man, an eccentric with high principles, a mass of unresolved contradictions . . . a vital role . . . was played by influential editors and their newspapers and by Lincoln's own knowledge of the press, and how to use it . . ." See, Tebbel and Watts, *op.cit.,* pp. 168–176. "Ray and Lincoln . . . co-authored the original Republican Party platform. Ray helped plan the Lincoln-Douglas debates, gave them national publicity, and presumed to coach Lincoln privately on both his argument and platform manner." See, Jay Monaghan, *The Man Who Elected Lincoln* (Indianapolis: Bobbs-Merrill, 1956) p. viii.

3. On March 6, 1857, just 2 days after the inauguration of James Buchanan as the 15th President, Roger B. Taney, Chief Justice of the Supreme Court, read for more than 2 hours the opinion of the Court in *Dred Scott v. Sanford.* Scott, a Negro slave, wanted to be a free man. The Court set in place two new rules interpreting the Constitution: 1) Negroes could not become U.S. citizens, or a state citizen; 2) Congress did not have the power to exclude slavery from the federal territories. For a thorough discussion of the case see, Don E. Fehrenbacher, *The Dred Scott Case: Its Significance in American Law and Politics* (New York: Oxford University Press, 1978).

4. It should be noted that these debates for the U.S. Senate included several references to the coming (1860) presidential election. For example, Lincoln was convinced that a Republican victory at the polls would, eventually, end the pro-slavery Supreme Court position. In the Galesburg debate Lincoln said, "It is my opinion that the Dred Scott decision, as it is, never would have been made in its present form if the [Democratic] party that made it had not been sustained previously by the elections. My own opinion is, that the new Dred Scott decision, deciding against the right of the people of the States to exclude slavery, will never be made, if that party is not sustained by the elections." *Debates of Lincoln and Douglas* (Columbus: Follett, Foster, 1860) p. 185.

5. These debates occurred as follows:
1st debate—Ottawa, August 21
2nd—Freeport, August 27
3rd—Jonesboro, September 15
4th—Charleston, September 18
5th—Galesburg, October 7
6th—Quincy, October 13
7th—Alton, October 15

6. See, for example, a discussion of the differences in preparations for the Lincoln–Douglas debates and those of the 1960 Kennedy–Nixon debates,

New York Times, September 26, 1960, p. 25. A comparison of the press coverage of the 1858 debates and those of today is in the next chapter, p. 77.

7. In 1964 Senator Barry Goldwater and his supporters vigorously tried to
involve President Johnson in debates, but the incumbent was at the peak of
his popularity and so ignored the appeals to debate. Likewise, for reasons of
political advantage by one candidate or the other, presidential elections in
1968 and 1972 were conducted without debates.

8. G. Bishop, R. Meadow, and M. Jackson-Beeck (Eds.), *The Presidential
Debates: Media, Electoral, and Policy Perspectives* (New York: Praeger, 1978); L.
Bitzer and T. Rueter, *Carter vs. Ford: The Counterfeit Debates of 1976* (Madison:
University of Wisconsin Press, 1980); S. Chaffee, "Presidential Debates—Are
They Helpful to Voters?" *Communication Monographs,* XLV (1978), 330–346;
S. Kraus (Ed.), *The Great Debates* (Bloomington: Indiana University Press,
1962); S. Kraus (Ed.), *The Great Debates: Carter vs. Ford, 1976* (Bloomington:
Indiana University Press, 1979); M. Martel, *Political Campaign Debates: Images,
Strategies, and Tactics* (New York: Longman, 1983); E. Mazo, M. Moos, H.
Hoffman, and H. Wheeler, *The Great Debates: An Occasional on the Role of the
Political Process in the Free Society* (Santa Barbara: Center for the Study of
Democratic Institutions, 1962); L. Mitchell, *With The Nation Watching: Report
of the Twentieth Century Fund Task Force on Televised Presidential Debates* (Lex-
ington, MA: Heath, 1979); *The Presidential Campaign, 1976: Vol. 3, The Debates*
(Washington, DC: Government Printing Office, 1979); A. Ranney (Ed.), *The
Past and Future of Presidential Debates* (Washington, DC: American Enterprise
Institute, 1979); W. Ritter (Ed.) *The 1980 Presidential Debates.* Special issue of
Speaker and Gavel, XVIII, 2 (1981); J. Swerdlow, *Beyond Debate: A Paper On
Televised Presidential Debates* (New York: The Twentieth Century Fund,
1984).

9. See chap. 4, endnote 2.

10. J. Auer, "The Counterfeit Debates," in Kraus (1962) p. 146; see also
Bitzer and Reuter.

11. L. Milic, "Grilling the Pols: Q & A at the Debates," in Kraus (1979) p.
205.

12. N. Polsby, "Debatable Thoughts on Presidential Debates," in A. Ranney (Ed.) p. 184.

13. Bitzer and Reuter, pp. 225–250.

14. J. Auer, "Great Myths About Great Debates," in Ritter (Ed.), (1981)
pp. 14–21.

15. See Bibliography.

16. M. Martel, "Debate Preparations in the Reagan Camp: An Insider's
View," in Ritter (Ed.) p. 46.

17. R. Sarnoff, "An NBC View," in Kraus (1962), p. 60. This article is
based on a speech delivered to the San Francisco Advertising Club, October 5,
1960.

18. F. Stanton, "A CBS View," in Kraus (1962), p. 70. This article is based
on a speech to the journalism fraternity, Sigma Delta Chi, New York, December 3, 1960.

19. U. S. Government Printing Office. *The Presidential Campaign, 1976: Volume Two, Part Two* (1979) p. 693.

20. *Ibid.*, pp. 704–705.

21. *Ibid.*, p. 705.

22. Letter to Sidney Kraus from Michael Raoul-Duval, Special Counsel to the President, October 27, 1976.

23. With candidates interested in winning the election, not educating the electorate, and with the League of Women Voters *Education* Fund involved, conflicts in format negotiations are inevitable.

24. S. Kraus (Ed.), "Presidential Debates Debriefing" (Unpublished manuscript Transcript of meeting at Crystal City Marriott Inn, Arlington, VA, Nov. 29–30, 1976) pp. 131–132.

25. *Ibid.*, p. 134.

26. In effect, this would have provided television audiences with three *different* formats of the same debate since the three individual network directors could select a variety of shots. Thus, as with any news event, the "editors" would decide which aspects, as the event proceeds, should receive attention. It was precisely this editorial prerogative that the networks defended and the candidates attacked.

27. Kraus, "Debriefing," p. 139.

28. See, for example, H. Terry and S. Kraus, "Legal and Political Aspects: Was Section 315 Circumvented," and R. Salant, "The Good But Not Great Nondebates: Some Random Personal Notes," in Kraus (1979) pp. 3–10 and 175–186, respectively.

29. Kraus, "Debriefing," pp. 114–117.

30. *Ibid.*, pp. 142–147.

31. E. Katz and J. Feldman, "The Debates in the Light of Research: A Survey of Surveys," in Kraus (1962) pp. 193–195; J. Robinson, "The Polls," in Kraus (1979) pp. 262–268.

32. Kraus, "Debriefing," pp. 100–101.

33. Mitchell, *With the Nation Watching* (1979).

34. Broadcast on NBC Radio Network, March 27, 1979.

35. Much of the materials for this and the following section was obtained through interviews and observations by the author as he witnessed the preparations for and attended the 1980 and 1984 presidential debates.

36. During that period the now famous Nashua (New Hampshire) debate between Bush and Reagan occurred. Reagan had just been upset by Bush in the Iowa caucuses. On the night of the debate the other Republican candidates, who had not been invited, began to stroll into the hall. The confusion resulted in a disorderly audience. Reagan began to introduce the other candidates and as the organizer attempted to cut off his microphone Reagan said, "I *paid* for this microphone, Mr. Green." This was indicative of the "new" Reagan who had taken command of his campaign and began to discuss issues.

Reagan said that he "paid for the microphones simply because of that decision by the Federal Election Commission . . . you realize that campaigning is now a government regulated industry and the government regulations prescribe that the paper could no longer sponsor it, and there would be no debate if we didn't put up the money." Transcribed from audio tape of Reagan press conference, Republican Convention, Detroit, July 17, 1980.

37. See, for example, discussions of journalistic and public opinion pre- and postresponses to John F. Kennedy's involvement in the Bay of Pigs and the Cuban missile crisis in David Halberstam, *The Powers That Be,* (New York: Alfred A. Knopf, 1979) pp. 385 and 447–448; and John Tebbel and Sarah Miles Watts, *The Press and the Presidency,* (New York: Oxford Univeristy Press, 1985) pp. 487–488.

38. There were five Republican televised debates between January and April in the primaries of Iowa, New Hampshire, South Carolina, Illinois, and Texas. The League sponsored the New Hampshire, Illinois, and Texas debates. The first primary debate (Iowa) was sponsored by the *Des Moines Register and Tribune.* The third debate (South Carolina) was sponsored by the University of South Carolina, Columbia, and the Columbia Newspapers, Inc. Essentially, the formats were the same as ever, with some modifications (i.e., proximity of candidates, informal and conversational). Carter's attention to Iranian hostages precluded Democratic primary debates. Republicans had seven viable candidates; Democrats had three.

39. "Symbolizing the more personal quality of network news is the relative attention given the debate about debates; first, the Reagan-Anderson debate in Baltimore and then the Carter-Reagan debate in Cleveland. The wire did not ignore the debate-debate issue; but it ranked fourth among all "issues" on UPI. But on CBS it ranked first, at least in hard news coverage. On "Evening News," there was more hard campaign news about the debate-debate than about the hostage "issue" or the economy." M. Robinson and M. Sheehan, *Over The Wire and On TV: CBS and UPI in Campaign '80* (New York: Russell Sage, 1983) p. 209.

40. "In the jockeying that normally preceded them and, even more, when one of the candidates declined to participate, the debates often appeared to become the major issue of the campaign. This was especially true in the sixties, when the 'empty chair debate' flowered as a form of political communication. This was the 'debate' form in which, to dramatize the refusal of an opponent to participate in a more traditional debate, the script called for the candidate to appear on television with an empty chair as a symbol and reminder of the opponent's cowardice." S. Becker and E. Lower, "Broadcasting in Presidential Campaigns, 1960–1976," in Kraus (Ed.) (1979) p. 16.

41. "Statement by Ruth Hinerfeld, Chair, League of Women Voters Education Fund," press release, September 17, 1980.

42. League President, Ruth J. Hinerfeld wrote: "I could find nothing in my notes to substantiate the claim that candidates' reps agreed candidates would question one another." Letter to Sidney Kraus, September 16, 1981.

43. New York *Daily News, Manhattan* magazine, November 15, 1980. See comments about Hanna's views in Swerdlow, *Beyond Debate,* p. 72, note 32.

44. The scene in Baltimore's Convention Center was chaotic. Among the hundreds of chores that remained to be completed in the few days before the

debate, many appeared to be trivial, but were linked to one or another's perception of their role in preparing for this debate. It was in this frenzied atmosphere that negotiations continued: Reagan's representatives forced the removal of 200 VIP seats (just before the debate they were reinstalled); the Baltimore Fire Department, invoking a state law prohibiting propane gas in the Center, forced the removal of two Winnebago motor homes that were brought in for the candidates (they were replaced by curtained areas that prompted Bill Carruthers, Reagan's television expert, to complain about the lack of a washroom facility for Reagan behind the stage)—a third draped room was installed in the event that Carter showed up; rumors circulated that Carter had agreed to a three-way debate in either Louisville or Portland; although Carter's absence alleviated the request for debate tickets, the League met for 4 hours on Saturday to discuss seating arrangements (decisions were made on Sunday); Frey complained to Mayor Schafer about ABC being charged $91 for each hotel room; and the entrance to the Center was being picketed while the press was being chauffeured to and from the Center, courtesy of the City of Baltimore.

45. Every broadcaster that was interviewed by the author supported reaction shots and cut aways as legitimate "copy" for the networks coverage of the debate. Marvin Schlenker, ABC pool director, felt that "the networks will deal responsibly with their requests [for such shots] and I see nothing out of the ordinary for making those requests. That's what broadcast news is about." Joseph Angotti, producer for NBC's coverage, agreed.

46. Interview with L. Hanna, Stouffer Inn, Cleveland, October 16, 1980.

47. *Newsweek* (April 21, 1981) p. 31.

48. Accusations were made that the briefing book was used to advise Reagan in his match with Carter. A House subcommittee and the Justice Department investigated the notion that there was a "mole" in the White House. Reagan supporters claimed that the Carter document was given to them unsolicited. For a complete discussion of this incident see, "Unauthorized Transfers Of NonPublic Information During The 1980 Presidential Election," Report prepared by the Subcommittee on Human Resources of the Committee on Post Office and Civil Service, House of Representatives, Part I and II, U. S. Government Printing Office, May 17, 1984.

49. This information was given to this writer by a board member of the Cleveland League of Women Voters.

50. D. Sears and S. Chaffee, "Uses and Effects of the 1976 Debates: An Overview of Empirical Studies," in S. Kraus (Ed.), *The Great Debates: Carter vs. Ford, 1976, op. cit.,* p. 247.

51. Most of the comments about the performances in the two presidential debates centered on *Reagan:* faltering as the "great communicator" in the first debate; recapturing his "old self" in the second. Less attention was given to Mondale's performance in the two debates taken together.

52. G. Pomper, *op.cit.,* p. 81.

53. In June, Mondale attended the NOW convention where its president, Judy Goldsmith, admonished the Mondale campaign: "We're saying, 'If there

isn't a woman, we don't win.' " Mondale began considering a woman candidate 6 weeks before the Democratic convention.

54. Although the Reverend Jesse Jackson's presidential candidacy did not represent the first time that a Black ran for the office (Representative Shirley Chisholm did so in 1972), his ability to command the public's attention made him an attractive candidate for the media to cover.

55. See, for example, N. W. Polsby, "Debatable Thoughts on Presidential Debates," in A. Ranney (Ed.), *The Past and Future of Presidential Debates,* (Washington, D.C.: American Enterprise Institute, 1979) pp. 175–190. For a fuller discussion of debates and polls see chap. 4.

56. Text of Senator Edward Kennedy's nomination speech before the Democrats' 1984 national convention at the Mascone Convention Center, July 19. Text verified with his television address.

57. Text of Walter F. Mondale's acceptance speech at the Democratic National Convention, July 19, 1984. Text verified with his television address.

58. A seasoned reporter has offered a different interpretation of Reagan's success with television:

> That Reagan had been an actor most of his life has been cited—beyond all previously known limits of redundancy—as the explanation for his success in communicating on television. In my minority opinion, acting background is an all-too-convenient, point-missing rationale for Reagan's effectiveness on camera and microphone . . . experience might help him . . . But what makes Ronald Reagan effective on television is that he is authentic.

See C. Corddry, "Television Politics: The Medium is the Revolution," in P. Duke (Ed.), *Beyond Reagan: The Politics of Upheaveal* (New York: Warner Books, 1986) p. 253.

59. A more generous explanation suggests that "In part, Reagan's decision reflected his love of political debate. He had won the 1980 debate with Carter and had a reputation as an effective verbal contestant. In part, too, Reagan's acceptance reflected his view of what is fair play in politics. Even though Mondale's attacks were not eroding support among voters, Reagan wanted a chance to answer." P. Light and C. Lake, "The Election: Candidates, Strategies, and Decisions," in M. Nelson, *The Elections of 1984* (Washington, DC: Congressional Quarterly Inc., 1985) p. 99.

60. League News Release, "Statement by Dorothy S. Ridings, President, League of Women Voters, At Press Conference Announcing 1984 Presidential Debate Plans, September 17, 1984," Washington, DC.

61. Local Leagues run major public relations campaigns to persuade the national office to select their cities as a site for one of the presidential debates. Often, these efforts include the enlisting of significant city leaders and a fundraising effort (see chap. 6).

62. Transcribed by author from his audio cassette recording at press conference in Galt Hotel, Louisville, KY, October 6, 1984.

63. For a fuller discussion of the selection of panelists in 1976 see Kraus

(1979), especially P. Lampl, "The Sponsor: The League of Women Voters Education Fund," pp. 98–101 and R. Salant, *op. cit.*, pp. 182–184. Salant was also irritated by the League's and candidates' insistence that TV broadcasters not be allowed to take audience reaction shots.

64. Estimates of the U.S. and worldwide audience for presidential debates have ranged from 200 to 250 million.

65. A. Hunt, "The Campaign and the Issues," in A. Ranney (Ed.), *The American Elections of 1984,* p. 150.

66. Quoted in *Broadcasting,* October 15, 1984, p. 37.

67. *Ibid.,* p. 36.

68. Reagan was played by Mondale's professor in law-school, Michael Sovern, and David Stockman, Reagan's budget director, was cast as Mondale.

69. "TV debates: pivotal points for politics," *Broadcasting,* October 15, 1984, p. 35.

70. The author, in attendance, observed both the press and the audience during the debate. Discussions among guests after the debate and subsequent media reports and interviews confirmed this observation. Several researchers and commentators have suggested that audiences watching the debate on television reacted much the same way as those in the Hall. For example: "Reagan was hesitant in his delivery and unsure of his facts, while Mondale gave the more confident and commanding performance." Thomas E. Patterson and Richard Davis, "The Media Campaign: Struggle for the Agenda," in Michael Nelson (Ed.), *The Elections of 1984,* (Washington, DC: Congressional Quarterly, Inc., 1985), p. 121; "inexplicably to all those closest to the President and to millions who admired him from a distance, that 90-minute televised confrontation with Mondale revealed a different Ronald Reagan. The Great Communicator was strangely awkward, halting, even confused before the cameras that had been major instruments in his success, first as an actor, later as a politician." J. Germond and J. Witcover, *Wake Us When It's Over: Presidential Politics of 1984,* (New York: Macmillan, 1985) p. 1.

71. Geraldine A. Ferraro, *Ferraro: My Story,* (New York: Bantom Books, 1985), p. 243. For Ford-Carter measurements see H. Seltz and D. Yoakam, "Production Diary of the Debates," in Kraus (1979) p. 122.

72. There is, however, evidence demonstrating that such factors may affect voter-viewers' decisions. For a brief review see, S. Kraus, "The Studies and The World Outside," in S. Kraus and R. Perloff, *Mass Media and Political Thought: An Information Processing Approach* (Beverly Hills: Sage, 1985) pp. 318–320.

73. J. Germond and J. Witcover, *Wake Us When It's Over,* p. 519.

74. There appears to be a tendency for the media to ask about the weight of debate briefing books (they have ranged from 6 to 12 pounds). For the media's handling of debate briefing activities see Chapter Four.

75. G. Ferraro, *Ferraro: My Story,* p. 247.

76. His persona was strikingly similar to Richard Nixon's in his first 1960 debate with John F. Kennedy in Chicago. Both were tired and drawn. Both

appeared to be struggling with portions of their answers. And both received low marks in the press and public opinion polls. Reagan, however, was elected to a second term as president; Nixon would have to wait 8 years for his first term.

77. See J. Germond and J. Witcover, *op. cit.,* pp. 2–3.

78. *Ibid.,* p. 3.

79. *Ibid.,* p. 2.

80. Given the fact that an incumbent aging president was running for another term, it was a legitimate issue for the press to explore. Their role in setting the "age agenda," however, raises questions about the relationship between the media and these debates. The topic of media's role in reporting and participating in presidential debates is detailed in the next chapter.

81. Germond and Witcover's chapter title, *op. cit.,* pp. 1–15.

82. *Ibid.,* p. 9.

83. Televised presidential debates have been assessed in many different ways by scholars, professionals, and other individuals and groups with varying interests and competencies. The first major debate debriefing conference occurred after the 1976 debates with representatives from the following: Carter, Ford, League of Women Voters, network television, journalists, scholars, FCC legal advisers, and the John and Mary R. Markle Foundation (S. Kraus, Chair, "Presidential Debates De-briefing," Crystal City Marriott, Arlington, Virginia, November 29–30, 1976, transcribed by N. W. Kramer, Brooklyn, New York).

4

DEBATE COVERAGE:
WHO'S WINNING

Dan Rather: *Do you think the election will be decided with the televised debates?*

Warren Mitofsky *(representing CBS/New York Times Carter-Ford debate poll): Yes. But with the provision that* a candidate has won the debate if they're told that by the reporters. I don't think the people have any view of this on their own without extra help.[1]

In the second debate of 1976 between Jimmy Carter and Gerald Ford, the incumbent President blundered when he twice insisted that Eastern Europeans were not under the domination of the Soviet Union.[2] Most media analysts concluded that Ford had lost the debate. It appeared as though the gaffe had cost Ford that leg of the race. But, in an important study, interviews with eligible voters within 12 hours after the debate revealed that Carter had lost and Ford won. Voters interviewed between 12 and 48 hours after the confrontation, however, gave the win to Carter. Thomas Patterson, a political scientist who conducted the study, concluded, "The passing of time required for the news to reach the public brought with it a virtual reversal of opinion."[3]

It was evident that the media thought Ford had lost the confrontation by the reaction of the press to the Eastern Europe comment on the night of the debate. Members of both the invited press and those in the working press room at the debate site[4] made such remarks as:

"This will cost Ford the election." "A major faux pas." "Now, they're even." "Ford not only fumbled, he made headlines." "Carter wasn't that sharp, but he didn't need to be. Ford lost it."[5] That night in the press room, many reporters thought Ford's remarks would damage his candidacy. A study of ethnic voters in Cleveland after the election found Eastern Europeans disapproving Ford's statement. The remark played an important part in the vote decisions of those who had watched the debate, but, those who heard of it from mediated sources were less impressed.[6]

Another study, this one of the first 1976 presidential debate, found that those watching the debate and free from outside influences (immediate response group) felt Carter was the winner, whereas viewers who responded a few days after the debate (mediated response group) claimed Ford had won. Lang and Lang concluded that:

> *The contaminated group must have been influenced by communications about the debate to which no one in the controlled-exposure condition could possibly have been exposed.* . . . over time. . . each persons impressions were constantly tested against those of others, including interpretative and analytic commentaries offered by authoritative mass media sources.[7]

These studies clearly show that media mediates between political events and the interpretation of them by voters. This should not surprise us, if for no other reason than voters have learned to depend on news media to inform them about events. It makes immanent sense that people look to credible news sources for selecting and interpreting current events. It may be surprising to some critics to learn that CBS News' "hard political coverage [in the 1980 presidential campaign] . . . was more personal; *more mediating;* more analytical; more 'political'; more critical; and more thematic" than the United Press International wire service.[8]

Notwithstanding Mitofsky's statement that people need extra help to determine debate winners, *reporters* may miscalculate initial public reactions to debates. Perhaps reporters' opinions, perceived as being authoritative, persuade voters with earlier contrary opinions to change. Jeff Greenfield, one of the more erudite political commentators, agreed with Mitofsky and explains Patterson's finding by declaring that:

> [M]any of the people watching the debates will not really know what they have seen until the next-day['s] notices tell them (Ford's Eastern Europe blunder, for example, was not understood as such by the bulk of the electorate until the commentators pointed out the foolishness of

Ford's no-Soviet-domination remark). Given the arcane nature of most debate questions and answers, the audience tends to be in the position of a theatergoer attending a preview, and saying, "I can't wait to read the reviews so I'll know what I thought about this."[9]

Without the "extra help" from the media the public apparently had made their initial assessments of the debate. With that "help" they changed their minds. Despite all of the 1976 debate commentaries, analyses, and research on the electorate, it has not been confirmed that the audience failed to understand, or was uncertain about Ford's comment until the press clarified it. What has been corroborated is that voters were persuaded by the media to change their minds. Media's calling of the race at that time in the election influenced voters' assessments of the candidates' debate performance, and may have had an effect on the outcome of the election.

Adam Clymer, Mitofsky's counterpart at the *New York Times,* takes a similar view about the mass media's influence: "Debates in 1960 and 1976 and the public opinion polls taken after them have suggested that the candidate who wins (or at least the one that newspapers and television say has won) gains, at least in the short run." He interpreted debate polling data and concluded that, "He who wins [the debate] gains [in the election]."[10]

Mitofsky's assertion of the relationship between reporters and voters (derived from his experience with polling for reactions to presidential debates), and Greenfield's declaration that most television viewers have difficulty in processing debate questions and answers, raises two important considerations about political reporting in a democratic society: (a) How do the media report on presidential debates? and (b) What are the effects of televised presidential debates on voters?

The second question is addressed in the next chapter. Here we are concerned with media coverage of televised debates. The exchange between Rather and Mitofsky is illustrative of *the* major component in media's coverage of presidential elections and debates—predicting and assessing winners and losers.

PREDICTING AND ASSESSING WINNERS AND LOSERS

Critics disdain televised presidential debates for: (a) creating in voters' minds a lasting impression of the personalities and images of candidates; (b) displaying a lack of concern for detailed discussions of substantive issues facing the country; (c) allowing a press panel to ask questions and permitting candidates to dodge them; (d) counterfeiting the classical debate format; (e) bringing about press reports on winners and losers; and (f) debasing what should be sacrosanct to the polity; and making an entertainment game of it all. It has been suggested that:

> [Media] *coverage focuses on identifying a winner while neglecting conflict over positions on issues. There is a real danger that the debates are becoming another campaign sideshow staged by and for the media to attract and entertain a politically apathetic audience.*[11]

As yet, no one has suggested a conspiracy among candidates, sponsors, and the media to maintain the televised debate in its current format, or to report debate items emphasizing the *race*. But some critics (opponents and conditionals) fail to consider, or refuse to accept, three basic factors about televised presidential debates. First, debates are expected to "gain an audience decision."[12] Second, they are part of a campaign that culminates in a winner and a loser. Third, televised presidential debate coverage is reflective of a society that largely enjoys a contest and wants to be entertained. One could argue, at least in light of these factors, that the media capture the quintessence of a presidential election by monitoring the race. This view of media coverage may be more symbolic of society's condition than exemplary of democracy's goals.

Presidential debates were born into an emerging television culture in 1960, and reborn in an established one in 1976. It will require some fundamental changes in the polity, reflected in mass information systems, to ameliorate several of the critics' objections. Still, it is important to consider some of these in the light of cultural experience and political history as we examine media debate coverage.

Americans are competitive and want to win. Winning and losing are ultimate measures of a variety of activities engaged in by Americans. Each week the media report on one race or another—game shows, lotteries, Miss America, sporting events, political races, and many more. We adulate the winners and disdain the losers. From early childhood on, many of us learn that recognition, acceptance, reward, and/or status can be achieved by doing something better than someone else, or better than we had done earlier. Elementary school students compete for grades and leadership in clubs. High school students compete in a variety of sports, and for admission to colleges. College and professional baseball, basketball, and football are followed assiduously by millions who, each week, cheer on their team to a hoped-for victory. Americans are *fans* who want to be *entertained*. Americans are socialized into *winning*. So are politicians and journalists.

And so were Americans in 1858, the year of the Lincoln–Douglas debates. These debates were held in an historic American period. They were and remain very important as a symbol of free elections and American political debate. They were also in a political campaign that was covered by a press with trappings, except for technology, not unlike those of today. In that respect it is relevant that this discussion of media coverage explore the mythology that persists today about those "Great Debates."

The Myth of the Lincoln–Douglas Debates

It has been an anathema to some critics that televised presidential debates have been called *Great Debates*. But it is interesting to note that in 1858 and in 1960 *Great* was used by the *media* to mark the debates *before* they occurred. Both debates were recommended by journalists. The senatorial debates between Lincoln and Douglas were first proposed by the *Chicago Tribune;* the idea for televised presidential debates also was suggested by a former journalist.[13]

Critics extol the debates between Lincoln and Douglas as exemplary of the American debate tradition. Critiques of presidential debates often include comparisons to the Lincoln–Douglas debates.[14] David Zarefsky pointed out that Mondale hoped to debate the issues "in as enlightened a tone as that of the Lincoln–Douglas debates." Zarefsky suggested that:

> His was not an isolated call. Especially since television debates have become commonplace, the 1858 encounters on the Illinois prairie are frequently held up as the paridgm case of what public political debate ought to be and as a measure of how far we have fallen from grace.[15]

With the possible exception of John F. Kennedy, none of the presidential debaters' use of language and argument approached that of both Lincoln and Douglas. However, presidential debates have not included issues of the magnitude of "Slavery and Freedom," except under abstract and general terms.[16]

Combining several of the criticisms, the comparision with televised versus the live Lincoln–Douglas debates and the arguments against the debates in their present form go somewhat like this:

- Lincoln–Douglas encounters were essentially *genuine* debates; televised presidential debates are *counterfeit*.

- Lincoln–Douglas faced each other, confronted each other, and were left to their own devices without a group of reporters intervening in the debate as they do presently.
- Change the format of the presidential debates in the direction of those in the Lincoln–Douglas encounters and voter-viewers will be impressed less by candidates' personalities and more by the their discussions of issues.
- Change the format and it is likely that changes in media's dominant coverage of winners and losers will follow.
- Change the format and the debate will not be perceived as entertainment, but as a bona fide news event.

The Lincoln–Douglas debates are held as representative of the kind of debate format that furthers democratic ideals and maintains the great American debate tradition. In an important way they have been a symbol of American democracy. They are renowned for rhetorical achievements rarely displayed in a political campaign. But the Lincoln legend so exalts the 1858 debates that some similarities between them and the current debates—between political debaters, their audiences, and the media then and now—have gone largely unnoticed. And "too often, the debates are considered wholly apart from the political struggles of which they are an important part."[17]

The objectives of this comparative analysis are fourfold: (a) demystify some aspects of the Lincoln–Douglas debates; (b) demonstrate that technology notwithstanding media coverage of the debates in 1858 was not all that different from what we see today; (c) display those behaviors of journalists, politicians, and members of the public that are idiosyncratic and permeate political events such as debates; and (d) decry suggestions that, if employed, the Lincoln–Douglas format would bring about more substantive, and less image, coverage of televised presidential debates.

The beginning of the previous chapter mentions Lincoln's relationship to some of his advisers, most notably two newspapermen, Joseph Medill and Dr. Charles H. Ray. Medill is a familiar name in newspaper history; he played an important role in Lincoln's political career. Dr. Ray, less well known, was editor in chief and (with Medill) one of the owners of the consolidated *Chicago Press and Tribune*.[18] Ray's contribution to Lincoln's participation in the debates is never mentioned when those debates are compared to presidential debates. It is instructive to review how the media (and Lincoln) played an important role in the 1858 debates; and to examine the relationship between candidates, their advisers and the press.

What went on then goes on now. For example, Ray, the newspaper editor, had suggested debate tactics to Lincoln, and engendered favorable publicity for him and negative publicity for Douglas. George Will, the newspaper columnist and television commentator, advised Ronald Reagan prior to the Cleveland debate, and then acclaimed his performance afterward (see chap. 3).

Lincoln was most astute in his relations with the press, some of whom became political operatives in his electoral pursuits.[19] He was an active participant in discussions of tactics to influence the press. Although he lost the 1858 Senate election to Douglas, the publicity generated by the debates propelled him into a prominent position for the Republican nomination in the presidential contest 2 years hence, and contributed to his election.[20]

The relationship between Lincoln and the press is explored in five historical accounts circumscribing the debates with Douglas: Don E. Fehrenbacher, *Prelude to Greatness: Lincoln in the 1850's;* Edwin E. Sparks, editor, *The Lincoln Douglas Debates of 1858;* Paul M. Angle, editor, *Created Equal? The Complete Lincoln Douglas Debates of 1858;* Robert S. Harper, *Lincoln and the Press;* and Jay Monaghan, *The Man Who Elected Lincoln.* Taken together these excellent studies, and a review of newspaper articles in 1858, provide a perspective on how media covered *the* Great Debates in 1858.

Monaghan examined Ray's personal papers, and concluded that "Ray and Lincoln were closely associated. They co-authored the original Republican Party platform. Ray helped plan the Lincoln–Douglas debates, gave them national publicity, and presumed to coach Lincoln privately on both his argument and platform manner."[21]

Media's active involvement with the Lincoln–Douglas debate was evident from the beginning. Monaghan wrote:

> On trains, in hotels, everywhere, Ray had been asked questions about this man who dared challenge Douglas. They wanted to know his age, profession, appearance, and every possible personal detail.
>
> The publicized challenge was finally accepted by Douglas on August 3, 1858. An exchange of letters specified arrangements for debates in the state's seven congressional districts. Lincoln's opportunity had come at last. He went into retirement to prepare his speeches. The *Press and Tribune* reorganized its staff in order that it might lead all other newspapers in reporting the campaign. To transcribe the arguments word for word, a shorthand expert, Robert R. Hitt [see later], was employed.
>
> The first debate was held at Ottawa on August 21, 1858, but the audience began to arrive the night before. Farmers came in wagons and on horseback. The hotels and private houses were crowded. Many people slept in their own bedding at the livery stables. Soon even these accommodations were filled, and latecomers camped by their carriages

along the river bottoms or beside the Illinois and Michigan Canal. Their campfires at midnight resembled any army bivouac. In the morning the crowd thronged the dusty streets and public square. Douglas had brought his charming wife to town. Other women had come by dozens to enjoy the gaiety. Booths for the sale of lemonade and watermelons lined the streets. Peddlers offered painkillers and ague cures. Jugglers tossed balls, then passed hats for coins. Beggars and pickpockets pushed their way through the throng. Brass bands made the air pulse with "Columbia the Gem of the Ocean."[22]

Most anyone who has examined the preparations for a presidential debate could, with minor emendations, describe them using much of Monaghan's depiction of the 1858 predebate events. Today, the media provide more details and more hype about debates than they did in 1858; that may be due to the difference in media technology—the ability to transmit information with "live" presentations instantly. Essentially, media cover the debates today as they did over a century ago, treating the event as a spectacle.

The Illinois press made a spectacle of the Ottawa debate. Harper found that, "The first debate was publicized as though it were a championship prizefight, and perspiring thousands converged on Ottawa that hot August Saturday."[23] Headlines indicated the press' concern with, and the public's interest in, who won or lost the debate. *Chicago's Press and Tribune* featured an article: DRED SCOTT CHAMPION PULVERIZED;[24] the other Chicago paper, the *Times*, described the fight in headlines:[25]

THE CAMPAIGN

Douglas Among the People.
Joint Discussion at Ottawa!
Lincoln Breaks Down.
Enthusiasms of the People!
Lincoln's Heart Fails Him!
Lincoln's Legs Fail Him!
Lincoln's Tongue Fail Him!
Lincoln's Arms Fail Him!
Lincoln Fails All Over!
The People Refuse to
Support Him!
The People Laugh at Him!
Douglas the Champion
of the People!

These assessments were typical of the media coverage of the encounters between Lincoln and Douglas. This kind of coverage—

emphasizing style and spectacle over substance—endures today.[26] Compare these headlines with this one from a *Washington Star* commentary by Russell Baker the day before the 1980 Reagan–Anderson debate in Baltimore:

SHOWDOWN IN BALTIMORE:
THE BOYS IN THE RING

Baker's alliterative lead (concocted, no doubt, for a clever, creative broadcasting boxing announcer) was: "The scene is set, ladies and gentlemen. The air is rife with intimidations of cataclysmic confrontation, yet the combatants are calm and composed as they contemplate the consequences that could concatenate upon failure to conquer fear Sunday night."[27]

In fact, one could argue that the media continue to be attracted by images of winners, but are more *discerning* in their coverage of presidential debates today than they were in Lincoln's generation.

Recording the Debates—Textual Accuracy. Consider just the task of establishing textual accuracy (verbatim recording of the debates), which in 1858 was largely left to the press.

First, there was the issue of bias, aggravated by the ideological positions of the newspapers. The *Chicago Press and Tribune*, identifying with the newly formed Republican Party, supported Lincoln. The newspaper's debate reporter was Horace White; he did not use shorthand. He was assigned to write about the debates and the candidates. Robert R. Hitt, hired by the paper and by Lincoln, was the "*verbatim* reporter, receiving the highest praise from Mr. Lincoln for the accuracy of his work."[28]

For much the same political reasons, Douglas and the Democrats had their journalists who could be counted on to render the "correct" version of a given speech. Henry Binmore invented his own system of phonographic reporting.[29] He was employed by the *Chicago Times*. He shared the debate "beat" with James B. Sheridan who had learned phonography early in its development and became a prominent *Philadelphia Press* reporter. Although he was a "recorder" of the debates, he also wrote descriptive articles for the *Press*.

These two teams—White–Hitt and Binmore–Sheridan—were touted as experts in verbatim "playbacks" of what was said at the debates. Without a detached, disinterested phonographer, and without modern recording devices and press facilities, the two teams of reporters were accused by opposing partisan newspapers of unfairness in reporting the debates. The debate about debate accuracy was common. Each "side" with its own reporters attempted to set the record straight. But often the record refused to be straightened out.

Today the debate "record" poses no problem for most debaters and recorders, and certainly not for the media.[30] Not so in Illinois in 1858, when it was difficult, if not impossible, to find impartiality in news about the Lincoln–Douglas debates.

For example, the *Galesburg Democrat,* after conducting a content analysis of the "reports of the speeches" headlined an article, OUTRAGEOUS FRAUDS, accusing the *Chicago Times* of altering Lincoln's speeches 180 times: "There is scarcely a correctly reported paragraph in the whole speech . . . ! the whole aim had been to . . . make him look like a booby, a half-witted numbskull."[31]

It was reported that Douglas' cohort, "a reporter named Sheridan [was charged with the responsibility] to garble the speeches of Mr. Lincoln and amend and elaborate those of Douglas for the *Times.*"[32] (Shades of *dirty tricks.*[33]) Hitt, recording the seven debates for Lincoln and the *Chicago Press and Tribune,* labored over his transcribed notes and manuscripts before they were set in print. He claimed that he made "no changes . . . except where there was 'some slight hiatus or evident mistake' in taking the speaker's exact words, owing to the turmoil about the reporter. He complained there was often confusion on the platform and that high winds also caused trouble."[34]

Covering the Lincoln–Douglas debates was arduous for reporters who found themselves "forced [into] a new role," frequently unable to adequately observe the contests.[35] Unlike today, it was difficult then to set aside "places," let alone seats, for the press. Local politicians at Illinois debates in 1858 would not be excluded from observing the event firsthand as they were, for example, in Baltimore in 1980.[36] The press attending presidential debates are provided with relatively comfortable facilities. Some of them (usually about 100 or so) sit in the audience along with invited guests and observe the debate directly. Others (usually about 1,500) watch the debate on a large television screen in an exclusive, specially equipped, press room near the debate auditorium. Debate audiences in 1858 were often disorderly and unmanageable, periodically interrupting the proceedings.

Before presidential debates began in 1976, 1980, and 1984 audiences were cautioned by sponsors, and later by moderators, not to display partisanship by laughing, clapping, or otherwise "commenting" on the proceedings. The League of Women Voters dreaded partisan reactions of audiences during televised presidential debates. The press, however, believes that such reactions are interesting and revealing commentaries on presidential candidates' behaviors. Television directors would be quite happy to be "allowed" to find those reactions.[37]

By and large, today's debates are held with much more decorum, are more easily understood by more people, at the debate and immediately afterwards, than were the Lincoln–Douglas debates.

Robert Harper provided a vivid account of the milieu at the earlier debates:

> Today's reporters will wonder how those on the Lincoln–Douglas assignment were able to do any kind of a job at all. Neither candidate spoke from manuscript, and they sometimes paused for asides. The platforms were jammed with local politicians until the reporters had scarcely room to work. The shouting of unruly crowds often made it difficult to hear the speaker. All meetings were held outdoors, regardless of weather conditions, and when the reporters were not choked with dust they were wet and muddy. Bands and fireworks added to the confusion; frightened horses ran away, and a fist fight was usually in progress on the edge of the throng.
>
> [Chester P.] Dewey of the New York *Evening Post* wrote from Freeport that crowds jammed the speaking platforms and 'The newspaper gentry have to fight a hand-to-hand conflict for even the meagerest chance for standing room'.[38]

Hardly an attentive audience. It has been suggested that, "The contemporary audience is probably unprepared to hear presidential candidates present such long speeches, even from Lincoln and Douglas."[39] So, apparently were those who crammed the platforms in 1858 (perhaps Shakespeare's groundlings felt similarly about a lot of words instead of action[40]).

Even delays in the 1858 debates involved the media and strike a somewhat familiar cord today. At the Freeport debate Lincoln was about to begin his speech when William "Deacon" Bross, editor of the *Chicago Democrat*, shouted out that Hitt was not on the platform and Lincoln's words would not be correctly recorded. Lincoln stopped and commented that indeed Hitt was not "here." Bross boomed, "If Hitt is in this crowd will he please come forward." Hitt was at the rear of the throng complaining that he could not get through to the platform. The debate was delayed while Hitt was carried over the heads of the crowd forward to where Bross was near Lincoln.[41]

In Philadelphia, during the first debate between Carter and Ford in 1976, the debate was delayed some 27 minutes because of the failure of a 25¢ audio chip (see chap. 3).

In both instances the debate was delayed because the media (print in 1858 and broadcasting in 1976) were unable to record or transmit the proceedings. Given the legal problems (third-party candidates' appeals) that were exacerbated by the audio failure in 1976, it is interesting to note the cause for delay in both situations was not, essentially, that the audience in attendance could not hear, but rather that the respective dominant media audience of the time would not be able to follow the debate.[42]

Political Public Relations.   Certainly, the political efforts associated with an election then were essentially the same as now. There were, of course, distinct differences in how the media were *able to cover* the debates then and now. Media technology, journalism, and public relations skills, however, are more sophisticated today than in Lincoln's day.

Although we can find facets of public relations in the writings of Greek theorists, and the concept of "opinion" in the ideas of the Romans (*vox populi, vox Dei:* "the voice of the people is the voice of God"), the origin of American public relations stems from the American Revolution. "The first clear beginnings of *the public presidential campaign* and of *the presidential press secretary's function* came in the era of Andrew Jackson and in the work of Amos Kendall."[43]

Lincoln and Douglas debated when the practice of political public relations in America was only about 35 years in its infancy. But both knew the value of information in creating sentiment in the electorate. Lincoln, for example, sought and maintained close relationships with editors and reporters so that his ideas would be disseminated and his policies could find support. He was an active participant in outlining strategies for the debates with Douglas. He sought out the opinions of editors, listened to constituents, and in the process gave testimony to the value of persuasion in developing public opinion. Lincoln recognized that to succeed politically in a democracy influencing public opinion was mandatory. He declared that, "In this age, and in this country public sentiment is everything. With it, nothing can fail; against it, nothing can succeed. Whoever molds public sentiment goes deeper than he who enacts statutes or pronounces judicial decisions. He makes possible the enforcement of them, else impossible."[44]

Lincoln's little remembered relationship with Dr. Charles Ray, (who, perhaps more than any other single individual helped Lincoln become president[45]) began after the Bloomington, Illinois Republican convention in 1854. Ray's role, a progenitor for today's political consultant-public relations-media advisers, was prompted by a dazzling abolitionist speech that Lincoln gave at the convention which impressed Ray (see footnote 35).

Some of the scathing criticisms of televised presidential debates probably comes about in deference to Lincoln, and to the format of the Lincoln–Douglas debates. His legacy to political rhetoric is legendary. It is cherished by scholars and political observers. None of our presidential candidates since then, and certainly none appearing in televised debates, has approached the great eloquent, persuasive rhetoric of Abraham Lincoln. It was a different time, a different setting, and a *different man*. Televised presidential debates will improve as candidates improve. Even then, it is likely that candidates will employ techniques designed for television by experts whose campaign activities closely resemble those used by Proctor and Gamble to influence consumers; and the press will follow the *race*.

Influencing opinion, creating a favorable impression, is ingrained in our society's notions about achieving success. The press plays a vital role in that process. Lincoln knew that, and candidates participating in debates understand that quite well. So do the cities that host debates. Promoting and achieving economic benefits from them were important in 1858 and still are today.

Preparations for the debate "crowd" by the League, special groups, and the business communities in cities hosting presidential debates are similar to, although more sweeping than, those of the Lincoln–Douglas debates. Baltimore in 1980 provided an excellent case study of what a city will do to get "good press" and a favorable image when hosting a presidential debate. Baltimore went "all-out" for the occasion to insure that the press covering the debate also covered *the city* favorably.

Baltimore.   The major story of the Baltimore debate was the refusal of President Carter to debate Ronald Reagan and John Anderson. Carter felt that although Anderson was "a very significant factor" in the election, his candidacy was "primarily a creation of the press."[46] The League threatened to keep an empty chair on the platform during the debate to emphasize Carter's absence;[47] later it reversed that decision. Libertarian presidential candidate, Ed Clark, lost his suit claiming that the city had violated his constitutional rights by excluding him from the free public facilities provided for the presidential debate.

But a good deal of the local (and national) media coverage was about the city: its public relations campaign; vignettes on personalities; stories on interesting events and people associated with the debate, and the media personnel who came to cover it. David Lightman of the *Baltimore Evening Sun* filed a report about the debate that appeared under the headline: DEBATE PROMISES LOTS OF HOOPLA. He noted, "When the media are greeted in lavish style by city officials at the Convention Center tomorrow night, it will launch a day and a half of hoopla scheduled to climax in Sunday's two-man presidential debate."[48] Baltimore's hotels were almost filled (recall Ottawa's livery stable), and as Lightman pointed out, that a "housing hotline" set up to find rooms for guests had been "largely quiet." He went on to describe rallies, receptions, and the difficulty in getting tickets and access to the debate.

Louis Azrael of *The News American* declared, "The show that will take place in Baltimore's Convention Center on Sunday will be just that: a show."[49] Chagrined that the debate might not bring the attention the city expected, the same paper featured a story under the headline: A DEBATE FOR DEBATE WEEKEND: WILL CITY PROMOTION EFFORT WIN? The lead asserted that Walter Cronkite, who had been invited to sail the Pride of Baltimore by Mayor William Schaefer, would not be in town for the debate. It detailed the city's public relations effort:

> The targets are representatives of nationwide news organizations who will be driven around town, sailed around the harbor, wined, dined and waited on by a cadre of volunteers.
> There will also be a grab bag of specially prepared city promotional information and tours of city renewal efforts.
> The premise of the city effort is simple: Representatives of the nation's press will be a captive audience, giving the city an opportunity to show off and possibly spark positive news coverage in the future.[50]

In addition to sailing on yachts, the press corps were chauffeured to restaurants, wined and dined with a "Maryland buffet" on a patio stocked with barbecued chicken, pit-roasted beef, crabs, oyster stew, and a raw fish bar. Sandy Banisky's article in the *Baltimore Sun:* CITY HUSTLES TO PREPARE FOR TOMORROW'S DEBATE detailed many of the city's specially created events for pursuing the press, including her paper's hosting of an "invitation-only party for about 300 business and Civic Leaders."[51]

Hoopla in Baltimore was planned, and was quite successful from the city's perspective. Preparations of the place where the debate would be held—Baltimore Convention Center—was in the hands of its executive director, James Smither, who found himself deluged with media requests for tours, interviews, and other contacts. A special staff member from the Mayor's office was put in charge of coordinating activities. Several of these were designed as media junkets, escorting the working press and elite media representatives to events, restaurants, and sightseeing the "Best of Baltimore."[52] Cars for the press and dignitaries were donated by auto dealers in the greater Baltimore area. Several hundred volunteer drivers came from the Jaycees. Owners of 29 yachts donated their boats and their time, making them-

selves available in the harbor for the press. There was a radio network
for the cars and the boats. Autos took the press to ethnic restaurants;
yachts sailed them to Fort McHenry. Advertising in commercial trade
journals a month afterward showed Reagan and Anderson in Baltimore for the presidential debate.

Although the expenses totalled some $250,000, most of the amount
was donated (e.g., $54,000 in cash from local firms). "We felt like we
were on a high after that debate. Bookings [for the Convention Center
and other facilities in Baltimore] were rolling in."[53] Wayne Chappell,
executive director of the Baltimore Convention Bureau, credits the
debate and the publicity the press provided as being largely responsible for the city's economic boost:

> We knew it meant a great deal and brought about increased bookings.
> We wanted to showcase the city's changes. We're dealing with images—
> a very mystical thing to change or create. Baltimore did not enjoy a
> good image. This was our opportunity. The nation would be watching.
> Baltimore would be on television. The ad campaign, after the debate,
> included a picture of Anderson and Reagan facing each other. The
> heading was: DON'T DEBATE. COME TO BALTIMORE. The copy asked the
> question, why was Baltimore chosen for the debate? Two days later, in
> Chicago with my sales staff at the "Meeting World" trade show, 90 per
> cent of the people there said, "We saw Baltimore in the debate. TV
> coverage was great!" In the six month period after the debate we in-
> creased our bookings by 22 per cent over what we did in the same
> period a year ago.[54]

Although Baltimore in 1980 had a larger population, faster trans-
portation, and more commerce and press, than Ottawa in 1858, the
preparations were, nevertheless, of the same order. Aside from format, rhetoric, and the office sought, Baltimore was the scion of Ottawa, as were the other 12 presidential debate cities.[55]

Furthermore, both the activities and the criticisms of the media are
much the same today as they were when Lincoln debated, and indeed
as far back as the beginning of our nation. Critics attacked newspapers
for their lack of substantive coverage of issues when our nation was
founded. Later, critics chastised radio, again for inane coverage. Today, television gets the brunt of the criticism. Two historical me-
dia/democracy propositions have been the heritage of critics and media theorists, denouncing the dominance of style over substance in
media's coverage of politics and candidates:

1. Issues equate with substance, and the public discussion of them
   is at the foundation of the democratic process.

2. Images, perceived from the personalities and styles of candidates and officials, are trivialities concocted largely by journalists
conforming to structural demands of media.

Nowhere in the literature of mass communication and politics have
these propositions been addressed with a more reasoned analysis of
the historical perspective on media and criticism than in the work of
Michael J. Robinson and Margaret A. Sheehan:

> Most media theorists assume that televison inherently fails as a serious
> mass medium.
>   The fact is if one goes back through the history of press criticism, a
> distinct pattern emerges: the most modern medium is always regarded
> as the most issueless, the most most frivolous—first, in print, then daily
> press, then radio, then television. It is, of course, possible that there is a
> casual relationship between modernity and superficiality, that the new-
> est medium inevitably behaves the most superficially. On the other
> hand, just as plausible is a causal relationship between modernity and
> criticism, the assumption that the newest medium inevitably attracts the
> loudest complaints.
>   [T]he historical comparisons . . . have forced us at least to consider
> the notion that the mass media change their emphasis and behavior less
> than the critics change theirs and that television behaves neither more
> nor less seriously than other media do or *have done*.[56]

Although some of us would have it otherwise, emphasizing candidate image and style in coverage of presidential debates conforms to
media's depiction of the overall race for the presidency as a sports
contest.

Debate as a Sports Contest

To report on the election media use a variety of information gathering techniques from person-on-the-street interviews to elite and public opinion polling. Reporters consistently question candidates, their
staffs, and voters in order to get a "tally" on how the candidates line-
up in the race. In election years, "won and lost" statistics appearing in
the news are presumably as interesting to the public as those that
appear in sports reporting. The analogies of politics as sporting events
and as entertainment are not new.[57] Incongruously, political reporters join in the "sporting event" giving the "debate scores" to the voters
and monitoring the election, while criticizing the process as being
similar to a sports contest.

Just as with sports, when they come together in an election campaign, candidates and reporters naturally presume that voters want
to keep tabs on the race, want to know who's ahead. Political jockeying
among candidates as they vie for media (hence, public) attention is
especially evident during presidential primaries. In the beginning
(which may be as early as 2 years before a presidential election)[58], and
as the race proceeds, journalists habitually "call" the winner—the
front-runner—as he or she rounds another political turn, or hurdles
over a political obstacle. In the end (which usually has been during the
first 30 minutes of the television network's election night coverage)
the media persist in making predictions much before the ballots
throughout the United States have been counted.[59] Thus, the American presidential election, the longest of all political races in Western
democracies, is concluded while the next one is not too far behind.

A politician in a race quickly learns that what gets on the campaign
schedule depends on one main consideration: Will the item help win
the election? Media personnel regularly recount, instruct, or debate
tactical decisions and maneuvers employed in political campaigns.[60]
Indeed, the spine of media campaign coverage—its continuity—is
rung with estimates of which candidates are winning (e.g., gaining in
the polls among voters) and which are losing.

The Horse Race. Advocates of election reform feel that giving this
much attention to the horse-race aspects of the campaign will be de-
leterious to our democracy. Horse-race reporting encourages reporters to look for stories that help explain why one candidate is ahead or
behind other candidates. That, in turn, leads to brief reports that
emphasize candidates' personalities over their positions on issues.

Some observers would have the process be a lesson giving life to
democratic theory—democracy in action—rather than simply a *contest*
for an elective office. They argue that an important protection for
democracy is an *informed* electorate. Voting, they assert, should be
based on a clear understanding of the issues and the candidates' views
about them. This process, it is thought, will culminate with the voter
having confidence that one of the candidates beliefs about issues
comes closer to his or her beliefs than the others. Society, it is argued,
also would benefit from a thorough discussion of issues.

It is an idealistic textbook model of what should influence voting
behavior that is worth striving for. But, it shuns other processes affecting voter decision making—processes primarily designed to utilize
aspects of persuasion, personality, and image development to gain
attention and support from voters. An election process filled with
personality, image, and horse-race journalism is unattractive to political

observers and other elites who feel that assessing the cognitive and leadership abilities of the candidates should be the main priority. Image and personality factors, they argue, fail to contribute significantly to that assessment; the horse-race contributes even less.

The public and reporters feel somewhat differently. They find that candidates' personalities reveal something about leadership; that candidate images are often "matched" with issues and voter preferences;[61] and that keeping tabs on the horse race (and who won the debate) establishes links with voters impressions of political events in campaigns.

David Broder, perhaps the most respected political journalist today, asserted "[That while] there are . . . things the press and televison can do to deepen the discussion of issues. . . . I would not concede that this is an argument against horse-race coverage. I [hold] the view that the public's interest in who is winning and who is lagging is inevitable and legitmate and human."[62] Though the media's concern with the race predominates presidential campaign news, issues are covered by the media. They are just covered less (or image and horse race more) than some critics would allow.

A recent major study, comparing a television network with a wire service in their coverage of the 1980 presidential campaign found that 59% of campaign news on CBS and 55% on UPI "failed to contain even one issue sentence."[63] What is more revealing is that horse-race items by far dominated the campaign news. Robinson and Sheehan explained that:

> At every level, in every phase, during each and every month, CBS and UPI allocated more newsspace [sic] to competition between candidates than to any other aspect of the campaign. Compared with time provided for news about policy or news about the candidate per se, "horse race" wins. . . . "Horse race" permeates almost everything the press does in covering elections and candidates.[64]

These findings confirm this writer's participant–observations of media coverage in presidential campaigns since 1976. As pointed out earlier in this chapter, the media coverage of presidential debates is mostly about winners and losers, as was revealed in Robinson and Sheehan's study of media reporting in campaigns. It is also about personality and image. In 1980,

> all the national media became more personal, especially the networks. Hard-core coverage of blunders, gaffes, scandals, and candidate issues consumed almost twice as much of the "Evening News" as the day

wire. . . . On "Evening News," there was more hard campaign news
about debate-debate than about the hostage "issue" or the economy.[65]

An election filled with interesting candidate personalities and images is attractive to many journalists because it helps them cover the
political "beat." It helps them to get a story. That kind of campaign
offers television journalists many different visual opportunities to cover the "same" story—"the race to the presidency," for example.[66] It is
also in keeping with journalists' notions about what readers and viewers want, ostensibly determined through a "transaction" with them.

Herbert J. Gans, presenting one of the most penetrating examinations of the journalism profession, found that:

> [J]ournalists strike a bargain with their audiences, especially the unin-
> terested one. They want viewers and readers to pay attention to impor-
> tant news because "people should know what is going on in the world";
> in exchange, they will supply interesting stories to please them. The
> essential provisions of this contract are already incorporated into the
> suitability considerations, *but journalists also make a special effort to find
> stories that will attract and then hold audience attention.*[67]

This writer's participant observations of the working press and electronic media as they covered political events, political party conventions, and debates were concordant with Gan's observations about
story selection.[68]

Reporters and editors feel that they give their audiences what they
want, which may not be what they *need.*[69] That is not to say that
television journalists ignore substantive discussions of issues. However, television news reporters and directors are particularly trained to
recognize visual aspects of a story. That training, reinforced by practice, "fits" television news' structural requirements calling for short
pictorial reports. Television news people insist that creating a "moving picture" depicting the essence or significance of a report, is far
more compelling than a "talking head." Getting the story on television
means *visualizing the story.*

Television news reporters covering the President are always concerned about their need for *visuals.* That need for visuals is, perhaps,
most evident in presidential press conferences. The "star" reporters
for ABC, CBS, and NBC, seated in the front row facing the President,
ask their one question (usually with a follow-up or two) for a newscast
that evening. Sam Donaldson, ABC's inveterate irritant of presidents,
feels "fortunate" that he has a producer with "an encyclopedia mind
for pictures, the thing television is all about."[70]

Who Won. In an election campaign the media follow the candidates' progress by assessing how well they are doing with voters. This means that the media must be in a position to monitor voter preferences continually. They do so in many ways: subscribing to established polling firms' political polls; commissioning polls; conducting polls; and through their usual reportorial practice of covering candidates in elections.

The crowning of a winner in a presidential debate preoccupies not only the press and the public, but survey researchers as well. Those who reviewed studies of the 1960 and 1976 presidential debates found that "The most commonly asked question was . . . which candidate people perceived as having won each debate."[71]

It should not come as a surprise, then, to find that the media are preoccupied with, and the public's interested in, *who won* a given presidential debate. Before the Cleveland debate (Reagan–Carter, 1980), Elizabeth Drew, writing for *The New Yorker,* said:

> [T]here is something wrong with the idea that the process of choosing a President should come down to a single television event. The press will be unable to resist casting the event in terms of "who won," turning it into one great sporting event. A debate does offer insights into the candidates' characters, but it tests only some of the things that are important in the White House.[72]

Taken together, the two debates between Mondale and Reagan in 1984 were described as a fight. Anticipating that the public would be "shocked by Reagan's halting performance" in Louisville, Sam Donaldson "said on the air afterward that the old champ had left the ring still on his feet, but the legs seemed a little wobbly."[73]

Two weeks later even the otherwise abstemious League of Women Voters, sponsor of most of the presidential debates in the general elections, entered the boxing arena by promoting the Kansas City debate as a prizefight. The League marketed a 36" × 24" poster with a photograph showing a pair of boxing gloves hanging from a microphone. One glove cuff had a patch with the name MONDALE on it; the other glove, REAGAN. Above the gloves was the heading: THE MAIN EVENT; below the gloves was the statement, KANSAS CITY WELCOMES YOU TO: A CELEBRATION OF AMERICAN DEMOCRACY.[74]

ENDNOTES

1. CBS Election Special, September 17, 1976. Warren Mitofsky is the director of the election and survey unit of CBS News. He and reporter Adam

Clymer from the *New York Times* were largely responsible for the joint CBS/*New York Times* poll. (emphasis added)

2. Panelist Max Frankel, associate editor of the *New York Times,* asked President Ford about our relationship with the Russians, and said, "We've virtually signed, in Helsinki, an agreement that the Russians have dominance in Eastern Europe." Ford, in his reply, said, "I can't under any circumstances believe that His Holiness, the Pope would agree by signing [the Helsinki] agreement that the 35 nations have turned over to the Warsaw Pact the domination of Eastern Europe." Frankel, interrupting the preplanned order of questioning the debaters, gave Ford a chance to correct his statement: "Did I understand you to say, sir, that the Russians are not using Eastern Europe as their own sphere of influence?" As part of his response, Ford said, "Each of these countries is independent, autonomous: it has its own territorial integrity and the United States does not concede that those countries are under the domination of the Soviet Union." For several discussions and references about this exchange see, S. Kraus (Ed.), *The Great Debates: Carter vs. Ford, 1976,* (Bloomington: Indiana University Press, 1979).

3. T. E. Patterson, *The Mass Media Election: How Americans Choose Their President* (New York: Praeger, 1980) p. 123. That Carter had "won" the second debate was clearly demonstrated in several studies reviewed by Sears and Chaffee. See S. Kraus (1979) pp. 237–240.

4. The second debate between Gerald Ford and Jimmy Carter, on the topic of foreign and domestic issues, was held in the Palace of Fine Arts Theatre in San Francisco on October 6, 1976. Essentially there were three distinct groupings for the media—(a) the working press and electronic media in the theatre actively involved with their jobs while the debate proceeded; (b) media representatives credentialed for the press room who were watching the debate on television in the Palace building; and (c) the invited press observing the live debate in the theatre.

5. From the research notes of the author who was invited to join the press observing the debate.

6. L. W. Jeffres and K. Kyoon Hur, "Impact of Ethnic Issues on Ethnic Voters," in S. Kraus (1979) pp. 437–445.

7. G. E. Lang and K. Lang, "Immediate and Mediate Responses: First Debate," in S. Kraus (1979) p. 311.

8. M. J. Robinson and M. A. Sheehan, *Over the Wire and On TV: CBS and UPI in Campaign '80,* (New York: Russell Sage, (1983), p. 209 (italics added).

9. J. Greenfield, Playing to Win: An Insiders Guide to Politics, (New York: Simon & Schuster, 1980) p. 215.

10. A. Clymer, "It's a Matter of Debate," *New York Times,* September 23, 1980, p. Y7.

11. D. K. Davis, (Review and Criticism Ed.) "Television and Political Debates," *Critical Studies In Mass Communication, 4*(2), 1987, p. 201. It should be noted that two debates in primaries were sponsored by newspapers and four debates in general elections were "staged" by the networks. For an interesting discussion of televised debates as television game shows see, S. J. Drucker and

J. P. Hunhold, "That's Entertainment," *Critical Studies In Mass Communication,* *4*(2), 1987, pp. 202–207.

12. Auer has identified five elements of a true debate: confrontation; equal and adequate time; matched contestants; stated proposition; audience decision. See J. Auer, "The Counterfeit Debates," in S. Kraus (1979) p. 146.

13. To the best of this writer's knowledge the phrase was originally coined by the *Chicago Press and Tribune* on August 18, 1858 (three days before the first debate) in the following article:

THE GREAT DEBATE AT OTTAWA

The first grand encounter between the champions of Slavery and Free-dom—Douglas and Lincoln—takes place at Ottawa on Saturday afternoon, Aug. 21st.

A special train will leave the Rock Island depot at 8 A. M., passing Blue Island at 8:45, Joliet at 9:55, Morris 10:50, and Ottawa at 11:45, which will give plenty of time for dinner, to arrange the preliminaries, and to prepare the polemic combatants for the contest. The train will leave Ottawa on its return at 6 P. M. and will be back to Chicago at 9:45.

Passengers will be carried the round trip for *half-fare* from all of the stations above named. How big a crowd is going from this city? The Lincoln boys should be on hand.

The idea for a televised presidential debate was suggested to Robert Sar-noff (Chairman of the Board, NBC) in July, 1952, by Blair Moody (a former reporter for the *Detroit News* and then a United States Senator from Michigan). To this writer's knowledge the expression, "Great Debate" was first ascribed to a televised presidential debate by Sarnoff in a telegram sent to Kennedy and Nixon "at the moment that the Republican Convention nominated Mr. Nixon for president." Sarnoff, in a speech to the San Francisco Advertising Club on October 5, 1960 (two days before the second Kennedy-Nixon debate), used *Great* to mark the occasion as a significant historical event, an important broadcasting event, and as the first such encounter between candidates for the office of the presidency:

This fall television has achieved another major milestone—a devel-opment that creates a valuable precedent not only for this young medi-um but for our nation and its political life. For the first time, the two major candidates for the presidency of the United States are meeting face to face in a systematic effort to exchange views on the great issues of the day. They are meeting before a forum as large as the American electorate itself—an audience far larger than any presidential candidate has been able to reach before.

This "Great Debate" is an event that concerns all of us as citizens. . .

The famous Lincoln–Douglas debates in 1858 have been cited as a precedent for the current encounters. However, there are fundamental differences. . .

See Robert Sarnoff, "An NBC View," in S. Kraus (Ed.), *The Great Debates, op. cit.,* pp. 56–64.

14. For example: "There once was a respectable tradition of debate on the American hustings, of which the Lincoln–Douglas debates of 1858 will serve as a classic exemplar. This is dead, how dead was pathetically demonstrated by the much bruited 'great debates' on television between Kennedy and Nixon in 1960 or the wooden performances of Carter and Ford in 1976." H. G. Nichols, *The Nature of American Politics*, (New York: Oxford University Press, 1980) p. 68.

15. David Zarefsky, "The Lincoln–Douglas Debates Revisited: The Evolution of Public Argument," *Quarterly Journal of Speech*, 72, 1986, p. 162.

16. Once could argue that we have had, and do have, such issues but they do not get on presidential debate agendas. For example, when Carter debated Reagon in Cleveland in 1980 the Iranians had the U.S. hostages confined, and we had failed in attempt to rescue them by force. Little was said, and certainly nothing was debated, about Iran, terrorism and the like. The apparent consensus was that any overt statement about the Iranian situation could interfere in their release, or result in harm to the hostages. No similar concern inhibited the discussion of slavery in the 1858 debates.

In the first debate of 1960 Senator Kennedy began his opening statement with a reference to Lincoln:

> Mr. [Howard K.] Smith. Mr. Nixon. In the election of 1860, Abraham Lincoln said the question was whether this nation could exist half slave or half free. In the election of 1960, and with the world around us, the question is whether the world will exist half slave or half free, whether it will move in the direction of freedom, in the direction of the road we are taking, or whether it will move in the direction of slavery.

See S. Kraus, (Ed.), *The Great Debates, op. cit.*, p. 348. In fact, Lincoln first used the phrase "half slave and half free" in his "House Divided" speech when he was nominated as the Republican candidate for the U.S. Senate on June 16, 1858, some 2 months before the first debate with Douglas at Ottawa, Illinois, and 2 years before his campaign for the presidency.

17. R. W. Johannsen, *The Lincoln–Douglas Debates of 1858* (New York: Oxford University Press, 1965) p. 9.

Another interesting Lincoln legend comment: "If Lincoln had been passed down to us only through painted portraits, perhaps his homeliness would have faded further with time. The rest of the Lincoln legend, however, including Lincoln's image as a dynamic speaker, continues to be preserved by the *lack* of recordings of his unusually high, thin voice, which rose even higher when he was nervous." See, J. Meyrowitz, *No Sense of Place*, op. cit., p. 275. For a description of Lincoln's voice see, W. E. Barton, *Lincoln at Gettysburg*, (Indianapolis: Bobbs-Merrill, 1930) p. 80.

Also, for a discussion of the arrangements for the Lincoln—Douglas and Kennedy–Nixon debates see *New York Times*, September 26, 1960, p. 25.

18. Historians associate Joseph Medill with the *Chicago Tribune*, yet it was Dr. Ray, another owner, who was editor in chief in the paper's policy setting days during the significant years of the Civil War period. Ray was one of the founders of the Chicago Historical Society.

19. ". . .the Chicago *Tribune*'s editors [Ray and Medill] and others worked the convention floor" to obtain the Republican presidential nomination for Lincoln. "Promises of offices in exchange for votes were traded freely, entirely without a candidate's knowledge. Ray told Medill, 'We are going to have Indiana for Old Abe, sure.' 'How did you get it?' Medill wanted to know. 'By the Lord, we promised them everything they asked,' Ray told him. J. Tebbel and S. M. Watts, *The Press and the Presidency: From George Washington to Ronald Reagan*, (New York: Oxford University Press, 1985) p. 175.

20. "[T]he story of Lincoln's rise to the presidency . . . is . . . underscore[d by] the vital role in it that was played by influential editors and their newspapers and by Lincoln's own knowledge of the press and how to use it, which was far greater than any of those who had preceded him. In fact, the intimate relationship with the press that Lincoln had already displayed was unprecedented, and there was much more to come [after he became the Democrats' nominee]." *Ibid.*, p. 176.

21. J. Monaghan, *The Man Who Elected Lincoln*, (Indianapolis: Bobbs-Merrill, 1956) p. viii.

22. *Ibid.*, p. 114.

23. R. S. Harper, *Lincoln and the Press*, (New York: McGraw-Hill, 1951) p. 24.

24. Quoted in Philip Kinsley, *The Chicago Tribune*, Vol. I, (New York: Alfred A. Knopf, 1943) pp. 84–85.

25. Chicago *Times*, August 22, 1858.

26. Politicians are advised to stress style over substance. Sam Donaldson, White House reporter for ABC, describes Jimmy Carter as a president who "thought that if he worked hard and did a good job, he didn't have to waste a lot of time on media events designed strictly to build his image. He was warned early in his term by his pollster, Pat Caddell, that politicians get defeated if they concentrate on substance at the expense of style, a mistake Reagan has never made." See Sam Donaldson, *Hold On, Mr. President*, (New York: Random House, 1987) p. 83.

27. Russell Baker, "Showdown in Baltimore: the Boys in the Ring," *Washington Star*, September 20, 1980, p. A-9.

28. E. E. Sparks, (Ed.), *The Lincoln Douglas Debates of 1858* (Springfield, IL: Illinois State Historical Library, 1908) pp. 77–78.

29. This was a "shorthand" system, not to be confused with the *phonograph* invented by Edison in 1877.

30. Some critics, however, feel that their rendition of textual accuracy should be preferred over others. See for example, L. Bitzer and T. Rueter, *Carter vs. Ford: The Counterfeit Debates of 1976*, (Madison: University of Wisconsin Press, 1980) pp. xi–xii. Even today the *New York Times*, the newspaper of record, falters in its *literal* accuracy. The problem of textual accuracy in 1858, however, was *political partisanship*. The problem today rests with research definitions and techniques of methodological precision, not with the employment of political propaganda techniques. Venerating the Lincoln–Douglas debates and castigating current presidential debates on the basis of *such* evidence is disingenous, dignifying a mythology while demeaning a potentially significant constituent in presidential elections.

31. Quoted in R. Harper, *Lincoln and the Press,op. cit.*, p. 25. See also *Galesburg Democrat*, October 13, 1858. Reprinted in Edwin E. Sparks, *The Lincoln–Douglas Debates of 1858*, Collections of the Illinois State Historical Library, Vol. III, Lincoln Series, Vol. I, Springfield Illinois, 1908.

32. Quoted in R. Harper, *Ibid.* See also, *Quincy Whig*, October 16, 1858. Reprinted in Sparks, *Ibid.*

33. "Before the October 28, 1980 debate between President Carter and Governor Reagan, the Reagan[–]Bush campaign obtained foreign policy and national defense briefing papers prepared to assist President Carter in that debate, and also acquired briefing papers on those subjects prepared for Vice President Mondale. . .

"The Carter debate briefing papers were used by persons connected with the Reagan[–]Bush campaign to enhance Governor Reagan's performance in the debates." See *Unauthorized Transfers of Nonpublic Information During the 1980 Presidential Election*, Report Prepared by the Subcommittee on Human Resources of the Committee on Post Office and Civil Service, House of Representatives, Washington, DC, May 17, 1984, p. 1.

34. R. S. Hopper, *Lincoln and the Press, op. cit.*, p. 25. See also, William H. Herndon and Jesse W. Weik, *Abraham Lincoln: The True Story of a Great Life*, Vol. II, (New York: Appleton, 1923) p. 89.

35. For a review of that new role see, Tom Reilly, "Lincoln–Douglas Debates of 1858 Forced New Role on the Press," *Journalism Quarterly*, Winter, 56(4), 1979, pp. 734–743.

36. Tickets to presidential debates are difficult to come by. After the candidates, League dignitaries, fundraisers, and the press get their tickets there are usually 200 or less tickets for the general public. See, Karen Hosler, "State, local politicians miffed at being shut out of debate," *Baltimore Sun*, September 21, 1980, p. B1.

37. Recall the heated discussions about unilateral cameras and reaction shots in debate negotiations (chap. 3).

One of the more interesting directing philosophies comes from Art Bloom, CBS director ("60 Minutes"). Bloom, who directed the 1976 San Francisco debate and the Des Moines debate in the 1980 primary, looks for cutaways, and reaction shots (if allowed), because he feels that he has editorial responsibility to make a debate interesting to the viewers. Although he takes on this "creative" function during a debate ("Visually it's my show.") he said that:

> I was never aware of it in San Francisco for the . . . debate, but they were counting the cutaways. And it turned out I had 25 of Carter and 26 of Ford or something. I never during the show kept count of that. I imagined that worked out probably because of my attention span and interest, looking for things in a certain period of time. You don't want to sit on someone forever . . . I don't think in my career that I've done anything that really editorialized. I may be wrong because maybe you say if you get a scowl from the other candidate that's editorializing. I look at that as being interesting to the viewers, of what's happening. . . . The point is that there is an audience here and they can see the reactions. Why shouldn't the person at home have the same right?

(From an interview with Mr. Bloom in Des Moines, Iowa, before the debate, January 4, 1980.)

38. R. Harper, *Lincoln and the Press, op. cit.,* p. 25. See also New York *Evening Post,* September 2, 1858; reprinted in Sparks, *op. cit.,* p. 193.

39. L. Bitzer and T. Reuter, *Carter vs. Ford: The Counterfeit Debates of 1976, op. cit.,* p. 237.

A politically active partisan audience would most likely be more receptive to long speeches by their cohorts than would an audience mixed with a range of political activity and interest. A case in point was the reaction to Lincoln's Bloomington, Illinois speech (mysteriously lost) to the Republican party convention a week after Sen. Douglas introduced the Kansas-Nebraska Act in 1854. John L. Scripps, editor of the Chicago *Press,* acclaimed the speech:

> . . . Never has it been our fortune to listen to a more eloquent and masterly presentation of a subject.
> . . . For an hour and a half he held the assemblage spell-bound by the power of his argument, the intense irony of his invective, and the deep earnestness and fervid brilliancy of his eloquence. When he concluded, the audience sprang to their feet, and cheer after cheer told how deeply their hearts had been touched, and their souls warmed up to a generous enthusiasm.

Quoted in J. Tebbel and S. M. Watts, *The Press and the Presidency, op. cit.,* p. 172.

40. Two Shakespearean scholars' observations shed some light on unseemly audience behaviors. Harley Granville-Barker felt it ". . . doubtless many of the audience for Shakespeare's new version of [*Hamlet*] only thought that he had spoiled a good story of a murder and revenge by adding too much talk to it." H. Granville-Barker, *Prefaces to Shakespeare,* (Princeton,. N.J.: Princeton University Press, 1947), footnote 4, p. 8.

J. Dover Wilson, commenting on Hamlet's quibbling, suggested that "much of it, with double or triple point, [is] beyond the comprehension of even the nimblest-witted among the groundlings. Its existence proves that Shakespeare could count upon a section of the audience at the Globe, nobles, inns-of-court men and the like, capable . . . of . . . sustained attention [and retention]." J. Dover Wilson, *What Happens in Hamlet,* (London: Cambridge University Press, 1951) p. 18.

Shakespeare commented through Hamlet that some members of his audience were "the unskilful" and prompts the "censure" of "the judicious" that will o'erweigh a whole theatre of others."

41. This account can be found in at least four references: New York *Evening Post,* August 29, 1858; *New York Herald,* May 29, 1904; reprinted in Sparks, *op. cit.,* p. 79 and 189; recounted in Harper, *op. cit.,* p. 25–26; and detailed in Monaghan, *op. cit.,* pp. 118–119.

42. As one of about 1,000 guests and press in the audience at the Walnut Street Theater, this writer, sitting in the balcony, could hear the debate with-

out the house audio (or the broadcasting audio which also ultimately supplied the house sound). The larger audience, however, was the approximately 70% of voters who watched the debate on television.

43. Scott M. Cutlip and Allen Center, *Effective Public Relations,* (Englewood Ciffs, N.J.: Prentice-Hall, 1982) p. 1. Kendall's contribution in the Jackson White House can be found in Arthur M. Schlesinger, Jr., *The Age of Jackson,* (Boston: Little, Brown, 1945).

44. A. Lincoln, *Notes for Speeches,* c. October 1, 1858.

45. Tebbel and Watts give equal credit to Medill and Ray: "Presumably [the Bloomington speech] convinced Joseph Medill and Charles Ray that Lincoln was a man to watch and to push to greater things. While many historians have given them short shrift in chronicling Lincoln's rise to the presidency, the evidence is impressive that it was their politicking and their *Tribune's* influence, more than anything else, that were responsible for Lincoln's nomination in 1860." L. Tebbel and S. M. Watts, *The Press and the Presidency, op. cit.,* p. 173.

Jay Monaghan, acknowledges Medill's influence, but claims that his name and reputation overshadowed Ray's, the man who was responsible for electing Lincoln. See, L. Monaghan, *The Man Who Elected Lincoln, op. cit.*

46. Hedrick Smith, "Anderson Receives Debate Invitation, So Carter Declines," *New York Times,* September 10, 1980, p. 1. Earlier, in the primary, Carter refused to debate Senator Edward Kennedy; he had remained in the Rose Garden in deference to the Iranian hostage situation.

47. There were dozens of articles and commentaries about "The Empty Chair." See, for example, Tom Wicker, "Carter's Empty Chair," *New York Times,* September 12, 1980, p. A23.

48. D. Lightman, "Debate Promises Lots of Hoopla,." *Baltimore Evening Sun,* September 19, 1980, p. A1.

49. L. Azreal, "Everybody Can Spout Opinions Freely," *The News American,* September 18, 1980, p. 15A.

50. R. Douglas, "A Debate For Debate Weekend: Will City Promotion Effort Win?", *The News American,* September 18, 1980, p. 1A.

51. S. Banisky, "City Hustles to Prepare for Tomorrow's Debate," *Baltimore Sun,* September 20, 1980, p. B2. The *Sunpapers* party was also opened to the press.

52. These events and several trips were announced to the press regularly. Although reporters were expected to pay for their own meals at restaurants, there were many other "freebees" for them.

53. Telephone interview with James Smithers, September 23, 1981. Smithers was head of the Baltimore Convention Center in 1980. It is interesting to note that four months after the debate Smithers moved on to head up a similar center in Kansas City, where the last of the 1984 Reagan–Mondale debates was held.

54. Telephone interview with Wayne Chappell, September 24, 1981.

55. The 1960 debates were held in television studios without an audience. Though there was hoopla, it was not on such a grand scale of those held subsequently.

56. M. J. Robinson and M. A. Sheehan, *Over the Wire and On TV, op. cit.,* pp. 141–144.

57. Three recent examples:

If politics were like a sporting event, there would be several virtues to attach to its name: clarity, honesty, excellence . . . If politics is like show business, then the idea is not to pursue excellence, clarity or honesty but to *appear* as if you are, which is another matter[: advertising]. From N. Postman, *Amusing Ourselves to Death: Public Discourse in the Age of Show Business,* (New York: Penguin Books, 1986) p. 126.

Even those who purport to report on politics often get caught in the web of performance and become part of the ritualized drama, just as sports commentators often become part of the ritual of sports. Both political and sports journalists speak of 'frontrunners' and 'dark horses,' of good losers and humble winners . . . Because politics is a dramatic ritual, it is ultimately impossible to separate the thread of reality from the thread of performance. From J. Meyrowitz, *No Sense of Place: The Impact of Electronic Media on Social Behavior,* (New York: Oxford University Press, 1986) p. 277.

"The political jargon is awash in the cliches of sports: winning or losing the game, campaign teams and their managers, public opinion polls handicapping the horse race, candidates (often called "horses") jockeying for position and so on. The similarities between politics and sports are striking and obvious.

An election is, first of all, a contest among competitiors striving for the same prize. If you work for one of them you are said to be, as in boxing, in his corner. In a debate, one candidate may score a knockout, or the event may be judged a draw. A single day on which several presidential primaries are held was originally called — what else? — Super Bowl Tuesday, now shortened to Super Tuesday. The language of the playing field or arena is too apropos to politics, and too integral, to be avoided in writing about a presidential campaign, and the reader will find this book no exception. From Jack W. Germond and Jules Witcover, *Wake Us When it's Over: Presidential Politics of 1984* (New York: Macmillan Publishing Co., 1985), p. xvi.

58. In November 1972, Hamilton Jordan, Jimmy Carter's campaign manager, wrote a memo to Carter in which he suggested that the "Eastern/liberal newspaper establishment['s] . . . recognition and acceptance of your candidacy as a viable force with some chance of success could establish you as serious contender worthy of financial support of major party contributors." Carter's campaign for the presidency had begun, 4 years before the election.

59. For the 1984 presidential general election, officials of the television networks agreed not to predict results of contests in a state until the polls of that state closed.

60. See, for example, Jeff Greenfield, *Playing To Win: An Insider's Guide to Politics* (New York: Simon & Schuster, 1980).

61. See, for example, S. Kraus and R. G. Smith, "Images and Issues," in S. Kraus (Ed.), *The Great Debates: Background, Perspective, Effects*, (Bloomington: Indiana University Press, 1962) pp. 307–308.

62. David S. Broder, *Behind the Front Page: A Candid Look at How the News Is Made* (New York: Simon & Schuster, 1987) p. 268. Mr. Boder includes a chapter entitled "Campaigns: Horse-race Journalism," (pp. 238–269).

63. M. J. Robinson and M. S. Sheehan, *Over the Wire and on TV: CBS and UPI in Campaign '80, op. cit.,* p. 146.

64. *Ibid.,* p. 148.

65. *Ibid.,* p. 209.

66. See James D. Barber, (Ed.) *Race for the Presidency: The Media and the Nominating Process,* (Englewood Cliffs, N.J.: Prentice-Hall, 1978).

67. H. J. Gans, *Deciding What's News,* (New York: Pantheon Books, 1979) p. 241 (italics added). Twenty years before, another researcher suggested that "the audience is made up of individuals who demand something from the communication to which they are exposed, and select those that are likely to be useful to them . . . A bargain is involved." See W. A. Davison, "On the Effect of Communication," *Public Opinion Quarterly,* 23 (1959): 360. For another study of the journalism profession see, John Johnstone, Edward Slawski, and William Bowman, *The News People: A Sociological Portrait of American Journalists and Their Work* (Urbana: University of Illinois Press, 1976).

68. The participant observations were conducted by this writer. For the most part, they are reported here for the first time; reference to previous reports are provided in the preface. Gans' data came from observations in 1965–1969, 1975, and "some last minute interviews" in 1978; Kraus' were gathered in 1976, 1980, 1984, and some re-checking interviews in 1986 and 1987. Gans, in his preface, observed that "the world had changed between my two field-work periods, but the way journalists work had not."

69. In another setting an editor of the *Minneapolis Star-Tribune,* argued that "voters don't get what they need, but they certainly get what they want." Conversation with Sidney Kraus, Radisson University Hotel, Minneapolis, MN., February 27, 1986.

70. S. Donaldson, *Hold On, Mr. President!, op. cit.,* p. 154.

71. Sears and Chaffee, p. 237 op. cit. See also, E. Katz and J. Feldman, "The Debates in the Light of Research: A Survey of Surveys," in S. Kraus (Ed.), *The Great Debates,* (Bloomington: Indiana University Press, 1962) pp. 173–223.

72. E. Drew, *Portrait of an Election: The 1980 Presidential Campaign,* (New York: Simon & Shuster, 1981) p. 312.

73. S. Donaldson, *Hold On, Mr. President!, op. cit.,* p. 171.

74. Printed by Constable Hodgins Printing. Photography R. C. Nible.

5

DEBATE EFFECTS:
VOTERS WIN

Which candidate won or lost the most Saturday night may not be clear. But we believe it is clear on this morning after that the voters are winners for having had a chance to make the kind of comparison that only this type of appearance permits.[1]

The media were not alone in their estimation of winners and losers; from the very beginning of televised presidential debates researchers were measuring such outcomes. Reviewing the studies of the 1960 and the 1976 debates, Katz and Feldman[2] and Sears and Chaffee,[3] noted the preoccupation of social scientists with the question, "Who won?". "In contrast to the paucity of questions concerning the format of the [1960] debates, it is surely revealing that so many of the studies asked, unabashedly, "Who won?"—or words to that effect."[4] Likewise in 1976, "The most commonly asked question in the surveys was, as in 1960, which candidate people perceived as having won each debate."[5] It is interesting to note that in 1960, debate studies were "consistent concerning the results" of winners and losers, and in 1976, "There [was] a remarkable consensus in the answers [to questions about who won]."[6] This pattern, evident again in 1980 and 1984, reveals an extraordinary faculty among debate viewers to agree on winners and losers among candidates.

These won and lost evaluations are usually concordant with debate audience members' prior preference of one candidate or another. It is not clear, however, whether these predispositions are altered or fluctuate during the debate and from debate to debate within a given election. Some analysts feel that there is a causal connection between candidates being called the winner and their winning votes.[7] But, that link may be explained by looking at the trend data in 1960: "changes in strength of commitment from debate to debate follow the pattern of evaluation of 'who won.'"[8] In any case, both journalists and social scientists assess candidates' debate performances to determine the winner. How they go about it is as important a consideration as what they find.

Assessing Debate Effects

Assessment of debate effects follows a research tradition in the study of mass communication and politics. The classical presidential voting studies of the 1940s and 1950s analyzed media coverage and monitored vote intentions in the months preceding presidential elections. Researchers investigated how voters made up their minds to vote for a given candidate, and the effect of media coverage in that process. By tracking voters during the campaign period, social scientists were able to determine when voters decided on their support for a candidate, what brought that support about, and how the media were utilized along the way to those decisions.

For the most part, journalists have relied on their past experience in reporting about the political process, and interviews with candidates and voters to make evaluations as the presidential campaign works its way to election day. For example, Samuel Lubell, a political and public opinion analyst who wrote a newspaper column, "The People Speak," gathered his "data" about political events from a few random intensive interviews with the electorate in different parts of the country:

> On the morning after the first TV debate I was interviewing in Freeborn County, in southern Minnesota. Near Bancroft one young farmer was fixing his plough when I drove into his farmyard. Asked whether he had heard the debate, he nodded and volunteered, "Before I tuned in I was afraid neither man was fit to be president. But they both handled themselves well. The country will be secure with either man."
>
> The reaction of this farmer points to one definitely constructive contribution of the TV debates—they made both candidates and the election result more acceptable to the electorate.[9]

In the last few decades, however, debate evaluators (social scientists and journalists) have benefited from the introduction of more sophisticated methods of assessing media and debate effects. Expanding technology and computing capabilities permit assessment to be made more quickly, accurately, and thoroughly. These advances have facilitated political events analyses by television networks, news magazines, and the larger newspapers.

The most significant bridge from social science's quantitative methodology to journalism's news gathering function emerged from sample survey techniques developed in the 1930s—*public opinion polling.* Opinion polling and survey research techniques are now accepted journalistic practice in evaluating the public's reaction to political events such as televised debates.[10]

Public Opinion Polling. The verb *polling* (stems from poll, to count heads) denotes the process by which we elect government officials and settle on issues (e.g., referenda). Since the 1930s, but especially after the second world war, polling has referred to scientific sample surveying used to assess the public's opinion on electoral candidates and issues.

Large scale electoral opinion assessment by the press began in the 19th century. Newspapers dispatched reporters who canvassed voters to estimate public sentiment on candidates and issues. These canvasses were *straw polls* of indigenous groups, usually not representative of the larger electorate the press wrote about in their subsequent reports.

Often, straw polls failed to account for political sub-groupings in their assessment of political opinion. For example, the *Harrisburg Pennsylvanian* tried to assess for whom the citizens in Wilmington, Delaware would vote in the presidential election of 1834. The newspaper reported that its "straw vote taken without discrimination of parties" disclosed that voters preferred Andrew Jackson over John Quincy Adams, Henry Clay, and William H. Crawford.[11]

Straw polls dramatically fell victim to the inadequacies of the market research techniques and sampling methods of the times when in 1936 the *Literary Digest* predicted that the Republican nominee, Alfred M. Landon, would win the presidency over Democrat Franklin Roosevelt. The *Digest's* poll was conducted by mailing millions of ballot cards to automobile and telephone owners, largely Republicans in households with higher incomes, many of whom supported Landon and returned their cards. These factors brought about a sampling error that over-predicted the support for the Republican presidential candidate.[12]

In 1933, with the knowledge that errors associated with sampling could be reduced by using probability techniques to measure public opinion, George Gallup founded the American Institute of Public

Opinion. "[W]ith the cooperation and support of a number of American newspapers,"[13] the Institute conducted weekly national polls and supplied the data with interpretation to newspapers. The press was eager to get objective measures of what people were thinking, and people seemed curious about the opinions of others. A market for *opinion* had been established. The Gallup Poll had arrived.

But as polls were reported disagreements were sometimes voiced. Criticism dogged poll results. Today, it is not unusual to hear a barrage of antipoll comments, or conflicting interpretations, on the opinion results of controversial issues, usually from individuals and groups who found their views reported not as significant as others. Pollsters have been accused of using the opinions of the "few" interviewed to represent the "many" not interviewed. Decrying errors of sampling, bias of questions, misrepresentation, and insisting that polling was a "threat to representative government and the democratic process," critics questioned the validity and reliability of polls.[14]

According to a recent analysis,[15] Gallup's margin of error (predicted compared to actual popular vote for the presidency) has decreased substantially since the 1936–1950 average error of 4 percentage points:

1950, 1954, 1958, 1960	less than 1%
1964	2.6
1968	0.4
1972	0.2
1976	2
1980	4.7 (John Anderson's candidacy muddles prediction)
1984	0.3

These impressive error percentages came after much criticism of survey techniques, prompting certain corrections. The "reformation" followed on the heels of the famous polling-press debacle in the 1948 Truman–Dewey presidential contest. On the second day in November the polls prompted the *Chicago Tribune* on election eve to go to press (Home edition, November 3) with the headline: DEWEY DEFEATS TRUMAN. Gallup missed the popular vote by -5.4%.[16] Still, the major polls—Gallup, Roper, Harris, and Field—are mostly valid and reliable, although often the butt of attacks by politicians and reporters.

Modern polling began as a circulation booster by newspapers. Today, however, it is a major tool of political reporting. The application of social and behavioral science research methods to the "precision" reporting of political events and the electorate's reactions to them is now customary in presidential campaigns. The term, *precision journalism,* was coined by Philip Meyer, who as a journalist learned quantitative research techniques and applied them in the coverage of political events.[17] Gallup and other polling organizations regularly conduct seminars for journalists in an effort to educate them in methods of gathering, analyzing, and reporting opinions.

Essentially, there are two kinds of polls used in presidential elections and campaigns—private polls and public polls. Private polls are those commissioned by candidates and political organizations for the purpose of guiding actions or policy. Candidates use polling to help develop campaign strategies: delineating the political constituency, determining the electorate's regard for the candidate, and defining the issues. They are useful in helping advisers prepare study documents for candidates participating in presidential debates.

These polls, of course, indicate the standings of candidates at a single point along a campaign time line. Private poll findings are either offered for publication or are "leaked," especially when favorable to the candidate. It is generally thought that good poll results translate into good publicity. But, the press have become more sophisticated in their understanding and use of polling, turning a private practice into a public podium. Polling, certainly polls, now plays an important part in newsrooms.

If the candidate uses polls to develop strategies, news organizations use them to develop stories. If the candidate uses polls to garner publicity, news organizations use them to ask candidates probing questions. In these and other ways, the interplay between public and private polls have altered campaigning and the structure of news gathering and reporting in presidential elections. Press polls are commonplace. Television networks have continuing alliances with newspapers and polling organizations, as this writer has noted:[18]

There are several "marriages" between pollsters and the media, and several "incestuous" relationships between media. For example, *Time* occasionally likes to use the research firm of Yankelovich, Skelly, and White, Inc.; *Newsweek* often commissions the Gallup Organization; ABC News has been wedded to the Louis Harris Organization, but has had romances with *Washington Post;* CBS News [it has a news election and survey unit] and the *New York Times* [it has a reporter experienced in opinion analysis] have had a long relationship; and NBC News and the Associated Press gave birth to several surveys in presidential campaigns. . .

NBC has also collaborated with the *Wall Street Journal,* and Cable News Network (CNN) has teamed up with *USA Today.* Although not without problems, these "polling teams" enable debate information to reach the public at least twice—immediately (on television) or within hours (in print).

A review of the effects of presidential debates as gleaned from polls begins the discussion of the impact of televised presidential debates.

DEBATE IMPACT

Polls

Increasingly, we have had polling surrounding presidential debates. Although there has been a good deal of discussion about the impact of polling on political, economic, and social issues, the discourse does not stem from a comprehensive study on the *impact* of polls on candidates and voters in presidential elections that have included televised debates.

One wonders, why? Both the Gallup and Roper polls have repositories that archive and study their respective data. The networks and other news organizations have debate polling data that, although not always readily available, usually can be retrieved (at least in table and report formats) for individual study. Perhaps, now that it appears that televised debates have been institutionalized in the presidential election process, such studies will emerge. Still, even without that extensive examination, several observations about polls and their effects may be derived from various sources.

Media sponsorship of polls has been increasing. C. Anthony Broh counted an increase of 15% in the number of media sponsored polls from 1976 (58%) to 1980 (73%).[19] *Newsweek, Time,* the *New York Times,* and the networks provide excellent examples of news polls that consistently examine the public's opinions about presidential candidates during elections. In elections with debates, polls are conspicuous. Usually they are fairly accurate. Sometimes they are downright wrong.

The worst of the "bad news" on polling came in 1980 when one television network got immersed in a controversial postdebate poll. Immediately after the Cleveland Carter–Reagan debate, Louis Harris conducted a poll for ABC that was intrinsically partial to Reagan.[20] The press' reaction was swift and hostile. Critics lambasted ABC in no uncertain terms. "ABC should be forced to put on all its news shows in the future a disclaimer that reads, 'This network is no longer in the news business but only seeks to use the news as a possible source of entertainment.' "[21] Researchers with apparent influence over policy makers put the reprimand in equally strong, but parental, voice: "We hope never to witness again a surprise pay-as-you-phone-in survey the likes of which ABC offered up immediately following the Carter–Reagan debate."[22]

The best of the "good news" confirms that throughout debate periods from 1960 through 1984 the public has anticipated encounters between candidates, responding positively to the idea of televised debates, while critically evaluating candidate performances in them. By and large, debate polls have served the public, the candidates, the media, and the political process in ways consistent with democratic tenets. Polls measuring how well the candidates handle themselves and the issues provide important feedback to candidates and voters.

Debate Strategies. It should be evident by now that polls play an important part in developing strategies and in preparing presidential candidates for televised debates. Less apparent is the part played by debate strategists' cumulative use of poll data over elections. Results of debate polls and analyses of candidate debate performances in one presidential election campaign may help interpret polls on televised debate strategies in another.

Patrick H. Caddell, Carter's pollster, wrote a 29-page memorandum, "Debate Strategy," a week before the 1980 Cleveland debate with Reagan.[23] At the very beginning, Caddell placed the upcoming debate in context with debates in 1960 and 1976. Moreover, he drew upon debate research in 1976 and 1980 that showed college educated and women voters the "two groups most affected by debates;"[24] referred to the 1976 foreign policy debate that, "contrary to conventional wisdom," it and the "Polish gaffe" did not hurt Ford (Carter can turn the "crisis management of foreign policy" to his favor);[25] and developed a debate strategy by comparing Reagan's probable composure to that of Carter's in 1976:

> Reagan is trying out for the biggest part of his life. That's the way he sees it. Whatever the veneer he will go into the beginning of this debate nervous, even scared. Remember Jimmy Carter at the first debate? *This is an advantage that the President must move to exploit in the first ten or fifteen minutes. We should plan well the opening of the debate.*[26]

But, strategies may or may not work. Caddell, Carter, and his advisers, of course, could not predict with certainty (even with polling data) that Reagan would be "nervous," let alone, "scared" in his match with Carter. Hindsight, of course, proved Caddell's strategy to be fallacious. One experienced observer noted:

> "Persona" did give another television advantage to Reagan, who won the critic's award for the outstanding performance by a leading actor in a dramatic series. . . . [A] candidate almost literally from "central casting," . . . Reagan's ease, poise, and warmth before the camera may have been most devastating to Carter, at the time of their debate.[27]

Whether debate strategies work, polling does have an effect on them. Perhaps an even greater effect on the preparation for the first televised debate in a presidential campaign than for the others.

First Debates. Determining the effect of first debates in presidential elections is most difficult. It seems plausible that the initial debate in the general election should have an impact similar to the first test (Iowa) in the primary. The initial debates of 1960 and 1976 were astonishingly similar in outcome—"Ford's victory over Carter [was] comparable to Kennedy's win over Nixon."—(in percent):[28]

1960		1976	
Kennedy	38	Ford	37
Nixon	21	Carter	24
No Winner	39	No Winner	39

But those comparisons are coincidences, anomalous findings, not found in other major polls of initial debates in presidential elections. Nonetheless, the first debates in 1960 and 1976 were important for the candidates because the results prompted the campaigns to look in a different way at how they stood with voters.

Defining a *first* debate may be troublesome, inhibiting the discovery of systematic effects of first debates. How should the Mondale–Dole (1976) or the Bush–Ferraro (1984) vice presidential debates be "counted?" Which debate, was *first* in 1980, Reagan–Anderson or Carter–Reagan? Neither? Both?

Still, in each of the debate years, before the first debate in the general election, voters' expectations heightened, and candidate campaigns were helped or harmed. Certainly, the momentum of the campaign was affected.

Anderson's Test. Actions circumscribing the first debate in 1980 demonstrated the portentous effect of polls in the political process. A strange and disputable feature entered into the annals of televised presidential debates—a candidate was invited to participate *provided he received 15% of voters' support in the major national polls.* Unable to otherwise resolve how *not* to invite the many nonmajor party candidates, on August 10 the League of Women Voters Education Fund set three criteria that presidential candidates had to satisfy before an invitation to debate would be extended. These edicts were: constitutional presidential eligibility; mathematically (on states' ballots) able to win the office; and by September 10, a 15% standing in major polls. Among the minor party candidates, only John Anderson could possibly have qualified, and did (see chap. 3).

This use of the polls in the political process is questionable. First, voters' responses to polling questions at any given time in an election reflects their opinions at a given *specific time.* A day or two before or after polling, opinions may change in magnitude. Further, fluctuations in results between polls may be accounted for by a variety of error sources. "Averaging" five polls may be acceptable practice for emphasizing front-runners in a journalistic report, but hardly for including or excluding a presidential candidate in a televised debate.

The League attempted to draw a narrow, but uncluttered, path between nonpartisanship (as measured by public institutions and legal entities—e.g., the Federal Election Commission and the Courts), and preference (as evidenced by their desire to mount debates that would be acceptable to the *leading* candidates and capture the attention of the public).[29] It was a vexing problem; an old problem with a new temporary "solution." The League had been taken to court by nonmajor party presidential candidates for excluding them in the 1976 debates (see chap. 3). Since then the issue of minor party candidate participation looms over discussions to mount debates. These discussions have been excited by Americans' sense of fairness toward minor party candidates displayed in public opinion polls.

Two items are interesting to note. Just 4 or 5 days after the League's deadline, the CBS News/*New York Times* Poll found "John Anderson [to be] the only candidate for President who is favorably regarded by more people than regard him unfavorably."[30] Less than a year later, Ruth J. Hinerfeld, President of the League, speaking at a colloquium on presidential selection reforms said:

> The conflicting views expressed on this subject here are indicative of the fact that the media and the candidates are at odds with one another. Over a long period of time, that makes for over-concentration on public opinion polls by both.[31]

Ferraro's Test. After the first debate in 1984, the polls indicated that Mondale had closed the gap among voters supporting Reagan and those supporting him.[32] The vice presidential debate was seen as pivotal. "Feisty" Ferraro, the first female candidate to participate in nationally televised debates in a presidential general election, would face a seasoned campaigner, Vice President George Bush.

As soon as Representative Geraldine Ferraro, was announced as Mondale's running mate, she was scrutinized by the media and by special interest groups. Her candidacy gave renewed life to the phrase, "Gender Gap." She recognized that in a debate she would be in a "fish bowl," thought of by some in the media as a curiosity that voters would scrutinize.

She envisioned media's and voters' interest in three aspects of her participation in the debates. First, as they appeared together in the debate she would be compared to Bush as presidential successors. Second, for some voters whose decisions turn on the consideration of who would succeed the president if a tragedy occurred, her performance in the debate would be enlightening. Last, but perhaps the most important aspect of the debate, voters' inquisitiveness would be piqued (either annoyed or excited) by a woman candidate for Vice President of the United States of America.

Ferraro saw the debate as an opportunity to expand the public's image of her, emphasizing her competence as an elected official and a lawyer, seriously bent on her candidacy, and capable of the task if elected.

League members in the audience on the night of the debate found it difficult to hold back their reactions to the contest.[33]

Afterwards, the polls were not kind. Bush led in all three network polls, with ABC voters giving the Vice President a 10-point margin. Men gave the debate to Bush; women to Ferraro. Ferraro credited the debate with "maintain[ing] the momentum of the campaign after Fritz's triumph over Reagan in their first debate." And Bush "boasted . . . that 'we tried to kick a little ass last night.'"[34]

Image

Some critics see polls as demanding quick answers to short questions, reinforcing what they insist are negative aspects of debates—a concentration on image and on "who won?". It is true that voters come away from the debate with certain notions about the debate and the candidates. For example, after the 1976 Carter–Ford debate the CBS/*New York Times* Poll found only 13% of the respondents whose one single impression of the candidates related to programs or issues.

When the CBS/*New York Times* Post-Election Poll asked voters, "What was the best thing Ronald Reagan did in this [1984] campaign?"—among those who had opinions—*personality* ranked first with 11% and *debates* was third at 6% on a list of 13. When asked, "What was the biggest mistake Ronald Reagan made in this campaign?" *debates* climbed to 29% for first ranking, whereas *personality* plummeted to a 5 way tie (2%) at the bottom of 10 "mistakes." Walter Mondale's "bests" were *debates* (ranked first) and *personality* (seventh); "mistakes" ranked *personality* fifth and *debates* seventh (*Ferraro* took first place).[35] Clearly, as far as voters were concerned, "one person's meat was the other person's poison." Candidate personalities are exposed in televised debates.

When critics discuss the relative value of televised debates in the presidential selection process many look for evidence that the debates provide information to voter-viewers about candidates' stands on *issues*. They eschew the idea that the *image* of the candidate (personality conveyed through television) has any place in the selection process. Others feel personalities are important in the selection of a president, and voters expect to gauge them in a campaign. Two scenarios can be composed.

Two Scenarios. Many serious students of the presidential election process would argue that the hoopla generated when the media treat debates as sporting events, identifying winners and losers, creates a frivolous election climate. Moreover, they would insist that the impact on the electorate cannot but reflect that kind of media coverage. Brought to its logical conclusion, the argument suggests a scenario in which voters will not learn about issues, at least not in a pithy way. Instead, they will be attracted or repelled by the candidate's style and personality. Candidate *charisma* becomes pivotal for voters as they process issue and image information and decide for whom to vote. In this scenario the televised presidential debate is the catalyst for voting on the basis of personality and not on issues. Critics disparage such a condition with the admonition: either change how we conduct and cover televised debates, or do without them. Viewed in this light, debates are spurious and dysfunctional for the democratic process of selecting a president.

Let us examine a different set of postulates. In the resulting scenario, citizens are not as involved in political matters as ideal democratic theory would urge. Their political interest is piqued only on urgent (mostly salient), personally relevant, issues. For the most part, voters rely on their feelings to determine their support for a candidate. They get impressions about the candidates. They form images about them. They like or dislike, trust or distrust, candidates. Candidates' demeanor, how they *act*, "tells" voters where to place their allegiance.

Televised presidential debates provide substance for voters' discussion and processing of particular information about candidates and issues as they arrive at a vote decision. Viewed in this light, debates further the democratic process of selecting a president.

Both scenarios are scripted in the extreme. Which one renders an accurate account of how televised presidential debates affect voters and their voting decisions? The reliable sketch may lay on a continuum somewhere between the two scenarios. To arrive at that point, it is necessary to examine and review what we have learned about images, their conveyance by the media, and their effect on voting.

Before Television. Effects on voters by media's coverage of candidates' personalities and images have been of concern to those who study the media and the election process. In 1940, investigators of a presidential campaign without television were curious about voters' perceptions of candidates' images. They wondered whether radio, the dominant mass medium, brought about particular effects on voting. Lazarsfeld and his associates asked voters, for example, if they agreed that "Roosevelt has great personal attractiveness, capacity for hard work, and keen intelligence."[36] Roosevelt had a magnetic radio voice, and is remembered by mass media students as being famous for his "Fireside Chats."[37]

When television first entered presidential elections in 1948, there were only 190,000 sets in use.[38] But even then, researchers continued to scrutinize media's (especially radio's) effect on voting behavior. With the hindsight provided by the research on the 1940 election, Berelson and others looked at how voters formed opinions about the 1948 presidential candidates. At four times during the election campaign they went to a sample of voters in Elmira, New York, asking various questions about their media use, and about how they perceived the candidates. In the second and third canvasses, they asked respondents, "Which of these words comes closest to describing the idea you have of [President Truman/Dewey]? Choose as many words as you think describe him." The words to pick from were: Courageous; Conservative; Weak; Honest; Inadequate; Sound; Confused; Efficient; Cold; Well-meaning; Thrifty; and Opportunist.[39]

After the election they explored why voters decided to vote the way they did. Once again they looked for the relationship between channels of communication and responses that tapped into images and issues as motivating factors in voting. Interviewers asked: "Please tell me if any of these [listed channels of communication] were particularly important in influencing you to make up your mind . . ." ; "Which of these were the two most important factors in making you decide to vote as you did?" Among the 11 possible responses were Dewey's and Truman's "stand on the issues"; "personality and ability"; and "The way [they] campaigned."[40]

For the most part, these early studies on media and voting behavior revealed that the media reinforced existing political predispositions. Fears that the media were all powerful were laid to rest. Researchers concluded that other political socializing agents had already made their lasting impressions before the voter came to the newspaper and radio in a presidential campaign (see chap. 2). These findings of benign media effects greeted television's debut in presidential elections.

Television. Before television became the foremost medium for political campaigning, voters were partisan "clones" of their parents. Essentially, they listened to, read, and remembered information that was compatible with their previously held political views, the influence of which could be traced back to their "political genes." Radio and newspapers did not alter those views. Television did. Especially, with events such as presidential debates.

Television brought the *long shot* and the *close-up* (the devices of film and moving pictures) into voters' homes. The former provided a moving visual panorama of political events; the latter supplied vivid, intimate *sketches* of candidates as they campaigned. Presidential election activities were no longer remote events that voters read and heard about. Voters became part of the events. Political events were staged for television coverage. Candidates performed for voters who, in turn, observed and formed impressions about them. Researchers and reporters gathered those impressions immediately after voters watched a specific political event on television. Never before had presidential candidates been so closely "monitored" by voters. The stuff of image had arrived in the home.

Evaluating Debaters. No doubt, the advent of television brought with it conditions that cultivated a penetrating press perspective from which voters could gauge the personalities of political candidates. Televised debates further sustain the process of evaluating candidate attributes in three fundamental ways. First, cameras focus on candidates, singly and together, capturing their mannerisms and reactions. Second, usually for 90 minutes, candidates *perform* on a *stage* and are observed by one of the largest American television audiences for *any* kind of programming. Third, the press and others *rate* candidates' in terms of how well they handle themselves and issues, and on the impact of their performances on voters.

It is this process of evaluating the impact of debating candidates on the electorate that motivates pollsters, politicians, social scientists, and journalists to *measure performance*. A most respected journalist's method for evaluating presidential candidates' performances in televised debates provides an excellent example of the extent to which one may go in evaluating presidential debaters.

David S. Broder systematically prepares for rating candidates in televised presidential debates:

> Before each debate I have covered, I have forced myself to write down—based on what I have learned from the two camps and my own sense of the strategic situation—what will constitute success or failure for each of the candidates.[41]

He also listed three "hurdles" that reporters must go through in order to "handle the debate assessment well." First, to make a "balanced judgment" debates should be scored much in the same way that prize fights are scored, by rounds. Second, weight should be given "to the candidates' accuracy and skill in answering policy questions." Finally, the reporter must decide which candidate seemed "more in command."[42]

Broder made it clear that television news formats have influenced the way print reporters look at and judge candidates in televised debates:

> [I]f you realize that television news shows will quickly capsulize the whole debate into that moment or two when one candidate or the other takes command, your attention can focus on recognizing that moment and can put it into context of the campaign situation.[43]

Although Broder questioned why reporters "bother calling the debates," he felt, "They test the candidates' skills, and we must judge how well they meet that test."[44]

Given this kind of attention, it is understandable (although perhaps not ignoble) that in television debate preparations, consultants scrutinize every minuscule detail that may help or hinder the candidacy. Hence, the structure of television and the practices of journalists make advisers anxious about production details which may affect the public picture of candidates' personalities (see chap. 3).

Candidate Personality and Public Pictures. In both theory and practice, it can be argued that the presidential candidate's skills in televised debating reveals his or her values and personality attributes. To begin with, the candidate wants to win the office. He or she has motives that are evident as he or she campaigns. These motives are related to some skills, else the candidacy would collapse (indeed, without that relationship, the candidacy could not be mounted in the first place). It is this combination of motives and skills that reaches voters as they form images about political personalities.

Twelve years before television entered politics, Harold Lasswell suggested that a mature political personality "combines certain motives with certain skills, fusing an emotional capacity to externalize impulses with enough skill to secure success."[45]

The link between Lasswell's theory of political personality and images resulting from presidential debates can be found in his writings of 1936 and 1962. In his discussion of personality, Lasswell suggested:

> The politician displaces his private motives upon public objects, and rationalizes the displacement in terms of public advantage. When this emotional and symbolic adjustment occurs in combination with facility in the acquisition of manipulative skill, the effective politician emerges.[46]

Introducing the research on the Kennedy–Nixon debates, Lasswell outlined what candidates should do in debates. First among several debate goals and values was the postulate that "contending *candidates conduct themselves in a manner that enables the electorate to arrive at an informed estimate of their competence to lead the nation.*" Lasswell continued by insisting that "facility in debate [is] an important skill for [candidates, and] that the asking and answering of key questions in public is a procedure of importance to democratic discipline."[47]

Lasswell saw Abraham Lincoln as a mature politician, personifying the "synthesis of motive and skill," and concluding that, "Inseparable from the public picture of Lincoln was his gentleness."[48] With the influence of newspapers, Lincoln projected an image that ultimately led voters to believe that he would make a good president. The character and personality projected by candidates are catalysts for voter support.

For some time, then, we have felt the necessity of scrutinizing the character and personality of those who seek the presidency. Although we should weigh the impact of that activity when taken to its extreme (as was evident in 1987 when presidential hopefuls were charged by the media with "womanizing"),[49] it is deemed an important component for assessing candidate qualifications by the press and the public.[50] Although it is evident that such publicity affects the public's perception of candidates, it is not clear to what extent evaluations of candidate morality enter into voters' assessments of their debate performances. Social scientists, however, have assessed the impact of candidate personality on voting behavior.

An instrument to evaluate voter attitudes toward presidential candidates, that has enjoyed wide acceptance in politics and scholarship, is The Semantic Differential.[51] It asks voters to rate candidates on a 7-point scale, the poles of which identify an adjectival opposite (e.g., good/bad, love/hate, strong/weak, and the like). The researcher ends up with a candidate profile covering various traits as rated by voters.

Utilizing this technique, Tannenbaum, Greenberg, and Silverman concluded that the first debate in 1960 induced modifications of voter images of Kennedy and Nixon, but overall the series of debates did not alter candidates images directly.[52] Kraus and Smith employed the semantic differential to determine the extent to which images of candidates held by voters were linked to their understanding of where the candidates stood on certain issues. They found that, for the most part, voters watching the 1960 debates formed decisive impressions about the candidates' personalities. These impressions were linked (rated on the semantic differential in a similar fashion) to their views of the issues.[53]

In 1972 Dan Nimmo and Robert Savage concluded that the mass media influenced voters' images of candidates. Images concerned with "liking or disliking [a candidate were] the single most important explanation for voting behavior in the presidential contest."[54]

Another study, investigating the 1972 Nixon/McGovern presidential campaigns, offers additional evidence that image of candidates held by voters is critical in determining their final vote choice. Harold Mendelsohn and Garrett O'Keefe asked a panel of voters to describe their feelings about Richard Nixon and George McGovern using the following adjectival opposite words and phrases:[55]

> Warm, Friendly ..... Cold, Unfriendly
> Strong .... Weak
> Smart .... Dumb
> Can Be Trusted ..... Cannot Be Trusted
> Safe .... Dangerous
> Effective .... Not Effective

Their results showed that considering issues, images, demographics, and political party affiliation, "the main predictors of [the panels'] actual vote were perceived image attributes."[56]

The "public pictures" of Presidents Kennedy and Carter were, to a large degree, framed by their performances in televised debates. It is important to note, however, that these pictures may be influenced by personal and political activities occurring prior to the candidate's participation in televised debates. Still, most observers feel that how candidates look and act during televised debates brings about favorable or unfavorable images in the minds of voters. "Indeed," wrote Thomas Patterson who conducted a study of media's impact during the 1976 election, "when only the voters' impressions about the candidates' personalities and leadership capacities are considered, television's impact is more apparent . . . though newspaper reading was more strongly and consistently related than television viewing to developing [such] impressions."[57]

Television's impact is more apparent. In the same election, CBS News/*New York Times* asked respondents who had just viewed the first debate "what single impression sticks most in your mind about Ford (Carter)?" Two combined image categories (Character Traits & Personality and Delivery of Thoughts & Appearance) led the lists of responses for *both* debaters.[58]

Measuring voters' attitudes toward candidates has become a staple in campaign research. Even as they prepare for debates, candidates are alerted to the images held by voters. Patrick Caddell was against Carter's debating Reagan in 1980. But a week before the debate, when it became apparent that public opinion would no longer permit Carter's ducking the encounter, Caddell prepared a memorandum on debate strategy.[59] Employing the semantic differential, Caddell "capsulized" key voter attitudes toward Carter and Reagan with eight adjectival opposites: warm/cold; effective/ineffective; trustworthy/ untrustworthy; decisive/wishy-washy; dedicated/opportunistic; strong/weak; thoughtful/impulsive; and qualified/unqualified. Carter had "edged" Reagan on five of the scales, but lost on effectiveness, decisiveness, and strength.[60] What Caddell found was the "public picture" of Carter, a portrait that could change just as campaign strategies change.

The impressions that formed the "public pictures" of Walter Mondale and Robert Dole were influenced by the vice presidential debate. People who watched the debate had different images of both Mondale and Dole than those who had not. Sears and Chaffee concluded "that viewing the debate did affect the organization [in voters' minds] of these impressions."[61]

Although these "pictures" of debating candidates are formed through images held by the public, *issues* are also part of the "picture" acquired from televised debates.

Issues

For purposes of emphasis, the two scenarios that introduced the previous section on image were cast without much consideration for *is-*

sues. Leaving the image discussion that way would be inaccurate. Issues are a part of the "picture," although perhaps not as much as some would demand before sanctioning televised presidential debates. It is important, however, to recognize that the distinction between the two scenarios is obfuscated by the fact that they were placed on a *continuum,* no part of which can be identified except by arbitrary separation. Each scenario, therefore, is importantly connected to the other. The import is found by identifying the *point* on the continuum where televised presidential debates lie. Although we have some help from discrete studies, *none has been designed to mark that point.*

In quoting arguments by Henry Steele Commager (against debates) and Stanley Kelley (for debates), Hennessy presented a deft representation of the extremes on the continuum.[62]

Commager's criticism was that the 1960 television debates "[did] not fulfill the most elementary political purposes of permitting the candidates to explore the vital issues."[63]

Stanley Kelley's praise of the same debates was that "they may help to identify for the voter those issues on which rival candidates do not disagree, making it easier for him to center his attention on those issues on which they do." He also noted that debates clarified "a number of issues that remained one-sided in [campaign] speeches." Kelley concluded that the 1960 debates were far better in revealing candidate issues than were other network news presentations.[64]

What do the studies say? Which position is supported by the data?

For the 1960 debates, Katz and Feldman's review of issue studies concluded:

> As far as issues are concerned, then, the debates seem to have (a) made some issues more salient rather than others (the issues made salient, of course, may or may not have been the most important ones); (b) caused some people to learn where the candidates stand (including the stand of the opposition candidate); (c) effected very few changes of opinions on issues; and (d) focused more on presentation and personality than on issues.[65]

For the 1976 debates, Sears and Chaffee's completed their review on issues in much the same way:

> In summary, then, the debates to some degree met the expectation that voters would learn where the candidates stood. The debates did not set any new agenda, but they did summarize the main on-going themes of the campaign in a way that gave their audience a clearer picture of the differences between the candidates on several key domestic issues.[66]

A simple inspection of transcribed debate texts will quickly reveal the serious attention candidates give to issues. Several studies, however, have analyzed that attention with great precision. Bitzer and Rueter found that in the three 1976 debates, a total of 26 specific issues were discussed, 11 raised by Ford and 15 by Carter.[67] The investigators examined Ford's and Carter's rhetoric in the 1976 debates and concluded that, "The [format] rules and conditions under which they spoke limited . . . how well the issues could be treated."[68]

For the 1976 debates, Riley, Hollihan, and Cooley,[69] and for those in 1980, Riley and Hollihan[70] compared candidate issues and the arguments used to support them. As part of the 1980 analyses, they looked at the percentage of issue-statements expressed by each candidate in eight issue categories (Energy, Foreign Relations, Economy, Big Government, Military, Symbolic America, Religion, and Presidential campaign and Presidential Leadership). There were differences in candidates' emphases of certain issues. For example, in the first 1980 debate, Reagan stressed "peace, prestige, nationalism, and the character of the American people [Symbolic America]" significantly more (17.4%) than did Anderson, who made such statements in only 2.1% of all his issues-statements.[71] Reagan and Anderson devoted about the same amount of statements to the economy (46.1% to 44.4%, respectively). But in the second debate, Reagan made significantly more economy statements (36.1%) than did Carter (21.8%).[72]

Both Bitzer and Rueter's and Riley and Hollihan's studies provide empirical evidence for the convention of challengers' attacking the record of incumbents in presidential debates. Carter, for example, was more aggressive with his arguments as a challenger in 1976 than he was in 1980 as an incumbent. That routine is not antithetical to democratic principles.

But another, more important, matter emerges when examining these studies: The debate format inhibits the ability of candidates to make their arguments forcefully. All critics would agree that the debate format ought to provide candidates with the opportunity to present their "credentials" for the presidency. Critics Bitzer and Rueter made a strong case that the *format* of the 1976 encounters was responsible for restricting the discussion of issues.[73] They claimed that the format favored Carter over Ford. A contributing factor was that the questioning forced more of Ford arguments (63%) to be directed to the panelists than to Carter (37%); Carter addressed his reasoning more in Ford's direction (57%) than in the panelists'.[74]

Riley and Hoolihan suggested that the 1976 debates differed from the 1960 and 1980 debates in three important ways. First was the change from 1976 to 1980, when Anderson, Carter, and Reagan used "direct responses" as Nixon and Kennedy had done in 1960. Second, the 1980 debaters relied "much more on evidence to support their claims than [Carter and Ford] had in 1976 debates." Third, as pointed out earlier, Carter challenged more in 1976 than he did in 1980.

Again, given these kinds of findings, it is understandable that candidates and their advisers jockey for the format position in the debate race. Unless both candidates are superb debaters in the classical sense, and all other considerations (political, tactical, etc.) are of equivalence in both campaigns, genuine debates may be difficult to come by.

Still it is important to discern the difference between debating format and skill, and voter comprehension of issues. It is probably true that better formats make for better discussions of issues (although we do not have the evidence, because we have not had genuine presidential debates). But, that proposition does not necessarily imply that formats' failing to measure up to classical debate standards prevents both the discussion of and learning about issues. Changes are certain to occur as presidential elections pass, but critics overstate the issue when claiming that without "reforms . . . as experience with debates accumulates, . . . ultimately [there will be] less information for voters and fewer insights into the candidates for the presidency."[75] Whatever the criticisms of presidential debate formats to date, the debates have contributed to the electorates' understanding of issues.

Overall, the debate studies of 1960, 1976, and 1980 confirm Stanley Kelley's position on issues. Scanning the data from at least three[76] presidential elections in which televised debates were held, by and large, the evidence is clear: (a) candidates discuss a variety of issues; (b) more often than not, candidates can be set apart by the issues; (c) voters learn about issues; (d) candidate issue positions are clarified; (e) some issues become more salient than others; and (f) voters remember the content of debates, especially as it relates to their own lives.[77] Whether the discussions of issues by candidates in debates prompt voters to take particular political actions is another question worthy of attention.

Activating the Electorate

One of the major concerns of democratic theorists and observers of the political system is the participation of American citizens in the electoral process. Historically, political participation was nurtured by a strong political party system that eventually gave power to small committees in cities and counties. These committees became "machines" headed by "bosses" who doled out political favors in exchange for political participation and votes.[78] Although these machines corrupted the tenets of good citizenship advocated by the Founding Fathers, they also served the poor by socializing them (and new immigrants) into the political process and providing jobs and other economic opportunities.

The weakening of the party structure in American politics can be traced to the middle-class Progressive movement that opposed the political machines in the late 19th century. However, the current decline in party affiliation and influence in presidential elections is due to a complex set of events—decline in trust for political institutions; increase in the number of young adults eligible to vote and decrease in their trust for institutions; increase in the number of independents, and decrease in party registration of voters; decline in organized labor; and the advent of *television campaigns.*[79]

Soon after television was introduced in presidential elections, it began to supplant the influence of political parties in the nomination process. Television coverage encouraged candidates to build their own campaign organizations, bypassing political parties, and influencing public opinion. So effective was the relationship between television and the campaign organization in the nomination process that state legislatures increased the number of presidential primaries from 17 in 1968 to 37 in 1980.

If television is the most significant political process innovation for candidates of the 20th century, televised presidential debates are the most useful political campaign innovation for the electorate since the Lincoln–Douglas debates in 1858. Clearly, presidential campaign innovations that offer opportunities for candidates to show their command of issues, to outline their agendas, and to reveal their personalities should be encouraged.

Televised presidential debates may be unparalleled in modern campaigning as an innovation that engages citizens in the political process by building large audiences, creating interest and discussion among voters, and influencing voting decisions.

Exposure, Interest, and Discussion. Public anticipation of presidential debates may be associated with several factors—interest in candidates, interest in issues, general interest in the campaign, and the desire to make up their minds. The evidence informs us that people generally watch part or all of a debate as much or more than they watch any other single television event, except perhaps, the football championship Super Bowl.

Given the political apathy displayed in low voter turnout for presidential elections, it is curious that televised debates receive so much

attention from Americans. In 1960 that attention was not very astonishing because all three networks carried the debates, leaving few
or no television alternatives. Also, the first presidential debates were
introduced into a "campaign which attracted unusually high interest
[with television] as the predominant source of campaign information."[80] Television still maintains that lofty position; even though additional ultra high frequency channels, videocassette recorders, and
cablevision were substantially available by 1976, virtually saturating
the market (along with pay TV and cassette rentals) by 1980 and 1984,
debate audiences remained among the highest for single televised
events.[81] The conservative exposure estimate in 1960 was:

> that at least 55 per cent of the total population watched or listened to
> each of the debates and, altogether, that upwards of 80 per cent of the
> population saw or heard at least one of the debates. The average debate
> viewer was in the audience for some 2 ½ hours—that is, for three of the
> debates. Surely, this is one of the *great* political assemblages of all time.[82]

When asked after viewing a debate, "Do you think that these face-
to-face meetings between Nixon and Kennedy are a good idea, bad
idea, or just what do you think?"[83] Or, "Do you feel that this kind of
debate between Presidential candidates is a good way or a poor way to
get the issues across to the American public?"[84] Or, "Are you glad you
[a Canadian citizen] had the chance of seeing the [fourth] debate on
TV, or would you rather have seen something else instead?"[85] Over-
whelmingly, and increasingly from debate to debate, (upwards of
70%) the response in the United States and in Canada was "yes!"

More political discussion than would probably have otherwise taken
place in 1960 occurred as a result of exposure to debates. In fact, one
study found a positive linear relationship between exposure and talking about the first debate: The more an individual was exposed to the
debate, the more likely he or she would be to talk about it. That
relationship obtained even when the number of people who were
indirectly exposed to the debate was included in the analyses with
those directly exposed. That exposure may account for the 87% of
those viewers exposed to media reports subsequent to the debate.[86]
Overall, the 1960 studies showed that about 50% of the "population
discussed the debates within 24 hours," listing them among those
events highly discussed up to that time.[87]

Philip E. Converse, a member of a well-known election survey research team,[88] pointed out that the Katz and Feldman review of televised debate studies provided evidence contradicting C. Wright Mills'
view that the mass media inhibit free discussion[89]:

Mills assumes quite directly that prior to the incursions of the mass media, people were *more* motivated to communicate informally about politics. Current data make this proposition hard to accept. Studies of the 1960 television debates, for example, suggest that these performances were responsible in the most direct way for lively spates of informal political discussion which undoubtedly would not otherwise have taken place.[90]

In 1976, voters expected the debates to (beginning with the highest expectation): (a) inform them about the positions the candidates took on issues, (b) learn about candidate personalities, and (c) help them with their voting decision. "other important reasons for watching . . . [were] keeping up with the campaign and otherwise doing one's civic duty." At the bottom of the list (21% in one study) was the "admission that there simply wasn't much else to watch on TV at the time."[91]

According to postelection data "at least one debate reached 83 percent of the public nationwide . . . and the Nielsen ratings estimated that 89 percent of households were tuned into at least one."[92] Political involvement was a "crucial underlying factor in debate exposure."[93] Voters reactions to the debate overall were extremely favorable, although "it appears that the media postdebate analyses made voters more negative about the debates and the candidates."[94] This latter finding is interesting to consider in light of Mitofsky's (CBS) contention that viewers of the second Ford–Carter debate were persuaded by media reports to change their minds about who they thought won (see chap. 4).

Studies in 1976 indicated that the debates induced much discussion, particularly the first debate. That debate "stimulated a good bit of talk,"[95] and "informed voters about the candidates' major domestic positions."[96] Postdebate discussions largely tended to confirm one's earlier voter preference.

Ronald Reagan's gains in voter preference, John Anderson's Independent candidacy, the prolonged confinement of U.S. hostages in Iran, and President Carter's White House "Rose Garden" campaign strategy, were important factors that affected audience exposure to the 1980 televised debates. With Carter refusing to participate in a three-way debate, The CBS/*New York Times* Poll found that less than half of the electorate saw the Reagan–Anderson Baltimore encounter.[97] However, once Reagan gave in to Carter's insistence for a debate without Anderson, exposure catapulted. Before the Cleveland debate, 83% of the electorate said they would watch; and 83% did watch or listen to the that debate.[98]

In 1984, voter interest in debates between President Reagan (the second incumbent to participate in debates) and Walter Mondale (the former Vice President who had selected Rep. Geraldine Ferraro as his running mate) was evident. Conservative exposure figures recorded for the 1984 televised debates were first debate, 66%; second debate, 57%.[99]

The public's anticipation of presidential debates is evident by the size of the audiences viewing them. They have been among the largest for televised events. Voters have been and remain interested in debates, and many use them as they make up their minds on voting.

Voting: Viewers and Nonviewers. For some observers and critics, the ultimate test—to keep debates in the election process—is the "effectiveness" of televised presidential debates in *changing* voters *predispositions* toward the candidates: Did the debate(s) *influence voting* behavior? Did voter-viewers *make-up* their *minds* as a result of the debate(s)? Did they *switch* their *voting intentions* after watching (or listening) to the debate(s)? These questions (and "Who won?") lead the debate effects inquiry in both the scientific and professional domains. Why these questions are paramount is as interesting as their answers.

As new technologies and their uses develop, scientists and other observers try to determine their impact on society. Among the first examinations are comparisons of the new technology or method with the old one. Often, traditionalists will argue, "If it ain't broke don't fix it!" or, "It's worked for us thus far. Why change it?". Although this conservative stance is probably an appropriate position to begin any review of an innovation affecting the presidential electoral campaign process, the final assessment should not rest only on matters of candidate custom and practice, it should address voter convenience and education as well.

It is important, therefore, that when we examine whether televised debates change voters' political predispositions, we consider *the voter and the way in which his or her information is obtained and processed,* and not only the *change,* or a lack of it. Hence, it is pertinent to determine if voters who view televised debates are affected differently than those who do not.

Just after the Kennedy–Nixon debates, Philip E. Converse reviewed studies of the national electorate to examine the relationship between the amount of information held by voters and the permanence of their partisan attitudes. With election data from 1952 through 1960, Converse investigated the "floating voter hypothesis" (i.e., voters who shift their political allegiances between two elections, or within an election). It was thought that these "voters tend to be those whose information about politics is relatively impoverished."[100]

One may infer from Converse's review that viewing televised presidential debates can affect predispositions and change vote intentions. He found that:

> The relatively small portion of the population that failed to see any of the television debates between Kennedy and Nixon . . . was made up of voters less likely to have revised their voting intentions before the final decision than were people who watched the debates.[101]

It should be added, however, that a study of the same debates conducted by the Opinion Research Corporation suggests that debate viewers changed their vote intentions *less* than did nonviewers. Katz and Feldman commented that, "This is not as surprising as it sounds considering the fact non-viewers were far less interested and far less committed to a candidate than the viewers."[102]

They also pointed out that both viewers and nonviewers who changed their voting intentions did so about equally for each candidate. However, viewing the first Kennedy–Nixon debate did change voting intentions with a net gain for Kennedy. The consensus of the findings in 1960 was that Kennedy gained significant Democratic support from viewers for his performance in the debate, but no definitive judgment can be made about the debates in general changing voting predispositions.

Sixteen years later, researchers did not attribute much influence on voting behavior to viewing the debates. Although there were changes in viewers' evaluations of Carter and Ford for each of the three debates, social scientists hesitated to ascribe those changes "solely to the debates." They suggested that viewing them had "no residual impact . . . on [voters'] net evaluations of, or preference between the candidates, when tested retrospectively from election-day or post election surveys."[103]

Viewing the debates in 1976, however, did provide voters with more information about the candidates than they had before. This information reception was most evident among the least informed voters, who may have wondered about "Carter, who?", and among those who may have been concerned with issues such as honesty, prompted by the Watergate investigation.[104]

Perhaps the most impressive effect of the debates is its impact on voters compared to that of other forms of televised political communication used in presidential campaigns. As previously discussed (chap. 2), voters learned more about candidates and their stands on issues from watching their political commercials than they did from the networks' nightly newscasts.[105] But the debates may have an even larger effect on voters than either news or ads. In a 1983 study of 2,530 voting-age Americans, ABC News and the John F. Kennedy School of Government noted that "voters and non-voters . . . [agree] that televised presidential debates are a good thing." They found that:

> Fifty-eight percent of the public says such debates are more helpful in deciding who to vote for than either television news reports or the candidate's own television ads.[106]

This finding is most profound given the political apathy the public has exhibited by their lack of involvement with, or simple attention to, many political events. An "active audience" for a major event in a presidential campaign bodes well for democratic theory, and for our understanding of voters' political information seeking and uses and gratifications of viewing television public affairs programming.[107]

Over half of the voting-age public rely on televised debates for decision making. Having them makes voters winners. How we have them in the future and what changes we should make are a few of the considerations that should be part of policy discussions to improve the political and presidential selection process.

ENDNOTES

1. "Who won? The Voters." Editorial, *The Des Moines Register*, January 6, 1980 (italics added).
2. Elihu Katz and Jacob J. Feldman, "The Debates in the Light of Research: A Survey of Surveys," in S. Kraus (Ed.), *The Great Debates* (Bloomington: Indiana University Press, 1962) pp. 173–223.
3. David O. Sears and Steven H. Chaffee, "Uses and Effects of the 1976 Debates: An Overview of Empirical Studies," in S. Kraus (Ed.), *The Great Debates: Carter vs. Ford, 1976* (Bloomington: Indiana University Press, 1979) pp. 223–261.
4. Katz and Feldman, *op. cit.*, p. 195.
5. Sears and Chaffee, *op. cit.*, p. 237.
6. *Ibid.*
7. See David S. Leuthold and David C. Valentine, "How Reagan 'Won' the Cleveland Debate: Audience Predispositions and Presidential Debate 'Winners,' *Speaker and Gavel*, vol. 18, no. 2, Winter, 1981, pp. 60. Two corollary findings: party leaders may be influenced by polls showing presidential front-runners (N. Polsby and A. Wildavsky, *Presidential Elections* (New York: Charles Scribner's Sons, 1964); and ". . . expectations of who will win a caucus shape opinions about who has won a primary." C. Anthony Broh, "Presidential

Preference Polls and Network News," in W. C. Adams, (Ed.), *Television Coverage of the 1980 Presidential Campaign* (Norwood, NJ: Ablex, 1983) p. 32.

8. Katz and Feldman, *op. cit.*, 0. 208.

9. S. Lubell, "Personalities vs. Issues," in S. Kraus (Ed.), *The Great Debates*, (1962) *op. cit.*, p. 151.

10. This writer maintains that, by and large, public opinion polling helps safeguard democratic precepts by providing a valid and reliable reading of constituents' and publics' views on events, issues, and personalities. For an opposing view see, John C. Ranney, "Do the Polls Serve Democracy?" *Public Opinion Quarterly 10*, 1946, pp. 349–360.

11. John M. Fenton, *In Your Opinion* (Boston: Little Brown, 1960) p. 3. Also cited in Bernard Hennessy, *Public Opinion* (Monterey, California: Brooks/Cole, 1985) p. 60–61. For other press examples see, Irving Crespi, "Polls as Journalism," *Public Opinion Quarterly 44*, 1980, pp. 462–476.

12. For a concise history of the *Literary Digest* and a discussion of straw polls see, B. Hennessy, *op. cit.*, pp. 60–64. See also, Claude E. Robinson, "Straw Votes," *Encyclopedia of the Social Sciences* (1937), 14: 417–419.

13. George Gallup and Saul Forbes Rae, *The Pulse of Democracy* (New York: Simon & Schuster, 1940) p. 46.

14. For the most pronounced attack see, Lindsay Rogers, *The Pollsters: Public Opinion, Politics, and Democratic Leadership* (New York: Knopf, 1949). The quotation is from the jacket of the book.

15. B. Hennessy, *op. cit.*, p. 390.

16. A month after the election, Lindsay Rogers commented:

> I regret that my criticism of the pollsters comes at a time when they are hiding their face in shame. I had rather that they could endeavor to defend their Copper Wares in respect of public opinion without the embarrassment of the Copper having proved Tin in respect of forecasting the result of an election.

L. Rogers, *op. cit.*, p. *vi–vii.*

17. P. Meyer, *Precision Journalism: A Reporter's Introduction to Social Science Methods* (Bloomington: Indiana University Press, 1979).

18. S. Kraus, "The Studies and the World Outside," in S. Kraus and R. M. Perloff (Eds.), *Mass Media and Political Thought: An Information Processing Approach* (Beverly Hills: Sage, 1985) p. 316. See also, S. Kraus, "The Volatility in Reporting Volatile Poll Results in Recent Presidential Elections: The Tail that Wags the Dog." Paper presented at the International Society of Political Psychology, June 24–27, Toronto, Canada. For an excellent look at the interactions of the press and the polls during a political crises see, G. E. Lang and K. Lang, *The Battle For Public Opinion: The President, the Press, and the Polls During Watergate* (New York: Columbia University Press, 1983).

19. C. Anthony Broh, "Horserace Journalism," *Public Opinion Quarterly*, *44*, 1980, p. 519.

20. ABC's national audience could vote for the "debate winner" by dialing one of two 900 numbers. The charge for the call was 50¢. Critics claimed that only those who could afford to make the call "voted." Because it was charged,

more Republicans than Democrats could afford to make the call, Reagan won by a margin of two to one.

21. John Sears, "How Presumptuous Can the Press Get," *Washington Post,* October 30, 1980, p. A23.

22. M. J. Robinson and M. A. Sheehan, *Over the Wire and On TV: CBS and UPI in Campaign '80* (New York: Russell Sage Foundation, 1983) p. 251.

23. Reprinted in E. Drew, *Portrait of an Election: The 1980 Presidential Campaign* (New York: Simon & Schuster, 1981) pp. 410–439.

24. *Ibid.,* p. 419.

25. *Ibid.,* p. 430.

26. *Ibid.,* p. 436.

27. W. C. Adams, "Media Power in Presidential Elections: An Exploratory Analysis, 1960–1980," W. C. Adams (Ed.), *Television Coverage of the 1980 Presidential Campaign* (Norwood, NJ: Ablex, 1983) p. 181.

28. CBS NEWS/*New York Times* Election Survey, September 24–25, 1976. These data and those of CBS cited later were provided by Warren Mitofsky, head of the election unit at CBS.

29. In 1960, Congress essentially gave their approval to exclude minor party candidates in presidential debates by suspending the equal time provision in Section 315 of the Communications Act. For the League's point of view see, "The 1980 Presidential Debates: Behind the Scenes," booklet, League of Women Voters Education Fund, Washington, DC, 1981, especially p. 5.

30. CBS/New York Times Poll, released 6:30 p.m., September 16, 1980.

31. F. Havelick, (Ed.), *Presidential Selection,* (Washington, DC: American Bar Association Special Committee on Election Law and Voter Participation, 1982) p. 140. This is the publication of the conference proceedings held in Racine Wisconsin, July, 1981.

32. Estimates differ. Over a 48-hour period (before and after the debate) CBS/*New York Times* Poll found the decrease of the spread went from a 26 point margin to 20. Ferraro reported the decrease "to a spread of 12 points, from 18 . . ." G. A. Ferraro, *Farraro: My Story,* (New York: Bantam Books, 1985) p. 240.

33. Observation of the author who was in the audience at the debate.

34. G. Ferraro, *Ferraro: My Story, op. cit.,* p. 266.

35. CBS News/*New York Times* Poll: Post-Election Poll, November 8–14, re-interview of 1,798 adults interviewed in preelection survey conducted October 31–November 2. Release, November 18, 1984, 6 p.m.

36. P. Lazarsfeld et al., *The People's Choice: How the Voter Makes Up His Mind in a Presidential Election,* 3rd ed., (New York: Columbia University Press, 1968) p. 179.

37. For historical precision it should be noted that Roosevelt developed his informal chatting radio style while he was governor of New York. See, James MacGregor Burns, *Roosevelt: The Lion and the Fox,* (New York: Harcourt, Brace & World, 1956); and J. Tebbel and S. M. Watts, *The Press and the Presidency: From George Washington to Ronald Reagan,* (New York: Oxford University Press, 1985) pp. 446–447. It also should be noted that in 1940 party identifi-

cation was related to media use: radio was the medium for democrats and newspapers commanded republicans' attentions. See Lazarsfeld et al., *op. cit.*, pp. 129–133.

38. See U.S. Census for that period; also, S. Kraus and D. Davis, *The Effects of Mass Communication on Political Behavior* (University Park: Pennsylvania State University Press, 1976) p. 49.

39. B. R. Berelson, P. F. Lazarsfeld, and W. N. McPhee, *Voting: A Study of Opinion Formation in a Presidential Campaign*, (Chicago: University of Chicago Press, 1954) pp. 356, 360.

40. *Ibid.*, p. 366.

41. D. S. Broder, *Beyond the Front Page: A Candid Look at How the News is Made*, (New York: Simon & Schuster, 1987) pp. 293–294. Broder is a syndicated columnist, and the national political correspondent and associate editor of *The Washington Post*. He won the Pulitzer Prize for Distinguished Commentary in 1974. Though he has not participated directly in the debates, he has written about them after close observation. In particular he has written "three general-election debate 'instant analysis' pieces" (p. 293).

42. *Ibid.*, p. 293. For a discussion of what a debate audience may feel is pertinent to the "who won?" evaluation see, D. Vancil and S. Pendell, (1984) Winning Presidential Debates: An Analysis of Criteria Influencing Audience Response. *Western Journal of Speech Communication, 48*(1), 62–74.

43. D. S. Broder, *op. cit.*, p. 293.

44. *Ibid.*, p. 294.

45. Harold Lasswell, *Politics: Who Gets What, When, How* (Cleveland: World Publishing, 1958) p. 132. Originally published by McGraw-Hill Book Co. in 1936.

46. *Ibid.*, p. 133.

47. H. Lasswell, "Introduction" in S. Kraus (Ed.) *The Great Debates, op. cit.*, p. 20.

48. H. Lasswell, *Politics: Who Gets What, When, How, op. cit.*, p. 133.

49. Former Senator Gary Hart, the leading Democrat running for the presidency, withdrew his candidacy in May, but re-entered the race in December and quit again in March; and in September, Ohio Governor Richard Celeste, who had been contemplating the race, decided not to run after a series of media reports that he had extramarital affairs.

50. Several important questions are: (a) Should the media inquire into the personal lives of presidential candidates? (b) Are such issues as a candidate's adulterous behavior related to his or her ability to hold office? (c) Do voters need such information about candidates in order to make an informed voting decision? (d) What are the ethical responsibilities of the press as they cover candidates seeking office? Answers to these questions form another continuum. At one extreme is moral anarchy. The other extreme would require the signing of a morality or fidelity oath (reminiscent of the 1950s when Senator Joe McCarthy demanded loyalty oaths from some American citizens) attesting to the fact that a candidate is virtuous—ethical, moral, righteous, and upright.

For the reader's resolution of some of these questions two helpful references are highly recommended: Walter Lippmann, *Public Opinion,* (New York: Macmillan, 1922, 1960); and David S. Broder, *Behind the Front Page: A Candid Look at How the News is Made,* (New York: Simon & Schuster, 1987).

51. This method of evaluating candidates was developed through research on language and meaning at the Institute of Communications Research and the Department of Psychology, University of Illinois in the 1950s. The major part of that work is reported in C. E. Osgood, G. J. Suci, and P. H. Tannenbaum, *The Measurement of Meaning* (Urbana: University of Illinois Press, 1957). Part of that research emphasized the development of three dimensions of cognitive response to political personalities (e.g., Roosevelt, Truman, and Eisenhower, p. 103)—activity, evaluative, and potency. The evaluative dimension correlates quite highly with other measures of attitude. Thus, this measurement technique has been used for many years to assess attitudes of voters toward the personalities traits of political candidates. See for example, S. Kraus (Ed.) *The Great Debates* (Bloomington: Indiana University Press, 1962) especially, P. H. Tannenbaum, B. S. Greenberg, and F. D. Silverman, "Candidate Images" (pp. 271–288) and S. Kraus and R. G. Smith, "Issues and Images" (pp. 289–312). See also, H. W. Simons and K. Liebowitz, "Shifts in Candidate Images," in S. Kraus, *The Great Debates: Carter vs. Ford, 1976* (Bloomington: Indiana University Press, 1979) pp. 398–404.

52. Tannenbaum, Greenberg, and Silverman, *op. cit.*

53. Kraus and Smith, *op. cit.*

54. D. Nimmo and R. L. Savage, *Candidates and Their Images: Concepts, Methods, and Findings,* (Pacific Palisades, CA: Goodyear, 1976) p. 206.

55. H. Mendelsohn and G. J. O'Keefe, *The People Choose a President: Influence on Voter Decision Making,* (New York: Praeger, 1976) p. 234.

56. *Ibid.,* p. 122.

57. T. Patterson, *The Mass Media Election: How Americans Choose Their President* (New York: Praeger, 1980) p. 143. Patterson did not use the semantic differential. "Respondents were given complete freedom to say what they wanted to say about the candidates." (Note, p. 143).

58. CBS NEWS/*New York Times* Election Survey, September 24–25, 1976, released by CBS NEWS, 6:30 p. m., September 26; *NYT,* September 27.

59. Memorandum II, Debate Strategy, Patrick Caddell, October 21, 1980, reprinted in E. Drew, *Portrait of an Election op. cit.,* pp. 410–439.

60. *Ibid.,* pp. 414–415.

61. Sears and Chaffee, *op. cit.,* p. 245.

62. B. Hennessy, *Public Opinion, op. cit.,* pp. 278–280. Presumably, Hennessy's discussion was intended to broadly outline televised presidential debates, not to illustrate any continuum.

63. Henry Steele Commager, "Washington Would Have Lost a Debate," *New York Times Magazine,* October 30, 1960.

64. Stanley Kelly, Jr., "Campaign Debates: Some facts and Issues," *Public Opinion Quarterly, 26,* 1962, pp. 360–362.

65. Katz and Feldman, *op. cit.,* p. 203.

66. Sears and Chaffee, *op. cit.*, p. 237.

67. Lloyd Bitzer and Theodore Rueter, *Carter vs Ford: The Counterfeit Debates of 1976* (Madison, WI: University of Wisconsin Press, 1980) pp. 99–113.

68. *Ibid.*, p. 224.

69. Patrica Riley, Thomas A. Hollihan, and David M. Cooley, "The 1976 Presidential Debates: An Analysis of the Issues and Arguments," paper presented at the Central States Speech Association Convention, Chicago, April, 1980.

70. Patricia Riley and Thomas Hollihan, "The 1980 Presidential Debates A Content Analysis of the Issues and Arguments," *Speaker and Gavel, 18*(2), 47–59.

71. *Ibid.*, pp. 50 and 53.

72. *Ibid.*, pp. 53 and 56.

73. Bitzer and Rueter, *op. cit.*, pp. 193–224.

74. *Ibid.*, pp. 113–144.

75. Robert G. Meadow, "Televised Campaign Debates as Whistle-Stop Speeches," in W. C. Adams (Ed.), *Television Coverage of the 1980 Presidential Campaign* (Norwood, NJ: Ablex, 1983) p. 101.

76. These are 1960, 1976, and 1980. The bibliography of debate literature reveals few studies published about the 1984 encounters.

77. For example, see Katz and Feldman, *op. cit.*, pp. 200–205; and Sears and Chaffee, *op. cit.*, pp. 233–237.

78. For a case (Chicago) in point see, Mike Royko, *Boss* (New York: The New American Library, 1971).

79. For a brief overview of each factor see, The Report of the Panel on the Electoral and Democratic Process of the President's Commission for a National Agenda for the Eighties, *The Electoral and Democratic Process in the Eighties* (Washington, DC: U.S. Government Printing Office, 1980, pp. 22–23.

80. Katz and Feldman, *op. cit.*, p. 193.

81. See the various studies in the Kraus edited volumes of the 1960 and 1976 debates. Consult the Gallup national polls beginning with their modified area sample of adults eligible to vote in 1960 just prior to the first debate.

82. Katz and Feldman, *op. cit.*, p. 190 (italics added).

83. National cross-study of 3,000 individuals with listed phone numbers, Sindlinger & Co. Reported in Katz and Feldman, *op. cit.*, p. 193.

84. The Calforina Poll. Reported in Katz and Feldman, *op. cit.*, p. 193.

85. Study of 4,800 citizens of English-speaking telephone households in seven major Canadian cities. Canadian Broadcasting Company. Reported in Katz and Feldman, *op. cit.*, p. 193.

86. Paul J. Deutschmann, "Viewing Conversation and Voting Intentions," in S. Kraus, *The Great Debates*, 1960, *op. cit.*, pp. 235–237. This study, sponsored by Scripps-Howard Research, included 159 members of a telephone panel initiated in 1958, and interviewed in five waves, the last two of which sandwiched the first Kennedy–Nixon debate.

87. Katz and Feldman, *op. cit.*, p. 194.

88. The others are Angus Campbell, Warren E. Miller and Donald L.

Stokes; all four were associated in the Survey Research Center, Institute for Social Research at the University of Michigan, where they conducted the classic election survey: *The American Voter.*

89. C. Wright Mills, *The Power Elite,* (New York: Oxford University Press, 1956) chap. 13.

90. P. E. Converse, "Information Flow and the Stability of Partisan Attitudes," in A. Campbell, et al., *Elections and the Political Order,* (New York: Wiley, 1966) p. 154. The studies referred to are from the review by Katz and Feldman, *op. cit.*

91. Sears and Chaffee, *op. cit.,* p. 228.

92. *Ibid.,* p. 230.

93. *Ibid.,* p. 232.

94. *Ibid.,* p. 251. See also, G. E. Lang and K. Lang, "Immediate and Mediated Responses: First Debate," in S. Kraus, *The Great Debates,* 1960, *op. cit.,* pp. 298–312.

95. Sear and Chaffee, *op. cit.,* p. 245.

96. *Ibid.,* p. 237.

97. CBS News/*New York Times* Poll, CBS release 6:30 p.m., September, 27, 1980; *NYT:* September 28, 1980.

98. CBS News Poll, CBS release 6:30 p.m., October 29, 1980.

99. CBS News/*New York Times* Poll, CBS News releases, 6:30 p.m., October 8 and 21, 1984.

100. P. Converse, "Information Flow and the Stability of Partisan Attitudes," *op. cit.,* p. 137.

101. P. E. Converse, *op. cit.,* pp. 146–147.

102. Katz and Feldman, *op. cit.,* p. 209.

103. Sears and Chaffee, *op. cit.,* p. 242.

104. *Ibid.,* p. 245.

105. T. Patterson and R. McClure, *The Unseeing Eye: The Myth of Television Power In National Elections* (New York: G. P. Putnam's Sons, 1976).

106. ABC News Poll, released Sunday, September 25, 1983. The study was conducted by telephone on June 29 through July 13 in preparation of the Symposium On American Voter Participation, sponsored by Harvard and the American Broadcasting Companies. The quotations are from unnumbered pp. 11 and 12.

107. The author is indebted to Professor Jennings Bryant for suggesting the interpretation of the ABC finding as providing evidence for an "active audience." The extention of the discussion to theoretical considerations of government and media rests with the author and may not reflect the intent of the suggestion.

6

DEBATE POLICY:
EVERY FOUR YEARS

*I would like to make the receipt of federal funding, as the law
now permits, available only to those candidates who agree that
they will participate in televised debates.*[1]

The previous discussions have detailed considerable evidence supporting the view that televised debates should be a standard part of
presidential elections. They have also revealed substantial criticism of
how the debates have been conducted. This concluding chapter reviews the significance of that support and criticism and suggests policy
options.

The most persuasive reason to include televised debates in presidential elections is that voters want them. Voters find something in
televised debates that confirms their previously held support for a
candidate, alters their support, or helps them decide on whom to
support. In that way voters, many of whom ordinarily are politically
inactive, at least participate minimally in the election. Televised presidential debates promote interest in the election. It is not surprising,
therefore, that many observers of the political system have urged the
institutionalization of presidential debates; some have even suggested
that presidential candidates should be required to debate. Mandating
presidential debates was first suggested by a network television executive in an exchange with a candidate's representative during a debriefing conference after the 1976 debates. Robert Chandler, vice president of CBS News said:

I was asking Mike [Michael Raoul-Duval, special counsel to President Ford] why he thought [mandating presidential debates], yesterday, had to be a constitutional amendment. One of the things that could be done is to make a commitment to debate a factor in eligibility for public financing, amend the public financing law, so that the presidential candidate is not entitled to public financing, unless he agrees to debate. He still has his option. He doesn't have to accept public financing, but if he does, he has to debate. I'm not even sure it's necessarily a good one, but the means does, I think, exist.[2]

In the discussions, disagreements centered on how debates could be institutionalized legally, and in a politically fair manner. Additionally, the debriefing conference explored the role of candidates and the League in the selection of panelists; scrutinized the decision of the League and the candidates not to allow unilateral cameras and audience reaction shots; and generally discussed the power of the candidates in the negotiations for the 1976 televised presidential debates. The conferees were the leading, behind-the-debates protagonists of the three major factions—candidates, sponsor, and the networks. Also, contributions to the discussion were made by legal experts in government positions, representatives from the media, and academic researchers (see chap. 3). The deliberations were candid and often heated. But they generally reflected a desire to continue televised debates, and to avoid another long hiatus before the next set of debates.

Although many of the problems remain, we have had debates in successive presidential elections since 1976. Some observers suggest that the debates have continued only because it was politically expedient for the respective candidates' campaigns. Others believed that they have occurred because they were already being institutionalized. That is, the debates were seen by the public, and by candidates, as political events that should regularly occur in presidential campaigns. Plans for improving debates should consider the *public interest*.

In planning for them, four major problem areas require examination—sponsors, candidate control versus the public interest, format, and public participation. These issues, and some ideas and recommendations to improve and broaden the scope and import of televised debates in the presidential election are discussed here.

Sponsors

Current discussions of who should sponsor televised presidential debates pit the League of Women Voters Education Fund against the two major political parties. As of this writing, the League, which has mounted a campaign for continued debate sponsorship, and the political parties, which have formed a bipartisan commission to sponsor televised debates in 1988, are holding firm to their positions.[3] Each has insisted that its structure can best serve the needs of the voters and the candidates. Each has criticized the other, claiming a more representative base from which to manage the debates than its competitor.

The League contends that its organization, a grassroots, nonpartisan amalgamation of women throughout the country, can be trusted to mount and manage presidential debates. Members cite the League's vast experience in local and state debates on a variety of issues. They also claim territorial rights as the planners and executors of three of the four sets of general election debates since 1960.

Essentially, League officials claim that their organization is better suited than the parties to sponsor debates, and reject the notion of even joint partnership with the Democrats and Republicans. The League's president, Nancy M. Neuman, asserted that the attempt by the major political parties to seize control of the general election debates shows that "they're trying to steal the debates from the American voters."[4]

As a matter of fact, after the 1976 debates there were disagreements among certain League officials about continuing as sponsor in subsequent presidential election years. When this writer put the question, "Do you want to [sponsor the debates] again?" to the League's president, Ruth Clusen, she responded:

> Well, we'd do it again, let's put it that way. One thing I'm sure of is that the financing would have to be different . . . we could do this once, by taking the money out of reserve, if need be . . . but we'd know how to do it better the next time. But obviously, anything that loosened up the relationship between any third-party and the people who are the media producers would be helpful, but to any organization, any outside body, anybody except the networks, money would be a problem unless the situation is changed.[5]

Peggy Lampl, executive director of the League, disagreed:

> I have a minority opinion. I think the League should not do it again, as Ruth knows. I'm kind of intrigued by public financing, some kind of restraint. I'm not sure that I think the networks should have sole control without some other factor. But I don't think . . . one other organization should do it again, although I feel they should be done.[6]

It is also interesting to note that the suggestion that major parties sponsor debates came first from a member of the League's presidential debates national advisory board, Newton Minow.[7]

For their part, Paul G. Kirk, the Democratic national chairman, and his Republican counterpart, Frank J. Fahrenkopf Jr., contended that their sponsorship would institutionalize presidential debates. Their remarks were more diplomatic than ingenuous. Kirk said:

> We believe the Democratic and Republican Parties are making history today by assuming their rightful responsibility for the single most effective voter education project.[8]

Fahrenkopf claimed that:

> The extremely competitive nature of the two parties will ensure that we will reach the best possible agreement for all concerned, most importantly for the voters of this nation.[9]

They argued that sponsoring the debates "would . . . strengthen the role of the political parties in the electoral process."[10] Ironically, it was a role that had been usurped by television. As presidential candidates used television to bring their campaigns directly to the electorate, the significance of the political parties in the electoral process diminished. Indeed, by the time of the nominating conventions, the public through television had, in effect, selected the nominees (see chap. 2). Apparently, sponsoring televised presidential debates would give back electoral meaning to the major parties, once again positioning them in a significant role in presidential elections. Even more of a role for the parties was suggested by Robert Squier, the campaign consultant, in a conference on government and campaign financing:

> I would propose we organize a system to give back to the political parties, nationally and locally, some power over the medium that has done them in. For instance, the Democratic and Republican national committees should be the place where equal time is taken care of for parties out of office.[11]

With the formation of the commission, it is apparent that the parties formally capitulated to television's dominant role in presidential elections.

It is claimed that each party's increased visibility as a sponsor during a presidential election would help to strengthen the two-party system. However, would the major parties' sponsorship of debates fortify the already powerful role of the candidates in controlling the debates? Probably. But, candidate control was there with the League as sponsor. And what happens to third and minor party candidates? These questions deserve the attention of policy makers.

Minor Party Candidates. This discussion begins with two positions. One, that a reasonable opportunity for television exposure should be provided to minor party candidates. Two, as this writer posited in 1977, "I personally regretted that Senator Eugene McCarthy was not given a chance to debate Ford and Carter. However, I would rather see only the major challengers debate on television than not see debates at all."[12] A similar view was found in a 1983 ABC-Harvard University Poll:

> A 57 percent majority of the public feels that if television networks sponsor national presidential debates they should include only the top two or three major candidates and not all candidates. Nevertheless, 39 percent think the debates should include all the candidates.
>
> Interestingly, the less likely you are to vote, the more likely you are to think all candidates should be concluded.[13]

Given that there are usually upwards of 100 qualified candidates running for the presidency, finding a reasonable and fair method for them to reach the electorate is a most difficult task. However, one of the determinants of debate sponsorship should be the ability and inclination of the potential sponsor to deal with such tasks.

Perhaps the League's most persuasive credential is its nonaffiliation with a political party, a position from which the League claims it can give assurance to "legitimate third-party candidates" that they would be included in debates.[14] The party chairmen were not disturbed by the criticism that third-party candidates would be excluded from debates held under the auspices of their organizations. In fact, Kirk wanted such exclusion; Fahrenkopf left that decision to the commission, but agreed that the inclusion of minor party candidates was unlikely.

Although both positions have merit, each is weakened by a serious flaw. The chairmen of the major political parties asks us to believe that a "bipartisan" commission composed largely of Democrats and Republicans[15] would be sympathetic to candidates from other parties who want to participate in debates, a highly improbable political event, unless, of course, the third-party candidate has considerable support. In negotiating aspects of presidential debates, what transpires between the parties and the candidates? As leaders of the major parties, candidates will most certainly want as much control over negotiations with these *new* sponsors as candidates have had in the past with the League.

The League claims that it will safeguard the interest of "legitimate third-party candidates," but that is questionable. What does *legitimate* mean? How is that term operationalized? In 1976 the League failed to consider the term seriously, and was sued by minor party candidates Eugene McCarthy and Shirley Chisholm. In 1980 it got entangled in a mess involving Carter (who had refused a three-candidate debate), Reagan (who debated Anderson and Carter separately), and Anderson, the minor party candidate who had to measure up to a certain standing in public opinion polls in order to participate in only one of two presidential debates (see chap. 3). Evidently, the League identifies a legitimate candidate eligible for debate participation as one who receives a certain percentage of voter support in public opinion polls.

With usually over 100 legally bona fide candidates seeking the presidency, determining minor party participation in debates is a difficult and vexing task.[16] David Broder's solution is to have the major parties guarantee debates with their candidates and exclude other parties' candidates from participating, but provide them with a different television format:

> First [each party] must lay down as a condition in its convention hall that the nominee of the party must be prepared to meet his major-party opponent, face-to-face, in genuine debate, say, three times in the fall campaign: in the third week of September and the first and third weeks of October.
>
> Second, they must be prepared jointly to defend the franchise of their mutually arranged debates, and insist that any other "debates" involving independent or third-party candidates under non-partisan auspices will be considered only as supplemental forums, with participation of the major-party nominees determined by their own tactical considerations.
>
> Without such a stand [there will be] no shred of a two-party system in the presidential contest.[17]

It is curious to note, in his several discussions about debates and about Anderson 7 years later, Broder does not mention the idea of politicians controlling preparations for televised presidential debates. To the contrary, in response to Lyn Nofziger's (ex-journalist; ex-Reagan press secretary) insistence that, "Winning an election means doing the things and having your candidate do the things that he can do most effectively and that will influence the most votes." Broder said: "I reject the Nofziger thesis. *The campaign is not the candidates' personal property. It is the public's hour of judgment.*"[18]

Broder's comments notwithstanding, it is clear that none of the potential debate sponsors thus far has proposed a fair and reasonable method for resolving the issue. One major newspaper exhorted that, "Neither [the League nor the parties] makes a persuasive case."[19] Its' solution is as follows:

> A reasonable way to protect such candidates would be for prospective debate sponsors—whether the League, the parties, the television networks or others—to issue guidelines or ground rules. These should cover among other things the criteria for including third candidates. Decisions might turn on objective popularity as measured by polls and on the subjective judgment of a blue-ribbon committee.[20]

The well-intentioned attempt by the League to use a specific percentage of public opinion support, below which a candidate would be excluded from a debate, failed to recognize error factors in polling, and the ephemeral state of the measurement itself. No one lowest percentage point, or even a minimal small range, could represent a candidate's probable public support or lack thereof *beyond the time the measurement was made*. If a candidate failed to get the specific percentage during 1 week, he or she may reach it the next. Hence, a candidate's eligibility for participating in debates depends on the timing of polling dates in conjunction with debating schedules. Taken to its extreme in the period from Labor Day to the election (just over 2 months) candidates could pop in and out of a number of debates depending on their standings in public opinion polls. The improbability of such an occurrence should not prevent us from rejecting the absurd procedure in the first place. The League could have met its responsibilities by making a considered judgment without employing polling results.

The notion of a relationship between public opinion polling and presidential debates can be in keeping with democratic theory, providing for voter involvement in the conduct of the presidential campaign and the election process (see following). But, its use as debate gatekeeper for minor party participation is questionable.

Minor party participation in debates could be decided by a formula not based on probability estimates but similar to that which qualifies presidential candidates to receive public funds under the Campaign Financing Act.[21] Under the law in effect for the 1980 presidential campaign, minor party candidates may be eligible for public funds provided that they receive between 5% and 25% of the general election vote. Anderson became eligible for $4.2 million after he received 6.5% of the popular vote. Although this method is not without problems, some adaptation of it would afford a more reasonable basis for assessing minor party public support than does the amalgamation of polling results. Still, some television opportunity for other candidates should be made available to them.

Candidate Control Versus Public Interest

Far more important than who sponsors the debates is the question of who controls them. Should control be in the hands of the candidates? The consequences of candidate control have been substantial (see chap. 3). Candidates have: (a) decided whether to participate in debates; (b) approved areas of discussion; (c) refused to debate without panelists; (d) had substantial influence in the panelists selection process; (e) restricted audience reaction shots, in effect, influencing how television covered them; (f) tactically determined when to hold debates; and (g) subtlety threatened not to participate or to pull out of debates if issues important to them were not acceded to. Broder's point about who "owns" the presidential campaign is pertinent here (paraphrasing): "Presidential debates are not the candidates' personal property. It is for the public's hour of judgment."

Although candidate control of debates is widely known and has received serious professional and scholarly discussion from the very beginning,[22] politicians and the media have not paid much attention to it. Some notable recent exceptions arose during a Harvard University conference on television and the presidential election process. One of the participants was Elizabeth Drew, a journalist with considerable experience covering presidential campaigns and debates. She regarded candidate control of televised presidential debates as being manipulative:

> A real question in the whole area of debates is not whether television organizations manage it or the league manages it, [or political parties manage it (?)] but to what degree the candidates themselves are succeeding in managing it and manipulating it.[23]

Drew observed that candidates' positioning debates advantageously for their campaigns may be disfunctional to the political process of electing a president. "Was it healthy," she queried, "to have only one debate in 1980, as close as possible to the election as one camp could get, therefore allowing for as little time for analysis as possible?"[24]

It is indeed an unhealthy political process that finds presidential candidates deciding on how, and on what, voters should judge them. Yet, it is in candidates' interests to seek and have control that circumscribes voters' judgments. It is in their interests to "manage and manipulate" presidential debates—to control them by including only those actions they deem will help their campaigns succeed, avoiding others that may be damaging.

It is in the candidates' interest to designate panelists, selecting names of journalists who are sympathetic to their candidacy and rejecting those who are not. Candidates in debates could not care less about the journalistic principle that a broadcast executive, Richard S. Salant, brought to their attention in 1976:

> The subject of an interview shall have no voice in the selection of the interviewer, nor, in any news coverage, should the subject of the coverage have any voice in the selection of the correspondent assigned to cover him/her on the story.[25]

Salant argued that "there are consequences that flow from the fact that these were not debates but were joint press interviews."[26] Salant's point is important. Violating that journalistic principle impairs more than just the debates, it risks impugning a variety of public interest issues (e.g., integrity of the press, bias, objectivity, and the like). Candidates for the presidency should recognize and accept the principle. Journalists should object to debate negotiations that compromise their integrity.

The Broder–Nafziger dispute illustrates two fundamentally different, if not opposing, theories of campaigning. David Broder, it appears, would have the presidential campaign be an educational one, in which voters' needs for decision making predominate the political agenda. His view is clearly within the scope of democratic theory that suggests that an informed citizen is better able to select competent, trustworthy leaders than one not so informed. Providing political communication is in the best interest of the voter, and preserves democratic values. Political journalism supports democratic institutions when its reports about them (favorable or unfavorable) enlighten the electorate. Broder's creed is: "I am not a [candidate's] advocate. . . . Professionally, I can't give a damn who wins or loses."[27]

Lyn Nofziger, Reagan's former "hired gun,"[28] "can't give a damn" about the press, or about political education, only the campaign. Our modern election process, Nofziger most likely would contend, includes three distinct participants with three specific roles. The press, whose job it "is to cover a campaign;" the voter, whose job it is to make up his mind and vote; and, the candidate and his or her campaign staff, whose jobs are to persuade a critical mass of the electorate and "win an election." These latter jobs fit aspects of economic, marketing, and mass persuasion theories. These theories are not concerned with teaching or educating voters, but rather with convincing voters to adopt a particular point of view, or pull a lever for a particular candidate. One is open to all ideas; the other is confined to one particular idea. Nofziger's creed is: Have a "candidate do the things . . . that will influence the most votes."[29]

Interestingly, these theories correspond to the primary functions of contending sponsors—the League, which professes to voter education, and the political parties, whose allegiance is to partisan persuasion. Although these groups' basic missions are different, they have a common interest in strengthening democratic values through the election process.

Are these interests (theories, if you will) incompatible with each other? Some observers submit that the information interests of the public and the campaign interests of candidates are reconcilable.[30] We should think of ways to join these seemingly disparate pursuits. Some portion of the presidential election could be "set aside" for voter educational functions carried out by the respective campaigns, including candidates, in conjunction with the combined efforts of the League and the political parties. For example, one televised presidential debate could be conducted with educational teaching techniques. Formats could be developed to serve both the candidate and the public.

Format

Coming to grips with sponsorship and control issues should bring about changes in format sought by many debate critics. Criticisms leveled against televised presidential debates invariably include comments about the *format,* the way in which debates are conducted. To some critics, a panel of journalists asking questions of candidates during a debate is not unlike reporters interrogating the president in a press conference at the White House. Critics sense that many panelists want to discover something sensational about the candidate, to check out their suspicions about one thing or another, to trap the debater, or to ask hostile questions.[31]

Why are these criticisms not acted upon? Let's review some of the conditions that appear to support the status quo. In this format of questions and answers, journalists and candidates vie for public attention. Candidates, seeking favorable media and voter attention, jockey for position in and out of debates (e.g., rehearsing and using phrases: "There you go, again!" and "Where's the beef?"). Journalists and city officials recognize that an association with a presidential debate brings publicity and prestige (see chap. 4). Many journalists covet an invitation to be a panelist in a nationwide televised debate. For journalists it has become a mark of recognition, if not achievement. More importantly, it is now seen as both a stamp of approval (acceptable to candidates and sponsors) and an object of criticism (journalists should cover the news, not make it).

Journalist-panelists become participant observers, tainting their role as watchdog in the political process. Candidates' responses often include stock phrases from speeches used in the campaign. Panelists attempt to set a debate agenda by asking certain questions. Indeed, on several occasions they have consulted on questions, occasionally deciding who should ask a given candidate a certain question. In turn, candidates attempt to avoid or not respond fully to questions, preferring to set their own agenda. The result is that panelists are sometimes criticized for asking nasty, testy questions, and candidates are chastised for being evasive.[32]

The substance of the debate is affected by the format. With a panelist format, candidates have few opportunities to present a position in *contrast* to their opponents'. Although the debates have been "thematic" (e.g., domestic issues, foreign affairs), candidates are usually barraged with a variety of questions on complicated issues. They have little time to develop a position, and virtually no time for rebuttal.

Even with these problems, the data support the conclusion that the public gains from having televised debates in presidential campaigns. Nevertheless, any change in format that enhances the presidential selection process should be seriously considered. We could *develop formats,* tailoring them to particular political races and contexts.

Developing Other Formats. Although in 1858 Lincoln and Douglas themselves negotiated their debate format without much concern for the media, the formats of modern presidential debates have been negotiated by candidate representatives and sponsors, with the inevitable presence of television executives. In 1960, the networks and the candidate representatives set the precedent for the panel formats (sometimes called *press conference formats*) that prevail today.

From the start of planning in 1976, Jim Karayn, project director for the League's presidential debates, believed that a format should engage the viewer. In his initial memorandum to the League's steering committee, Karayn reviewed the 1960 format negotiations and concluded that the League "may well show the pattern for the future."[33] Karayn's view of presidential debates was that they should be distinctive, and uniquely placed among political communications in the election campaign:

> The task is to devise a format where the viewer/voter can come away with some insights and knowledge about the candidates he would not have gotten from his other "exposures" to them, be it the nightly news

campaign reports, the Sunday afternoon panel show appearances, the paid political spots, or what others write about them.[34]

Karayn thought that the "pure" face-to-face format required a "narrow, clear-cut issue on which the debaters can take definite stands." He saw such 1-hour encounters as "too limiting," and candidates as "too deferential," making "for dull viewing."[35]

About a week later, Karayn sent another memorandum in which he was optimistic that the candidates would accept "questioning each other," but insisted that "candidates need the stimulation of incisive questions to get their juices flowing."[36] Among observers there may be disagreement about the incisiveness of the questions asked in the Carter–Ford debates, and skepticism about the flow of candidates' juices, but Karayn's reasons for suggesting that the 1976 format should be considered along with other criteria to guide the development of future formats makes sense.

There are many texts that outline and examine different formats. One discussion of presidential debate formats is that included in a study of the Carter–Ford encounters.[37]

Bitzer and Rueter made several severe criticisms, underscoring flaws in the "press conference" format: a "third-party" (panelists) in the debates; order effects in speaking, questioning and answering; and a "lack of adequate time." These and other factors, they maintained, allowed panelists to set a deficient agenda.[38] They argued that the central flaw of the format has been its infrastructure that has prevented candidates from adequately answering panelists questions, and displaying deftness in debate.[39] Bitzer and Rueter proposed four basic formats for future presidential debates beginning in 1980—news interview, modified Ford–Carter, Lincoln–Douglas, and policy address. They insisted that these "options exhaust the desireable possibilities" in that:[40]

> The news interview format provides for discussion and inquiry. If they debate, they either do so face-to-face or at a distance. The policy address format provides for the latter. If they debate face-to-face, they cover either many issues or a few critical issues. The modified Ford–Carter format meets the first option; and the Lincoln–Douglas format meets the second. The conditions of genuine debate are built into each debate format.

Apparently, the formats were suggested by Bitzer and Rueter because they concluded that those of the 1960 and 1976 debates were inadequate. Although their alternative models contain elements that should be useful in developing formats for presidential debates, none of the models gained support of the candidates in 1980 and 1984, years in which the "press conference" model was repeated.[41]

Several of the Bitzer–Rueter ideas have been around for some time. They were either "laid on the table" in the negotiations for the Kennedy–Nixon and Ford–Carter debates, or were part of an external attempt to influence them. In 1960 and 1976, attempts to bring about face-to-face debates, even as part of the panel format, failed.[42] For example, Sig Mickelson, President, CBS News, Inc., suggested that Kennedy and Nixon question each other in the "Oregon Debate" style,[43] but the candidate representatives would have none of that format.[44] And in 1976 the League tried three times to get Carter and Ford to "cross-examine" each other, but was rebuffed because "the idea was 'a dud,' since neither candidate would want to look as if he were 'beating hell' out of the other."[45]

Originators and supporters of these and other suggestions for improving televised presidential debates recognize that unless candidates perceive potential changes as being in their interest (i.e., election to the presidency) adoption of them is unlikely. Public opinion may persuade candidates to make certain changes, or prompt them to adopt some new formats. Most likely, however, someone or some institution interested enough in debates will be needed to mount such efforts.

In any case, one important presidential debate policy objective should be the public's involvement with them. According to communication and electoral research, and even some passive measures of the public's interest in debates (e.g., televison audience measurement), debates may be able to increase the public's involvement in the presidential election process (e.g., voter turnout). Proposals for mandating debates and efforts to affect their agendas, part of earlier suggestions, seek to expand the involvement of the public in debates as well as improve their quality.

Public Participation

An important policy question in this assessment is what contribution can televised presidential debates make that would increase the electorate's interest and participation in the presidential selection process? Asked another way—can the debates help reform the political process of electing a president—the question inevitably turns to tinkering with the system. This is not the case in this instance. Here, we look at those aspects of televised debates, and those of the electorate's use of political television, to determine ways in which the debates can better serve voters.

Voter Turnout. In this section we are concerned with Americans' participation in voting, not their voting choice. To what extent can televised debates help get more voters to the polls in a presidential election? Although there are incidental and fragmentary data from which the relationship between televised presidential debates and its effect on voter turnout may be inferred, no investigation centering on that relationship has been uncovered by this writer. Some surveys have poll results nudging at that relationship, but none has captured it in a definitive manner. To gain some insight, we turn to voter surveys conducted by CBS/*New York Times* in 1976 and 1984, and ABC-Harvard University in 1983.

The notion that low voter turnout in presidential elections is due to an alienated electorate appears to have been inaccurate in 1976:

> The CBS/New York Times survey of adults who didn't vote found relatively little indication of alienation from politicians in general or dissatisfaction with the choice of candidates as a factor in the failure to vote. Moreover, a battery of questions designed to measure "alienation" produced no more acceptance among nonvoters than among voters. People who held these "alienated" views voted about as heavily as did adults nationwide (55%).
>
> Most adults who didn't vote were unable to because they weren't registered.[46]

Similar results were found in the 1984 presidential election. When asked, "Why didn't you vote for President this year?" 39% of registered nonvoters said they were too busy or work interfered, and about 50% of the nonvoters were not registered. "Disenchantment with the electoral process as a whole was mentioned by only 6% [of registered nonvoters and nonvoters]."[47] This suggests that the campaign interest level for nonvoters was not significantly different from voters. Indeed, only 12% of those who did not vote were not interested in politics.[48] Maintaining the electorate's interest in election campaigns is a prerequisite for political involvement. Televised debates appear to do just that.

The ABC News-Harvard University voter turnout study found that "everybody—voters and nonvoters alike—agree[d] that televised presidential debates are a good thing."[49] It is interesting to find that nonvoters have a positive attitude about televised debates. The study concludes that:

> Since so many say televised debates are useful in decision making, perhaps more of them would help engage more citizens in the campaign process and thereby increase voter turnout.[50]

Plans to increase voter turnout may need to distinguish between registered voters who can, but fail to vote, and nonregistered voters who, unless activated during a campaign, cannot. This latter group may require long-term attention (i.e., educational programs that are aimed at increasing political involvement, and provide for voter registration). Both groups of nonvoters, however, can be reached *within* the presidential election campaign period, especially during the more salient spans of primaries and conventions, and in the general election after Labor Day.

Any plan to increase voter turnout through televised debate viewing needs additional system support. That support should involve the political parties, although support must also come from nonpartisan groups, such as the League. The rallying call for building a strong democratic political system in the 1980s appears to be, "Strengthen the major political parties." President Carter's panel's 1980 report on the electoral and democratic process details ways in which the parties may be strengthened. To increase political participation, for example, it suggested that free television time should be given to the major parties and to those minor parties reaching "a threshold of voter support in the previous national election."[51] The panel also recommended making voter registration "easier," and creating "holidays of the Presidential primary day and the general election day."[52] Nonvoters in the 1983 ABC News-Harvard University Poll (recall that they were debate supporters) were in favor of an election holiday because it "reduce[d] . . . logistical problems."[53]

Three ideas that could sustain public participation, and help increase voter turnout, have been advanced: (a) in 1975 by Marjorie and Charles Benton and Gene Pokorny (citizen-directed political education program), and (b) by Daniel Yankelovich and Cyrus Vance (public agenda issues analysis), and (c) after the 1976 debates by Jim Karayn ("*Agenda of Events*"). These ideas (parts of which have been implemented in the past) are reexamined here in view of the wide acceptance of televised presidential debates among voters, and among registered nonvoters and those not registered to vote.

Citizen-Directed Political Education. The Bentons and Pokorny thought that the 1976 presidential election offered a unique opportunity for citizens to celebrate the nation's Bicentennial. They suggested the Presidential Forum Project, which was to include about 10 "town meetings" (forums) with citizens and presidential candidates. Although the League sponsored four forums in 1976, which, incidently, set the precedent for candidates debating on television in primaries, much of the citizens' participation initially conceived was not realized. It was an opportunity to begin a voter education program, but the anticipation that after 16 years there would be presidential debates in the general election all but consumed the effort.

Although politicians talk about voter education, they neither have the time nor the inclination to engage in a political education public program. Candidates are too ego involved in their own campaigns to mount an educational campaign for voters. Understandably, they are preoccupied with persuasion, not education.

Televised presidential debates are major campaign events that could be the cornerstone of a public voter education effort.

Public Agenda. Like the Presidential Forums, an experiment in issues analysis began as a result of discussions among dedicated concerned individuals. In 1976 Yankelovich and Vance were concerned about four developments: "1) *The rapid increase in the number of presidential primaries;* 2) *The large number of serious primary candidates expected;* 3) *The dramatic increase in the number of independent voters;* 4) *The absence of any systematic attempt to discuss and deal with important public policy issues from the point of view of reconciling expert opinion with public attitudes.*" Yankelovich and Vance thought that these four developments would add to the usual "distractions" in a presidential campaign and "obscure" candidates position on "critical national issues."[54]

They formed the Public Agenda Foundation, a nonprofit, nonpartisan research organization to:

> (1) . . . identify several critical national issues that were likely to be pivotal to the outcome of the 1976 presidential election; (2) analyze each of these issues [utilizing] expert opinion and public attitudes . . . (3) make available the completed analyses to both presidential candidates . . . the media and the voters.

The experiment brought together elite and public views about the salient issues in 1976 that were ultimately formulated into three issue research reports—inflation and unemployment, moral leadership in government, and U.S. foreign policy. The Public Agenda staff established contact with the League as the latter sought to sponsor the 1976 Carter–Ford Debates. The three-issue research reports were given to the candidates as they prepared for the debates.

Perhaps the most innovative and sophisticated adjunct activity of the 1976 presidential debates was the Public Agenda Foundation's effort to influence the issues discussed in the debates. An attempt such as this to set the issues agenda in the campaign, and especially in presidential debates, widens the sphere of public involvement in the election and increases the credibility of the election campaign.

An issues agenda could be accompanied by an events agenda similar to one suggested by Jim Karayn, the League's first debate director.

Agenda of Events. After the hectic experience that allowed only 35 days to mount the League's 1976 debates, Karayn appealed for a "kind of calm, reasonable planning [for debates]." He envisioned "an *Agenda of Events,* a formal schedule of campaign activities among candidates, not exclusively confined to a series of face-to-face encounters or debates."[55]

Karayn suggested that in January of the election year the Democratic and Republican candidates for the top two offices agree to "participate in a specific timetable of events, if they received their party's nomination."[56] He suggested a 9- or 10-week agenda with these major events beginning with Labor Day:[57]

Week 1   Back-to-back addresses by the two candidates.
Week 2   Presidential debate 1.
Week 4   Presidential debate 2.
Week 5   Individual interviews with presidential candidates.
Week 6   Vice-presidential debate.
Week 7   Presidential debate 3.
Week 8   Minority candidates' debate.
         Appearances by candidate advisors.
Last week before election—Presidential debate 4.

To set an agenda, Karayn would establish a national debate commission chartered by Congress and funded by them or through the Federal Election Commission.

A bold, perhaps too structured, election campaign innovation, the Agenda of Events does not seek to eliminate the usual candidate campaign activities, but may reduce the number of them. More importantly, the agenda includes events that along with peripheral activities could promote public participation and involvement in presidential elections.

Debate Public Funding. Charles Benton helped launch the Forums in the 1976 primaries with a $50,000 grant from the foundation he heads. Very little, if any, of that money was available for the grassroots political education plan that had been originally envisioned. The Yankelovich–Vance issues agenda was supported with $150,000 contributed by individuals, foundations, and corporations. Much of the effort was completed by volunteers. Karayn's Agenda funding plan would require congressional action. These ideas, all geared to promote public participation, have fiscal implications. Introducing campaign reforms would doubtless increase the already financially expensive presidential campaign.

The economics and politics of funding political campaigns have received much attention.[58] In addition to the obvious concern of politicians, individuals and organizations committed to supporting and improving democratic institutions are concerned with the increasing costs of election campaigns. Election campaign reforms will be inhibited unless funding sources are available. One participant in a national conference reviewing the 10-year experience with the Federal Election Campaign Act cautioned that, "By reforming the reforms we risk creating yet another series of unforseen results."[59] The conference concluded that:

> Political reform . . . should encourage participation, including financial participation, in the political process. It should open up opportunities for individual citizens to serve their parties and their candidates, rather than restrain such voluntary activity . . . [O]ur nation's political campaign laws [should] encourage citizen participation in the election campaign process.[60]

Instead, in 1976 campaign funding laws were interpreted in such a way as to *discourage* participation. In 1977, the League filed suit against the Federal Election Commission (FEC), requesting judicial review of a Policy Statement that eliminated corporate and union funding for the 1976 debates.[61] The FEC allowed that Political Action Committee (PAC) funds could be used to help defray debate costs. The League refused PAC funds because they considered those to be political and partisan. On the other hand, they argued that union and corporate funds would support a political education information program—the presidential debates. That Policy Statement prohibited the League's Education Fund from accepting already committed corporate foundation funding, forcing it to mount a fundraising campaign among individuals, and ending up using its own money without recovering debate costs.[62]

An exemption to the law now permits corporations to contribute money as long as at least two candidates debate. But solving one problem may have brought about another. Professor John G. Murphy of Georgetown Law Center maintained that, "One would have to be a fool to think that doesn't have some adverse effect on the candidates who are not included."[63]

But, there are other ways to finance debates, some of which have been rejected out of hand. These and other ideas may prove useful as future debates are organized.

IDEAS AND RECOMMENDATIONS

Here are some ideas that may promote public participation, and help improve televised debates and some aspects of election campaigning.

Corporate Advertising and Public Appeals. One recommendation for raising money to mount presidential televised debates proposed corporate solicitations to "advertise" just before and immediately after the actual debate, much like the current PBS "sponsors." Another recommendation advanced a plan appealing to citizen-viewers and listeners to contribute funds to support the debate. Each of these recommendations was informally rejected by League officials as being too commercial and not in keeping with the occasion.[64] Contributors, however, have been listed in the printed program given to the invited guests in the audience at the debates.

Tailored corporate listings as "sponsors ex officio," and tastefully constructed appeals for funds by the debate sponsor or the moderator, should not interfer with the dignity of the occasion. Indeed, with proper "historical" incentives, the fundraising among the mass audience could further public participation in the election.

Notes and Audio Visuals. Most formats have rules that are rigidly applied during the debate. Ostensibly, the rules are there to help ensure that each candidate is treated exactly the same, has the same opportunity for advancing his or her position, and that each will be perceived by the public has having been treated fairly. This rigidity takes on absurd proportions. For example, notes may not be brought into the debate, but notes may be taken during the debate. Why the restriction? If a candidate wants to build a particular case *beforehand* why shouldn't he or she be allowed to? Probably, the reason is that predebate notes may encourage unresponsiveness to the panelists' questions. For the most part, under the present rules they are unresponsive,[65] or they lay in waiting to get their points across, or to rebut. Notes brought into the debate should be allowed. Also, during the debate audio visual aids should be permitted. Unless it can be supported that by maintaining a specific rigid format for all debates candidates are able to get their views across *and* voters benefit, formats should vary from debate to debate.

Candidates should be given the latitude necessary to present their views. Candidates should be able to say and do as they please, restricted by time allotment only. Negotiations should begin with such freedom to express points of view. Formats should enhance such freedoms, not repress them.

Political and Legal Issues. All branches of government—executive, legislative, and judicial—have been involved with one or another aspect of presidential debates. Issues relating to the role of the debate sponsor and its activities, candidates and their campaigns, the media (especially television and the networks), and the election process generally, have affected televised presidential debates.

Since 1960, two vexing questions persist: (a) Should televised debates be a part of presidential elections? (b) If so, which candidates may participate? The answer to the first question appears to be in the affirmative. The answer to the second one, however, has not been satisfactorily resolved. The Federal Communication Commission, Federal Election Commission, Congress, and the courts have had to decide on the efficacy and legality of allowing televised presidential debates with the major party candidates only, excluding, for the most part, third and minor party candidates. The issue has been resolved for expediency as related to circumstances surrounding a given election. Neither the Congress, the regulatory agencies, nor the courts have been able to resolve the issue so that both law and practice are fair to candidates and voters while benefiting the electoral process.

It may prove helpful to create a bipartisan commission whose task would be to draft for consideration by Congress a bill that resolves the issue of eleigibility of candidates to participate in televised presidential debates.[66]

Mandatory Participation. That commission could also consider whether candidates should be required to debate. The evidence reviewed herein clearly shows that voters want debates in presidential elections. Suggestions of compelling candidates to debate by making it a qualifying condition to receive public funds under the Federal Election Campaign Act of 1971 should receive serious consideration. The argument advanced is that the Revenue Act of 1971 provides a tax checkoff to help finance campaigns in presidential general elections, and since the *public wants presidential debates* those who receive funds should debate. Candidates may refuse to debate, but they would not receive public funds.

Research and Experiments. Televised presidential debates have been the subject of inquiry for university-based researchers, professional research organizations, media, and candidates' campaigns. The accumulation of that body of information presents a sizeable bibliography that has been appended to this discussion.

Most of the debate studies considered the impact or effects of the debates on voters and presidential campaigns. They have also added much to our understanding of how political information is diffused and reacted to in a democratic society. Few studies have been conducted that especially seek to improve the debates, and fewer have sought to experiment with the debates and various effects on voters.[67]

It is clear that the media have direct effects on the political process of electing presidents. The National Science Foundation, which traditionally has funded the expert election studies conducted at the University of Michigan, should help finance studies that help us to understand and improve television's role, and the role of debates, in presidential general elections.

Some concerns and some research questions:

1. How do voters use televised presidential debates in making up their minds?
2. In 1960, radio listeners thought Richard Nixon came off better than John Kennedy, whereas television viewers found Kennedy to be the better debater. Does it matter from which channel of communication voters receive political information? If so, how does it matter? Do voters learn more through one medium than through another? Are voters more impressed by visual and image characteristics of candidates than by their stands on issues?
3. What kinds of debate formats produce more issue learning than others?
4. What are the consequences to the election process of the concern among the media and academic researchers with "who won?"
5. What do voters want to see during televised presidential debates? How does that match with their views of what a president should be?
6. Are there election reforms that can be aided by televised presidential debates? How?
7. What are the negative system effects of televised debates?
8. What is the role of public opinion in a presidential election from just after Labor Day to election day? Is that role affected by televised presidential debates?
9. How can the televised debates be used to increase voter turnout and participation generally?
10. Does televised presidential debates influence how children and adolescents learn about politics?

We have discussed partial answers to some of these questions. But, even if some of them were answered in the past, it may prove quite useful to ask them again. Monitoring the debates, sponsors and candidates, and observing new voter cohorts as they emerge in presidential election years, will help raise our general understanding of these unique political events—televised presidential debates.

ENDNOTES

1. John B. Anderson, "The Third Party Candidate's View of the System," in Franklin J. Havelick, (Ed.), *Presidential Selection* (Washington, DC: American Bar Association, 1982) p. 31.

2. From the transcript, S. Kraus, Chairman, Presidential Debates De-Briefing, Crystal City Marriott, Arlington, Virginia, November 30, 1976, p. 69. In 1980, Senator Robert Dole (R-Kansas), evidently irritated by President Carter ducking debates, attempted to amend legislation on campaign financing, essentially in keeping with Chandler's idea. Part of the amendment that failed included the statement, "No debate, no dollars." See Dole's press release, "Dole Amendment Would Force Candidates to Debate or Give Up Federal Funds," September 18, 1980.

3. P. Gailey, "Two Major Parties Form Panel To Sponsor Debates in 1988," *New York Times*, Thursday, February 19, 1987, p. Y 11.

4. *Ibid.*

5. From the transcript, S. Kraus, Chairman, Presidential Debates De-Briefing, *op. cit.*, pp. 70–71.

6. *Ibid.*, p. 71.

7. His advocacy for major party sponsorship came just after the 1984 fracas between the League and candidates' representatives over the panelists selection process.

8. P. Gailey, "Two Major Parties Form Panel To Sponsor Debates in 1988," *op. cit.*

9. *Ibid.*

10. *Ibid.* Another supplication advocates a broader exposure for the major parties by their sponsorship of debates at all levels:

"We recommend that the political parties at all levels take the initiative for such activities as candidate debates and policy forums. Such undertakings are certainly appropriate to the parties and are potentially invaluable means of building institutional party consciousness in the public mind. Cable television, including the possibility of party channels, offers a potential for exposure of candidates for those lesser offices which tend to be overlooked by the media attention given to the major national and state races." From an undated pamphlet, *The Future of American Political Parties*, highlighting recommendations included in, Joel L. Fleishman, *The Future of American Political Parties: The Challenge of Governance* (Englewood Cliffs, NJ: Prentice Hall, 1982).

11. Herbert E. Alexander and Brian A. Haggerty, *The Federal Election Campaign Act: After a Decade of Political Reform*, (Los Angeles: Citizens' Research Foundation, 1981) p. 99.

12. Sidney Kraus, Testimony to the Federal Election Commission on Pro-

posed Regulations for Federal Candidates: Sponsorship and Financing of Public Debates, Washington, DC, September 12, 1977.

13. ABC News-Harvard University Poll, "Analysis of Special Voter Turn-out Survey Shows Deep-Rooted Problems, Needed Reforms," released on September 25, 1983, p. 11.

14. P. Gailey, *op. cit.*

15. The 1988 debates commission members: Frank J. Fahrenkopf Jr., Republican National Committee Chairman; Sen. Pete Wilson, R-Calif.; Gov. Kay Orr, R-Neb.; Rep. Barbara Vucanovich, R-Nev.; David Norcross, Republican National Committee adviser; Paul Kirk, Democratic National Committee Chairman; former Sen. John Culver, D-Iowa; Richard Moe, Democratic National Committee adviser; Vernon Jordan, former president of the Urban League; and Pamela Harriman, Democratic Fundraiser.

16. The potential legal obstacles (sponsorship, television coverage, and the equal time provision of the Communications Act) have apparently been resolved with the Aspen Ruling and subsequent action by the Federal Communications Commission and the Federal Election Commission (see chap. 3).

17. David Broder, "There Will Be Many Andersons Unless the Parties Make a Stand," Baltimore *News American*, September 21, 1980.

18. D. S. Broder, *Behind the Front Page: A Candid Look at How the News is Made,* (New York: Simon & Schuster, 1987) p. 299 (italics added).

19. Editorial, "The Debate Debate," *New York Times*, Sunday, February 22, 1987, p. E 22.

20. *Ibid.*

21. Charles Benton, President of the William Benton Foundation, suggests that "eligibility criteria for public financing could be applied as well to the debate setting. This would ensure that substantial constituencies will have their points of view expressed." Statement at the Federal Election Commission Hearings, September 12, 1977.

22. See S. Kraus, *The Great Debates,* (Bloomington, IN: Indiana University Press, 1962) pp. 19–169.

23. M. Linsky, *Television and the Presidential Elections,* (Lexington, MA: D. C. Heath, 1983) p. 108.

24. *Ibid.*

25. Richard S. Salant, "The Good But Not Great Nondebates: Some Random Personal Notes," in S. Kraus, *The Great Debates: Carter vs. Ford, 1976,* (Bloomington: Indiana University Press, 1979) p. 183. Salant was quoting from the CBS News Standards.

26. *Ibid.*

27. D. Broder, *Behind the Front Page: A Candid Look at How the News is Made, op. cit.,* p. 300.

28. Broder "once described a consultant in a particular mayoral campaign as a 'hired gun'." *Ibid.,* p. 299.

29. *Ibid.* For discussion of persuasion and mass communication persuasion theories see, John C. Maloney, "Advertising Research and an Emerging Science of Mass Persuasion," *Journalism Quarterly,* XLI, No. 4 (Autumn, 1964), 517–28; Dan Nimmo, *The Political Persuaders: The Techniques of Modern Election Campaigns,* (Englewood Cliffs, NJ: Prentice-Hall, 1970), pp. 1–33 and 111–

162; Melvin L. De Fleur and Sandra Ball-Rokeach, *Theories of Mass Communication,* (New York: Longman, 1982); and Alexis S. Tan, *Mass Communication Theories and Research,* (New York: Macmillan, 1986).

30. "[O]ne may hope that the ideal of sound political discourse will serve as a regulative principle forceful enough to lead candidates and sponsors to select a format which serves truth and the public interest, as well as the political ends of the candidates." Lloyd Bitzer and Theodore Rueter, *Carter vs. Ford: The Counterfeit Debates of 1976,* (Madison: University of Wisconsin Press, 1980) p. 226.

". . . [I]t *is* possible to identify what is in the public interest, and to make this coincide with what the candidates will perceive to be in their interest." Joel L, Swerdlow, *Beyond Debate: A Paper on Televised Presidential Debates,* (New York: The Twentieth Century Fund, 1984) p. 60.

31. One extensive study found that of the questions asked by panelists in the 1976 debates well over half were hostile. See L. Bitzer and T. Rueter, *Carter vs. Ford: The Counterfeit Debates of 1976, op. cit.,* p. 65.

32. Louis T. Milic, "Grilling the Pols: Q & A at the Debates," In S. Kraus, *The Great Debates: Carter vs. Ford, 1976, op. cit.,* pp. 187–208.

33. From a document that Karayn wrote for the League's debate steering committee, "A Position Paper on the Staging, Structure, and Format of the Debates," undated, p. 1. Given to this writer by Karayn with the notation: sometime between August 10–15, 1976.

34. *Ibid.,* p. 3.

35. *Ibid.*

36. J. Karayn, memorandum to steering committee re: Format, August 24, 1976. Also quoted in Peggy Lampl, "The Sponsor: The League of Women Voters Education Fund," in S. Kraus, *The Great Debates, op. cit.,* pp. 91–92.

37. L. Bitzer and T. Rueter, *Carter vs. Ford: The Counterfeit Debates of 1976, op. cit.,* pp. 193–250.

38. *Ibid.,* pp. 193–224.

39. *Ibid.,* pp. 197–217.

40. *Ibid.,* pp. 245–246.

41. It is not unusual for presidential candidates to ignore ideas for improving televised debates. For example, on at least three occasions it was suggested that a moderator replace the panelists, eliminate the questions, and introduce different propositions for the candidates to debate. See S. Kraus, "Presidential Debates in 1964," *Quarterly Journal of Speech,* 50 (1964), p. 22; J. W. Germond and J. Witcover, Presidential Debates: An Overview," in A. Ranney (Ed.), *The Past and Future of Presidential Debates* (Washington, D.C.: American Enterprise Institute for Public Policy Research, 1979), p. 201; and S. A. Hellweg and S. L. Phillips, "Form and Substance: A Comparative Analysis of Five Formats used in the 1980 Presidential Debates," *Speaker and Gavel,* 18:2 (1981), pp. 75–76.

42. See S. Kraus, *The Great Debates, op. cit.* and *The Great Debates: Carter vs. Ford, 1976, op. cit.* Also see chapter 3.

43. See Samuel L. Becker and Elmer Lower, "Broadcasting in Presidential Campaigns," S. Kraus, *The Great Debates,* (1962), *op. cit.,* pp. 39–40. See also, "The Oregon Plan of Debating," *Quarterly Journal of Speech,* XII (April, 1926), pp. 176–180.

44. See Herbert A. Seltz and Richard D. Yoakam, "Production Diary of the Debates," in S. Kraus, *The Great Debates*, (1962), *op. cit.*, p. 77. Also, in Frank Stanton's (President, CBS) testimony, Senate Interstate and Foreign Commerce Committee, January 31, 1961.

45. P. Lampl, "The Sponsor: The League of Women Voters Education Fund," in S. Kraus, *The Great Debates*, (1979), *op. cit.*, p. 94.

46. CBS/*New York Times* Election Survey, November 4–8, 1976, pp. 1–2.

47. CBS News/*New York Times* Poll, November 14–18, 1984, released on November 18, 1984, p. 6.

48. CBS News/*New York Times* Poll, November 4–8, 1976. It is interesting to note that in 1956 12% of the electorate held negative evaluations of the political parties. See, Norman H. Nie, Sidney Verba, and John R. Petrocik, *The Changing American Voter*, (Cambridge, MA: Harvard University Press, 1979) p. 32.

49. ABC News-Harvard University Poll, *op. cit.*, p. 12.

50. *Ibid.*

51. President's Commission For a National Agenda For the Eighties, Report of the Panel on the Electoral and Democratic Process, *The Electoral and Democratic Process in the Eighties*, (Washington, DC: U.S. Government Printing Office, 1980) p.30.

52. *Ibid.*

53. ABC News-Harvard University Poll, *op. cit.*, p. 13.

54. Richard L. Cohen, "The Public Agenda Foundation: An Experiment in Issues Analysis," in S. Kraus (Ed.), *The Great Debates*, (1979), *op. cit.*, pp. 55–56 (italics his).

55. J. Karayn, "Presidential Debates: A Plan for the Future," in S. Kraus (Ed.), *The Great Debates*, (1979), *op. cit.*, pp. 210–211.

56. *Ibid.*, p. 211.

57. *Ibid.*, p. 218.

58. See Herbert E. Alexander, *Financing the 1972 Election* (Lexington, MA: D. C. Heath, 1976); H. E. Alexander, *Financing the 1976 Election* (Washington, DC: Congressional Quarterly Press, 1979); H. E. Alexander, *Financing Politics: Money Elections and Political Reform*, 2nd ed. (Washington, DC: Congressional Quarterly Press, 1980); H. E. Alexander and B. A. Haggerty, *The Federal Election Campaign Act, op. cit.*; and Institute of Politics, Harvard University, *Financing Presidential Campaigns: An examination of the ongoing effects of the federal election campaign laws upon the conduct of presidential campaigns*, A research report by the Campaign Finance Study Group to the Committee on Rules and Administration of the United States Senate, January, 1982.

59. Attributed to Joseph diGenova, staff director of the Senate Committee on Rules and Administration (jurisdiction over federal election laws) in H. E. Alexander and B. A. Haggerty, *The Federal Election Campaign Act, op. cit.*, p. 124.

60. *Ibid.*, p. 125.

61. See Ruth C. Clusen, "Statement Before the Federal Election Commission Sponsorship and Financing of Public Debates," League of Women Voters Education Fund, September 12, 1977.

62. *Ibid.*, p. 5.

63. Quoted in H. E. Alexander and B. A. Haggerty, *The Federal Election Campaign Act, op. cit.,* pp. 52–53.

64. These recommendations were made by the author to League presidents and public relations personnel in 1976, 1977, and 1980. In 1976 and 1977 the League's reaction may have been affected by their involvement in litigations.

65. See Louis T. Milic, "Grilling the Pols: Q & A at the Debates," in S. Kraus (Ed.), *The Great Debates,* (1979), *op. cit.,* pp. 187–208.

66. Perhaps this commission could serve as a bipartisan public trustee for the Federal Election Commission, similar in relationship to that between the United States Advisory Committee on Public Diplomacy and the U. S. International Communication Agency. See Report of the United States Advisory Commission on Public Diplomacy, 1982, Leonard L. Silverstein, Chairman, Washington DC 20547

67. Perhaps the first experimental study of this type was George F. Bishop, Robert W. Oldendick, and Alfred J. Tuchfarber, "The Presidential Debates as a Device for Increasing the 'Rationality' of Electoral Behavior," in G. Bishop, R. Meadow, and M. Jackson-Beeck (Eds.), *The Presidential Debates: Media, Electoral and Policy Perspectives* (New York: Praeger, 1978) pp. 179–196.

BIBLIOGRAPHY

This bibliography lists those books, book chapters, articles, government documents, academic conference presentations, and other materials on presidential debates. Some nonpresidential debate entries have been included for their import as precedents; others have been selected for historical reference. Although an attempt has been made to be comprehensive, certain judgmental decisions were made (e.g., representativeness; contribution to the larger research domain of political communication; significance for a particular debate, election, or campaign; and the like).

Abramowitz, A. (1977). *The first debate: A study of attitude change.* Unpublished manuscript, College of William and Mary, Baltimore, MD.
Abramowitz, A. (1978). The impact of a presidential debate on voter rationality. *American Journal of Political Science, 22,* 680–690.
Alexander, H., & Margolis, J. (1978). The making of the debates. In G. Bishop, R. Meadow, & M. Jackson-Beeck (Eds.), *The presidential debates: Media, electoral, and policy perspectives* (pp. 18–32). New York: Praeger.
American Political Science Association (1964). *Report of the Commission on Presidential Campaign Debates.* Washington, DC: author.
Atkin, C., Hocking, J., & McDermott, S. (1979). Home state voter response and secondary media coverage. In S. Kraus (Ed.), *The great debates: Carter vs. Ford, 1976* (pp. 429–436). Bloomington, IN: Indiana University Press.
Auer, J. J. (1962). The counterfeit debates. In S. Kraus (Ed.), *The great debates: Background, perspective, effects* (pp. 142–150). Bloomington, IN: Indiana University Press.

Auer, J. J. (1981). Great myths about the great debates. *Speaker and Gavel, 18*(2), 14–21.

Baker, K. L., Norpoth, H., & Schoenbach, K. (1980, August). Television debates and popular evaluations of parties and leaders in West Germany, 1972–1980. Paper presented at the meeting of the American Political Science Association.

Baker, K. L., & Norpoth, H. (1981). "Candidates on television: The 1972 electoral debates in West Germany," *Public Opinion Quarterly, 45,* 329–345.

Baker, K., & Walter, O. (1977, April). *The 1976 presidential debates and political behavior in Wyoming.* Paper presented at the meeting of Western Pocial Science Association, Denver, CO.

Barrow, L. (1961). Factors related to attention to the first Kennedy–Nixon debate. *Journal of Broadcasting, 5,* 229–238.

Barrow, R. L. (1977). Presidential debates of 1976: Toward a two party political system. *University of Cincinnati Law Review, 46,* 123–149.

Bechtolt, W., Hilyard, J., & Bybee, C. (1977). Agenda control in the 1976 debates: A content analysis. *Journalism Quarterly, 54,* 674–681.

Becker, L., Sobowale, I., Cobby, R., & Eyal, C. (1978). Debates' effect on voters' understanding of candidates and issues. In G. Bishop, R. Meadow, & M. Jackson-Beeck (Eds.), *The presidential debates: Media, electoral, and policy perspectives* (pp. 126–139). New York: Praeger.

Becker, L., Weaver, D., Graber, D., & McCombs, M. (1979). Influence on public agendas. In S. Kraus (Ed.), *The great debates: Carter vs. Ford, 1976* (pp. 418–428). Bloomington, IN: Indiana University Press.

Becker, S., & Lower, E. (1962). Broadcasting in presidential campaigns. In S. Kraus (Ed.), *The great debates: Background, perspective, effects* (pp. 25–55). Bloomington, IN: Indiana University Press.

Becker, S., & Lower, E. (1979). Broadcasting in presidential campaigns, 1960–1976. In S. Kraus (Ed.), *The great debates: Carter vs. Ford, 1976* (pp. 11–40). Bloomington, IN: Indiana University Press.

Becker, S., Pepper, R., Wenner, L., & Kim, J. (1979). Presidential debates, information flow, and the shaping of meaning. In S. Kraus (Ed.), *The great debates: Carter vs. Ford, 1976* (pp. 384–397). Bloomington, IN: Indiana University Press.

Benenson, R. (1984). News media and presidential campaigns. *Editorial Research Reports,* October 12, 759–776.

Benton, C., & Pokorny, G. (1979). The presidential forums. In S. Kraus (Ed.), *The great debates: Carter vs. Ford, 1976* (pp. 68–82). Bloomington, IN: Indiana University Press.

Ben-Zeev, S., & White, I. (1962). Effects and implications. In S. Kraus (Ed.), *The great debates: Background, perspective, effects* (pp. 331–337). Bloomington, IN: Indiana University Press.

Berquist, G. F. (1960, September). The Kennedy–Humphrey debate: To talk sense or to talk politics. *Today's Speech, 8,* pp. 2–3, 31.

Berquist, G. F., & Golden, J. L. (1981). Media rhetoric, criticism, and the public perception of the 1980 presidential debate. *Quarterly Journal of Speech, 67*(2), 125–137.

Bishop, G., Meadow, R., & Jackson-Beeck, M. (Eds.). (1978). *The presidential debates: Media, electoral and policy perspectives.* New York: Praeger.

Bishop, G., Oldendick, R., & Tuchfarber, A. (1978). Debate watching and the acquisition of political knowledge. *Journal of Communication, 28,* 99–113.

Bishop, G., Oldendick, R., & Tuchfarber, A. (1978). The presidential debates as a device for increasing the "rationality" of electoral behavior. In G. Bishop, R. Meadow, & M. Jackson-Beeck (Eds.), *The presidential debates: Media, electoral and policy perspectives* (pp. 179–196). New York: Praeger.

Bishop, G. (1980). Review of *The great debates: Carter vs. Ford, 1976. Public Opinion Quarterly, 44,* 598–600.

Bitzer, L., & Rueter, T. (1980). *Carter vs. Ford: The counterfeit debates of 1976.* Madison, WI: The University of Wisconsin Press.

Blankenship, J., & Kang, J. G. (1987, May). *The 1984 presidential and vice presidential debates: The printed press and "construction" by metaphor.* Paper presented at meeting of the International Communication Association, Montreal, Canada.

Bothwell, R. K., & Brigham, J. C. (1983). Selective evaluation and recall during the 1980 Reagan–Carter debate. *Journal of Applied Social Psychology, 13,* 427–442.

Bowes, J., & Strentz, A. (1978, April). *Candidate images: Stereotyping and the 1976 debates.* Paper presented at the meeting of the International Communication Association, Chicago, IL.

Brydon, S. R. (1985). The two faces of Jimmy Carter: The transformation of a presidential debater, 1976 and 1980. *Central States Speech Journal, 36,* 138–151.

Cantrell, W., Colella, M., & Monroe, A. (1976, November). *The great debates of 1976: A quasi-experimental analysis of audience effects.* Paper presented at the meeting of the Midwest Association for Public Opinion Research, Chicago, IL.

Cantrell, W. R. (1977). *The impact of the 1976 presidential debates on a student population.* Unpublished manuscript, Illinois State University, Normal, IL.

Carter, R. (1962). Some effects of the debates. In S. Kraus (Ed.), *The great debates: Background, perspective, effects* (pp. 253–270). Bloomington, IN: Indiana University Press.

Carter, R. (1978). A very peculiar horse race. In G. Bishop, R. Meadow, & M. Jackson-Beeck (Eds.), *The presidential debates: Media, electoral, and policy perspectives* (3–17). New York: Praeger.

Casey, G., & Fitzgerald, M. (1977, October). *Candidate images and the 1976 presidential debates.* Paper presented at the meeting of the Midwest Association for Public Opinion Research, Chicago IL.

Cater, D. (1962). Notes from backstage. In S. Kraus (Ed.), *The great debates: Background, perspective, effects* (pp. 127–131). Bloomington, IN: Indiana University Press.

Center for the Study of Democratic Institutions (1962). *The great debates.* Santa Barbara: Author.

Chaffee, S. (1978). Presidential debates: Are they helpful to voters? *Communication Monographs, 45,* 330–346.

Chaffee, S., & Choe, S. (1980). Time of decision and media use during the Ford-Carter campaign. *Public Opinion Quarterly, 44*(1), 53–69.

Chaffee, S., & Dennis, J. (1979). Presidential debates: An empirical assessment. In A. Ranney (Ed.), *The past and future of presidential debates* (pp. 75–106). Washington, DC: American Enterprise Institute for Public Policy Research.

Cheney, R. (1979). The 1976 presidential debates: A republican perspective. In A. Ranney (Ed.), *The past and future of presidential debates* (pp. 107–136). Washington, DC: American Enterprise Institute for Public Policy Research.

Clevenger, T., Parson, D., & Polisky, J. (1962). The problem of textual accuracy. In S. Kraus (Ed.), *The great debates: Background, perspective, effects* (pp. 341–347). Bloomington, IN: Indiana University Press.

Cohen, R. (1979). The public agenda foundation: An experiment in issues analysis. In S. Kraus (Ed.), *The great debates: Carter vs. Ford, 1976* (pp. 54–67). Bloomington, IN: Indiana University Press.

Cross, M. (1976). First debate: Many barbs, no clear winner. *Congressional Quarterly Weekly Report, 34,* 2583–2587.

Cross, M. (1976). Second debate: Tough Carter, angry Ford. *Congressional Quarterly Weekly Report, 34,* 2901–2903.

Cross, M. (1976). TV debates: One down, two to go. *Congressional Quarterly Weekly Report, 34,* 2695–2697.

Danders, R. (1961). *The great debates* (Freedom of Information Center Publication No. 67). Columbia, MO: University of Missouri School of Journalism.

Davis, D. (1979). Influence on vote decision. In S. Kraus (Ed.), *The great debates: Carter vs. Ford, 1976* (pp. 331–347). Bloomington, IN: Indiana University Press.

Davis, D., & Kraus, S. (1982). Public communication and televised presidential debates. In M. Burgoon (Ed.), *Communication Yearbook 6* (pp. 289–303). Beverly Hill, CA: Sage.

Davis, L. (1978). Camera eye-contact by the candidates in presidential debates of 1976. *Journalism Quarterly, 55*(3), 431–437–455.

Davis, M. H. (1982). Voting intentions and the 1980 Carter-Reagan debate. *Journal of Applied Social Psychology, 12,* 481–492.

deBock, H. (1978). The influence of the Ford-Carter debates on the Dutch television audience. *Journalism Quarterly, 55,* 583–585.

Dennis, J., & Chaffee, S. H. (1978). Legitimation in the 1976 U. S. presidential election campaign. *Communication Research, 5,* 371–394.

Dennis, J., Chaffee, S., & Choe, S. (1979). Impact upon partisan: Image and issue voting. In S. Kraus (Ed.), *The great debates: Carter vs. Ford, 1976* (pp. 314–330). Bloomington, IN: Indiana University Press.

Desmond, R., & Donohue, T. (1981). The role of the 1976 televised presidential debates in the political socialization of adolescents. *Communication Quarterly, 29,* 302–308.

Deutschmann, P. (1962). Viewing, conversation, and voting intentions. In S. Kraus (Ed.), *The great debates: Background, perspective, effects* (pp. 232–252). Bloomington, IN: Indiana University Press.

Donnelly, H. (1984a). Presidential debates usually aid challenger. *Congressional Quarterly Weekly Report, 42*, 2313–2314.

Donnelly, H. (1984b). Mondale outpoints Reagan; Ferraro and Bush break even. *Congressional Quarterly Weekly Report, 42*, 2625.

Donnelly, H. (1984c). Reagan–Mondale, round 2: No clear-cut win. *Congressional Quarterly Weekly Report, 42*, 2827.

Drucker, S. J., & Hunhold, J. P. (1987). The debating game. *Critical Studies In Mass Communication, 4*(1), 202–207.

Ellsworth, J. (1965). Rationality and campaigning: A content analysis of the 1960 presidential campaign debates. *Western Political Quarterly, 18*, 794–802.

Ericson, E. (1984). Some debate. *The Reformed Journal, 34*(3), 2–3.

Freely, A. (1961). The presidential debates and the speech profession. *Quarterly Journal of Speech, 47*(1), 60–64.

Friedenberg, R. V. (1979). We are present here today for the purpose of having a joint discussion: The conditions requisite for political debates. *Journal of the American Forensic Association, 16*(3), 1–9.

Friedenberg, R. V. (1981). "Selfish interests," or the prerequisites for political debate: An analysis of the 1980 presidential debate and its implications for future campaigns. *Journal of the American Forensic Association, 18*(1), 91–98.

Gadziala, S., & Becker, L. (1983). A new look at agenda-setting in the 1976 election debates. *Journalism Quarterly, 60*(1), 122–125.

Gans, H. J. (1977). Lessons 1976 can offer 1980. *Columbia Journalism Review, 15*(5), 25–28.

Gantz, W., & Petrie, C. (1977). *The politics of non-exposure: A comparison of viewers and non-viewers of the 1976 presidential debates.* Unpublished manuscript, State University of New York at Buffalo, Buffalo.

Garramone, G. M. (1985). Motivation and selective attention to political information formats. *Journalism Quarterly, 62*(1), 37–44.

Germond, J., & Witcover, J. (1979). Presidential debates: An overview. In A. Ranney (Ed.), *The past and future of presidential debates* (pp. 191–214). Washington, DC: American Enterprise Institute for Public Policy Research.

Gilbert, R. E. (1982). Television debates and presidential elections: The United States and France. *Journal of Social, Political and Economic Studies, 7*, 411–429.

Goldhaber, G. M., Frye, J. K., Porter, D. T., & Yates, M. P. (1976). *The image of the candidates: A communication analysis of the Ford/Carter debates, I, II and III.* Unpublished manuscript, State University of New York at Buffalo, Buffalo.

Gottlieb, S. E. (1978). Role of law in the broadcast of political debate. *Federal Bar Journal, 37*(1), 1–24.

Graber, D. (1977, May). *Measuring audience effects of the 1976 presidential debates: Some methodological problems.* Paper presented at the meeting of the Annenberg Research Conference on the Presidential Debates, Philadelphia, PA.

Graber, D. (1978). Problems in measuring audience effects in the 1976 debates. In R. Meadow, M. Jackson-Beeck, & G. Bishop (Eds.), *The presidential debates: Media, electoral, and policy perspectives* (pp. 105–125). New York: Praeger.

Graber, D., & Kim, Y. (1977). *The 1976 presidential debates and patterns of political learning.* Paper presented at meeting of the Association for Education in Journalism, Madison, WI.

Graber, D., & Kim, Y. (1978). Why John Q. voter did not learn much from the 1976 presidential debates. In B. Ruben (Ed.), *Communication yearbook 2* (pp. 407–421). New Brunswick, NJ: Transaction Books.

Hagner, P., & Orman, J. (1977, September). *A panel study of the impact of the first 1976 presidential debate: Media-events, "rootless voters" and campaign learning.* Paper presented at the meeting of the American Political Science Association, Washington, DC.

Hagner, P., & Rieselbach, L. (1978). The impact of the 1976 presidential debates: Conversion or reinforcement? In G. Bishop, R. Meadow, & M. Jackson-Beeck (Eds.), *The presidential debates: Media, electoral, and policy perspectives* (pp. 157–178). New York: Praeger.

Hawkins, R., Pingree, S., Smith, K., & Bechtolt, W., Jr. (1976). Adolescents' responses to the issues and images of the debates. In S. Kraus (Ed.), *The great debates: Carter vs. Ford, 1976* (pp. 368–383). Bloomington, IN: Indiana University Press.

Hellweg, S. A., & Phillips, S. L. (1981a). A verbal and visual analysis of the 1980 Houston republican presidential primary debate. *Southern Speech Communication Journal, 47*:1, 23–38.

Hellweg, S. A., & Phillips, S. L. (1981b). Form and substance: A comparative analysis of five formats used in the 1980 presidential debates. *Speaker & Gavel, 18,* 67–76.

Hemsley, G. D., & Doob, A. M. (1974). The effect of looking behavior on perceptions of a communicator's credibility. *Journal of Applied Social Psychology, 8,* 136–144.

Institute for Communication Research (1960). *"The great debates" and the 1960 presidential campaign.* Stanford, CA: Stanford University.

Jackson-Beeck, M., & Meadow, R. (1977a, August). *Content analysis of presidential debates as communication events.* Paper presented at the meeting of the Association for Education in Journalism, Madison, WI.

Jackson-Beeck, M., & Meadow, R. (1977b, October). *Issue evolution: Parameters in presidential debate and public perceptions.* Paper presented at the meeting of the Midwest Association for Public Opinion Research, Chicago, IL.

Jackson-Beeck, M., & Meadow, R. (1979a). Content analysis of televised communication events: The presidential debates. *Communication Research, 6,* 295–320.

Jackson-Beeck, M., & Meadow, R. (1979b). The triple agenda of presidential debates. *Public Opinion Quarterly, 43,* 173–180.

Jackson-Beeck, M., & Meadow, R. (1979c). Ascertainment and analysis of debate content. In G. Bishop, R. Meadow, & M. Jackson-Beeck (Eds.), *The presidential debates: Media, electoral and policy perspectives* (pp. 205–210). New York: Praeger.

Jacoby, J. (1986). Viewer miscomprehension of the 1980 presidential debate—A research note. *Political Psychology, 7,* 297–308.

Jeffres, L., & Hur, K. (1979). Impact of ethnic issues on ethnic voters. In S. Kraus (Ed.), *The great debates: Carter vs. Ford, 1976* (pp. 437–445). Bloomington, IN: Indiana University Press.

Joslyn, R. A. (1977). *Voter belief and attitude change and 1976 debates.* Unpublished manuscript, Temple University, Philadelphia, PA.

Karayn, J. (1979). Presidential debates: A plan for the future. In S. Kraus (Ed.), *The great debates: Carter vs. Ford, 1976* (pp. 209–219). Bloomington, IN: Indiana University Press.

Karayn, J. (1979). The case for permanent presidential debates. In A. Ranney (Ed.), *The past and future of presidential debates* (pp. 155–174). Washington, DC: American Enterprise Institute for Public Policy Research.

Katz, E., & Feldman, J. (1962). The debates in light of research: A survey of surveys. In S. Kraus (Ed.), *The great debates: Background, perspective, effects* (pp. 173–223). Bloomington, IN: Indiana University Press.

Kay, J. (1981, November). *Campaign debate formats: The non-presidential level.* Paper presented at the meeting of the Speech Communication Association, Anaheim, CA.

Kelley, S., Jr. (1962). Campaign debates: Some facts and issues. *Public Opinion Quarterly, 26,* 351–366.

Kerr, H. (1961). The great debates in a new perspective. *Today's Speech, 9*(4), 9–11.

Kinder, D., Denney, W., & Wagner, R. (1977, May). *Media impact on candidate image: Exploring the generality of the law of minimal consequences.* Paper presented at the meeting of the American Association for Public Opinion Research, Buck Hills Falls, PA.

Kirkpatrick, E. M. (1979). Presidential candidate debates: What can we learn from 1960? In A. Ranney (Ed.), *The past and future of presidential debates* (pp. 1–55). Washington, DC: American Enterprise Institute for Public Policy Research.

Kraus, S. (Ed.). (1962). *The great debates: Background, perspective, effects.* Bloomington, IN: Indiana University Press. Reissued in paperback, 1977, as *The Great Debates: Kennedy vs. Nixon, 1960.*

Kraus, S. (1964). Presidential debates in 1964. *Quarterly Journal of Speech, 50*(1), 19–23.

Kraus, S. (Ed.). (1976). "Presidential debates de-briefing," transcripts of conference held at Crystal City Marriott, Arlington, Virginia, November, 29–30, unpublished transcript.

Kraus, S. (1977a, May). *Presidential debates and public policy.* Paper presented at the meeting of the Annenberg Research Conference on the Presidential Debates, Philadelphia, PA.

Kraus, S. (1977b). Testimony to the Federal Election Commission on Proposed Regulations for Federal Candidates: Sponsorship and Financing of Public Debates, 12 September.

Kraus, S. (Ed.). (1979a). *The great debates: Carter vs. Ford, 1976.* Bloomington, IN: Indiana University Press.

Kraus, S. (1979b). Presidential debates: Political option or public decree? In S. Kraus (Ed.), *The great debates: Carter vs. Ford, 1976* (pp. 3–10). Bloomington, IN: Indiana University Press.

Kraus, S. (1979c). Candidate briefings. In S. Kraus (Ed.), *The great debates: Carter vs. Ford, 1976* (pp. 105–108). Bloomington, IN: Indiana University Press.

Kraus, S. (1987). Voters win. *Critical Studies in Mass Communication, 4,* pp. 214–216.

Kraus, S., & Davis, D. (1982a). Political debates. In D. Nimmo & K. Sanders (Eds.), *The handbook of political communication* (pp. 273–296). Beverly Hills, CA: Sage.

Kraus, S., & Davis, D. (1982b). Political debates: The negotiated format. *Gamut: A Journal of Ideas and Information, 5,* 102–112.

Kraus, S., & Smith, R. (1962). Images and issues. In S. Kraus (Ed.), *The great debates: Background, perspective, effects* (pp. 289–312). Bloomington, IN: Indiana University Press.

Lampl, P. (1979). The sponsor: The League of Women Voters Education Fund. In S. Kraus (Ed.), *The great debates: Carter vs. Ford, 1976* (pp. 83–104). Bloomington, IN: Indiana University Press.

Lang, G. E. (1987). Still seeking answers. *Critical Studies in Mass Communication, 4,* pp. 211–214.

Lang, G. E., & Lang, K. (1978a). The formation of public opinion: Direct and mediated effects of the first debate. In G. Bishop, R. Meadow, & M. Jackson-Beeck (Eds.), *The presidential debates: Media, electoral, and policy perspectives* (pp. 61–80). New York: Praeger.

Lang, G. E., & Lang, K. (1978b). The first debate and the coverage gap. *Journal of Communication, 28*(4), 93–98.

Lang, G. E., & Lang, K. (1978c). Immediate and delayed responses to a Carter–Ford debate: Assessing public opinion. *Public Opinion Quarterly, 42,* 322–341.

Lang, G. E., & Lang, K. (1979a). Making the least of it? Television coverage of the audio gap. In S. Kraus (Ed.), *The great debates: Carter vs. Ford, 1976* (pp. 158–174). Bloomington, IN: Indiana University Press.

Lang, G. E., & Lang, K. (1979b). Immediate and mediated responses: Reaction to the first debate. In S. Kraus (Ed.), *The great debates: Carter vs. Ford, 1976* (pp. 298–313). Bloomington, IN: Indiana University Press.

Lang, G. E., & Lang, K. (1984). *Politics and television: Reviewed.* Beverly Hill, CA: Sage.

Lang, K., & Lang, G. E. (1961). Ordeal by debate: Viewer reactions. *Public Opinion Quarterly, 25,* 277–288.

Lang, K., & Lang, G. E. (1962). Reactions of viewers. In S. Kraus (Ed.), *The great debates: Background, perspective, effects* (pp. 313–330). Bloomington, IN: Indiana University Press.

Lasswell, H. (1962). Introduction. In S. Kraus (Ed.), *The great debates: Background, perspective, effects* (pp. 19–24). Bloomington, IN: Indiana University Press.

League of Women Voters' Education Fund (1977). *Effect of the debates on the 1976 campaign and election.* Washington, DC: Author.

League of Women Voters' Education Fund (1981). *The 1980 presidential debates: Behind the scenes.* Washington, DC: Author.

Lemert, J. B., Elliott, W. R., Nestvold, K.-J., & Rarick, G. R. (1983). Effects of viewing a presidential debate: An experiment. *Communication Research, 10,* 155–173.

Lesher, S. (with Caddell, P., & Rafshoon, G.) (1979). Did the debates help Jimmy Carter? In A. Ranney (Ed.), *The past and future of presidential debates* (pp. 137–154). Washington, DC: American Enterprise Institute for Public Policy Research.

Leuthold, D., & Valentine, D. (1981). How Reagan "won" the Cleveland debate: Audience predispositions and presidential debate "winners." *Speaker and Gavel, 18,* 60–66.

Lichtenstein, A. (1982). Differences in impact between local and national televised political candidates' debates. *Western Journal of Speech Communication, 46,* 291–298.

Light, L. (1980a). Reagan and Anderson accentuate differences in campaign's first debate. *Congressional Quarterly Weekly Report, 38,* 2831–2832.

Light, L. (1980b). The debate: Campaign's critical moment? *Congressional Quarterly Weekly Report, 38,* 3232.

Lubell, S. (1962). Personalities vs. issues. In S. Kraus (Ed.), *The great debates: Background, perspective, effects* (pp. 151–162). Bloomington, IN: Indiana University Press.

Lupfer, M. B., & Wald, K. (1977, May). *An experimental study of the first Carter–Ford debate.* Paper presented at the meeting of the American Association for Public Opinion Research, Buck Hill Falls, PA.

Martel, M. (1981). Debate preparations in the Reagan camp: An insider's view. *Speaker and Gavel, 18,* 34–46.

Martel, M. (1983). *Political campaign debates: Images, strategies, and tactics.* New York: Longman.

Martel, M. (1984). Political campaign debates: Images, strategies, and tactics. *Campaigns and Elections, 4,* 13–27.

Mazo, E., Moos, M., Hoffman, H., & Wheeler, H. (1962). *The great debates: An occasional paper on the role of the political process in the free society.* Santa Barbara: Center for the Study of Democratic Institutions.

McLeod, J., Bybee, C., & Durall, J. (1979). Equivalence of informed political participation: The 1976 presidential debates as a source of influence. *Communication Research, 6,* 463–487.

McLeod, J., Bybee, C., Durall, J., & Ziemke, D. (1977). *The 1976 debates as forms of political communication.* Paper presented at the meeting of the Association for Education in Journalism, Madison, WI.

McLeod, J., Durall, J., Ziemke, D., & Bybee, C. (1979). Reactions of young and older voters: Expanding the context of effects. In S. Kraus (Ed.), *The great debates: Carter vs. Ford, 1976* (pp. 348–367). Bloomington, IN: Indiana University Press.

Meadow, R. (1983). Televised campaign debates as whistle-stop speeches. In W. Adams (Ed.), *Television coverage of the 1980 presidential campaign* (pp. 89–102). Norwood, NJ: Ablex.

Meadow, R. (1987). A speech by any other name. *Critical Studies in Mass Communication, 4,* 207–210.

Meadow, R., & Jackson-Beeck, M. (1978a). A comparative perspective on television debates: Issue evolution in 1960 and 1976. In G. Bishop, R. Meadow, and M. Jackson-Beeck (Eds.), *The presidential debates: Media, electoral, and policy perspectives* (pp. 33–58). New York: Praeger.

Meadow, R., & Jackson-Beeck, M. (1978b). Issue evolution: A new perspective on presidential debates. *Journal of Communication, 28*(4), 84–92.

Meadow, R. G., & Jackson-Beeck, M. (1980). Candidate political philosophy: Revelations in the 1960 and 1976 debates. *Presidential Studies Quarterly, 10,* 234–243.

Mears, W. (1977). The debates: A view from the inside. *Columbia Journalism Review, 15*(5), 21–25.

Mehling, R., Kraus, S., & Yoakam, R. (1962). Pre-debate campaign interest and media use. In S. Kraus (Ed.), *The great debates: Background, perspective, effects* (pp. 224–231). Bloomington, IN: Indiana University Press.

Messaris, P., Eckman, B., & Grumpert, G. (1979). Editing structure in the televised versions of the 1976 presidential debates. *Journal of Broadcasting, 23,* 359–369.

Middleton, R. (1962). National TV debates and presidential voting decisions. *Public Opinion Quarterly, 26,* 426–429.

Miller, A., & MacKuen, M. (1979a). Learning about the candidates: The 1976 presidential debates. *Public Opinion Quarterly, 43,* 326–346.

Miller, A., & MacKuen, M. (1979b). Informing the electorate: Effects of the 1976 presidential debates. In S. Kraus (Ed.), *The great debates: Carter vs. Ford, 1976* (pp. 269–297). Bloomington, IN: Indiana University Press.

Milic, L. (1979). Grilling the pols: Q & A at the debates. In S. Kraus (Ed.), *The great debates: Carter vs. Ford, 1976* (pp. 187–208). Bloomington, IN: Indiana University Press.

Mitchell, L. (1979). *With the whole nation watching: Report of the Twentieth Century Fund task force on televised presidential debates.* Lexington, MA: D. C. Heath.

Mitofosky, W. J. (1977, September). *1976 presidential debate effects: A hit or myth.* Paper presented at the meeting of the American Political Science Association, Washington, DC.

Morrison, A., Steeper, F., & Greendale, S. (1977, May). *The first 1976 presidential debate: The voters win.* Paper presented at the meeting of the American Association for Public Opinion Research, Buck Hill Falls, PA.

Morrow, G. R. (1977). Changes in perceptions of Ford and Carter following the first presidential debate. *Perceptual and Motor Skills, 45,* 423–429.

Mulder, R. D. (1978). The political effects of the Carter-Ford debate: An experimental analysis. *Sociological Focus, 11*(1), 33–45.

Myers, S. L., Kaid, L. L., & Towers, W. M. (1979, May). *An experimental approach to the uses and effects of televised political debates.* Paper presented at the meeting of the Speech Communication Association, San Antonio, TX.

Neuman, W. R. (1977). *The visual impact of presidential television: A study of the first Ford-Carter debate.* Unpublished manuscript, Yale University, New Haven, CT.

Nimmo, D., & Mansfield, M. (1985, May). *Change and persistence in candidate images: Presidential debates across 1976, 1980, and 1984.* Paper presented at the meeting of the Speech Communication Association, Denver, Colorado.

Nimmo, D., Mansfield, M., & Curry, J. (1978). Persistence and change in candidate images. In G. Bishop, R. Meadow, & M. Jackson-Beeck (Eds.), *The presidential debates: Media, electoral, and policy perspectives* (pp. 140–156). New York: Praeger.

O'Keefe, G., & Mendelsohn, H. (1979). Media influences and their anticipation. In S. Kraus (Ed.), *The greate debates: Carter vs. Ford, 1976* (pp. 405–417). Bloomington, IN: Indiana University Press.

Pfau, M. (1981, November). *Criteria and format to optimize political debates: An analysis of South Dakota's "election 80" series.* Paper presented at the meeting of the Speech Communication Association, Anaheim, CA.

Polsby, N. (1979). Debatable thoughts on presidential debates. In A. Ranney (Ed.), *The past and future of presidential debates* (pp. 175–190). Washington, DC: American Enterprise Institute for Public Policy Research.

Prentice, D. B., Larson, J. K., & Sobnosky, M. J. (1981, November). *The Carter-Reagan debate: A comparison of clash in the dual format.* Paper presented at the meeting of the Speech Communication Association, Anaheim, CA.

Ranney, A. (Ed.). (1979). *The past and future of presidential debates.* Washington, DC: American Enterprise Institute for Public Policy Research.

Ray, R. F. (1961). Thomas E. Dewey: The great Oregon debate of 1948. In R. Reid (Ed.), *American public address: Studies in honor of Albert Craig Baird* (pp. 245–270). Columbia, MO: University of Missouri Press.

Riley, P., & Hollihan, T. A. (1981). The 1980 presidential debates: A content analysis of the issues and arguments. *Speaker and Gavel, 18,* 47–59.

Riley, P., Hollihan, T. A., & Cooley, D. (1980, April). *The 1976 presidential debates: An analysis of the issues and arguments.* Paper presented at the meeting of the Central States Speech Association, Chicago, IL.

Ritter, K. W. (Ed. Special Edition). (1981). The 1980 presidential debates. *Speaker and Gavel, 18,* 12–13.

Robinson, J. (1979). Poll results on the debates. In S. Kraus (Ed.), *The great debates: Carter vs. Ford, 1976* (pp. 262–268). Bloomington, IN: Indiana University Press.

Rogers, E., Dozier, D., & Barton, D. (1977). *Changes in candidate images as a result of the debates.* Unpublished manuscript, Stanford University, Stanford, CA.

Rose, D. D. (1979). Citizen uses of the Ford–Carter debates. *Journal of Politics, 41,* 214–221.

Rotzoll, K., & Tinkham, S. (1977). *A Ford/Carter panel study from a Sherifian perspective.* Unpublished manuscript, University of Illinois, Urbana, IL.

Salant, R. (1962). The television debates: A revolution that deserves a future. *Public Opinion Quarterly, 26,* 335–350.

Salant, R. (1979). The good but not great numbers: Some random personal notes. In S. Kraus (Ed.), *The great debates: Carter vs. Ford, 1976* (pp. 175–186). Bloomington, IN: Indiana University Press.

Samovar, L. A. (1962). Ambiguity and unequivocation in the Kennedy-Nixon television debates. *Quarterly Journal of Speech, 48,* 277–279.

Sarnoff, R. (1962). An NBC view. In S. Kraus (Ed.), *The great debates: Background, perspective, effects* (pp. 56–64). Bloomington, IN: Indiana University Press.

Schrott, P. R. (1986). The West German television debates, 1972–1983: Candidate strategies and voter response, unpublished Ph.D. dissertation.

Scott, R. L. (1981). You cannot not debate: The debate over the 1980 presidential debates. *Speaker and Gavel, 18,* 28–33.

Sears, D. (1977, September). *The debates in the light of research: An overview of the effects.* Paper presented at the meeting of the American Political Science Association, Washington, DC.

Sears, D., & Chaffee, S. (1978). Uses and effects of the 1976 debates: An overview of empirical studies. In S. Kraus (Ed.), *The great debates: Carter vs. Ford, 1976* (pp. 223–261). Bloomington, IN: Indiana University Press.

Sebold, H. (1962). Limitations of communication: Mechanisms of image maintenance in the form of selective perception, selective memory, and selective distortion. *Journal of Communication, 12*(3), 142–149.

Seldes, G. (1962). The future of national debates. In S. Kraus (Ed.), *The great debates: Background, perspective, effects* (pp. 163–169). Bloomington, IN: Indiana University Press.

Seltz, H., & Yoakam, R. (1962). Production diary of the debates. In S. Kraus (Ed.), *The great debates: Background, perspective, effects* (pp. 73–126). Bloomington, IN: Indiana University Press.

Seltz, H., & Yoakam, R. (1979). Production diary of the debates. In S. Kraus (Ed.), *The great debates: Carter vs. Ford, 1976* (pp. 110–157). Bloomington, IN: Indiana University Press.

Shilds, S. A., & MacDowell, K. A. (1987). "Appropriate" emotion in politics: Judgments of a televised debate. *Journal of Communication, 37*(2), 78–89.

Siepmann, C. (1962). Were they great? In S. Kraus (Ed.), *The great debates: Background, perspective, effects* (pp. 132–141). Bloomington, IN: Indiana University Press.

Sigelman, L., & Sigelman, C. K. (1984). Judgments of the Carter-Reagan debate: The eyes of the beholders. *Public Opinion Quarterly, 48,* 426–429.

Simons, H., & Leibowitz, K. (1979). Shifts in candidate images. In S. Kraus (Ed.), *The great debates: Carter vs. Ford, 1976* (pp. 398–404). Bloomington, IN: Indiana University Press.

Sloan, L. (1977, May). *Biasing effects of news analyses of the 1976 presidential debates.* Paper presented at the meeting of the American Association for Public Opinion Research, Buck Hill Falls, PA.

Smith, R. G. (1977). The Carter-Ford debates: Some perceptions from academe. *Central States Speech Journal, 28,* 250–257.

Stanton, F. (1962). A CBS view. In S. Kraus (Ed.), *The great debates: Background, perspective, effects* (pp. 65–72). Bloomington, IN: Indiana University Press.

Stephan, F. (1962). Review of *The Great Debates: Background, Perspective, Effects.* *Public Opinion Quarterly, 26,* 524–526.

Steeper, F. (1977, May). *Effects of the second presidential debate.* Paper presented at the meeting of the American Association of Public Opinion Research, Buck Hill Falls, PA.

Steeper, F. (1978). Public response to Gerald Ford's statements on Eastern Europe in the second debate. In G. Bishop, R. Meadow, & M. Jackson-Beeck (Eds.), *The presidential debates: Media, electoral, and policy perspectives* (pp. 81–101). New York: Praeger.

Swanson, L. L., & Swanson, D. L. (1978). The agenda-setting function of the first Ford-Carter debate. *Communication Monographs, 45,* 347–353.

Swerdlow, J. L. (1984). *Beyond debate: A paper on televised presidential debates.* New York: The Twentieth Century Fund.

Swerdlow, J. L. (Ed.). (in press). *Presidential debates: 1988 and beyond.* Washington, DC: Congressional Quarterly Press.

Tannenbaum, P., Greenberg, B., & Silverman, F. (1962). Candidate images. In S. Kraus (Ed.), *The great debates: Background, perspective, effects* (pp. 271–288). Bloomington, IN: Indiana University Press.

Terry, H., & Kraus, S. (1979). Legal and political aspects: Was section 315 circumvented? In S. Kraus (Ed.), *The great debates: Carter vs. Ford, 1976* (pp. 41–53). Bloomington, IN: Indiana University Press.

The Joint Appearances of Senator John F. Kennedy and Vice President Richard M. Nixon: Presidential Campaign of 1960 (1961). Washington, DC: Government Printing Office.

Tiemens, R. K. (1978). Television's portrayal of the 1976 presidential debates: An analysis of the visual content. *Communication Monographs, 45,* 362–370.

Tiemans, R. K., Hellweg, S. A., Kipper, P., & Phillips, S. L. (1985). An integrative verbal and visual analysis of the Carter-Reagan debate. *Communication Quarterly, 33*(1), 34–42.

Vancil, D., & Pendell, S. (1984). Winning presidential debates: An analysis of criteria influencing audience response. *Western Journal of Speech Communication, 48*(1), 62–74.

Wald, K., & Lupfer, M. (1978). The presidential debate as a civics lesson. *Public Opinion Quarterly, 42,* 342–353.

Weiss, R. O. (1981). The presidential debates in their political context: The issue-image interface in the 1980 campaign. *Speaker and Gavel, 18,* 22–27.

White, F. (1976, September). *Presidential debate of 1976.* Paper presented at the meeting of the American Political Science Association, Chicago, IL.

Whitney, D. C., & Goldman, S. B. (1985). Media use and time of vote decision: A study of the 1980 presidential election. *Communication Research, 12,* 511–529.

Yoder, J., & Mims, H. (1979). The significance of written texts. In S. Kraus (Ed.), *The great debates: Carter vs. Ford, 1976* (pp. 449–452). Bloomington, IN: Indiana University Press.

Zapple, N. (1979). Historical evolution of section 315. In A. Ranney (Ed.), *The past and future of presidential debates* (pp. 56–74). Washington, DC: American Enterprise Institute for Public Policy Research.

SELECTIVE RELATED PUBLICATIONS

Adams, W. C. (Ed.). (1983). *Television coverage of the 1980 presidential campaign.* Norwood, NJ: Ablex.

Basler, R. P. (1980). *The Lincoln legend: A study in changing conceptions.* New York: Farrar, Straus & Giroux.

Berelson, B., Lazarsfeld, P., & McPhee, W. (1954). *Voting: A study of opinion formation in a presidential campaign.* Chicago: University of Chicago Press.

Boller, P. F. Jr. (1984). *Presidential campaigns.* New York: Oxford University Press.

Broder, D. S. (1987). *Behind the front page: A candid look at how the news is made.* New York: Simon & Schuster.

Campbell, A., Converse, P. E., Miller, W. E., & Stokes, D. E. (1960). *The American voter.* New York: Wiley.

Campbell, A., Converse, P. E., Miller, W. E., & Stokes, D. E. (1966). *Elections and the political order.* New York: Wiley.

Campbell, A., Gurin, G., & Miller, W. E. (1954). *The Voter Decides.* Evanston, Ill.: Row, Peterson.

David, P. T. (Ed.). (1961). *The presidential election and transition: 1960–1961.* Washington, DC: The Brookings Institution.

Drew, E. (1981). *Portrait of an election: The 1980 presidential campaign.* New York: Simon & Schuster.

Gans, H. J. (1979). *Deciding what's news: A study of CBS Evening News, NBC Nightly News, Newsweek, and Time.* New York: Pantheon Books.

Germond, J. W., & Witcover, J. (1985). *Wake us when it's over: Presidential politics of 1984.* New York: Macmillan.

Graber, D. (1980). *Mass media and American politics.* Washington, DC: Congressional Quarterly Press.

Greenfield, J. (1980). *Playing to win: An insider's guide to politics.* New York: Simon & Schuster.

Harper, R. S. (1951). *Lincoln and the press.* New York: McGraw-Hill.

Havelick, F. J. (Ed.). (1981). *Presidential selection.* Washington, DC: American Bar Association Special Committee on Election Law and Voter Participation.

Jamieson, K. H. (1984). *Packaging the presidency: A history and criticism of presidential campaign advertising.* New York: Oxford University Press.

Johannsen, R. W. (Ed.). (1965). *The Lincoln-Douglas debates of 1858.* New York: Oxford University Press.

Kessel, J. (1980, 1984). *Presidential campaign politics: Coalition strategies and citizen response.* Homewood, Ill.: Dorsey Press.

Key, V. O. Jr. (with the assistance of Cummings, M. C. Jr.). (1965). *The responsible electorate.* Cambridge, Mass.: Harvard University Press.

Kraus, S., & Davis, D. (1976). *The effects of mass communication on political behavior.* University Park, PA: Pennsylvania University Press.

Kraus, S., & Perloff, R. (Eds.). (1985). *Mass media and political thought: An information processing approach.* Beverly Hills, CA: Sage.

Lazarsfeld, P., Berelson, B., & Gaudet, H. (1944). *The people's choice.* New York: Columbia University Press.

Linsky, M. (Ed.). (1983). *Television and the presidential elections: Self interest and the public interest.* Lexington, MA: D. C. Heath.

McGinnis, J. (1969). *Selling of the president, 1968.* New York: Trident Press.

Meyrowitz, J. (1985). *No sense of place: The impact of electronic media on social behavior.* New York: Oxford University Press.

Minow, N. N., Martin, J. B., & Mitchell, L. M. (1973). *Presidential television.* New York: Basic Books.

Monaghan, J. (1956). *The man who elected Lincoln.* Indianapolis: Bobbs-Merrill.

Nelson, M. (Ed.). (1985). *The elections of 1984.* Washington, DC: Congressional Quarterly.

Nimmo, D., & Savage, R. L. (1976). *Candidates and their images: Concepts, methods, and findings.* Pacific Palisades, CA: Goodyear.

Neuman, R. W. (1986). *The paradox of mass politics: Knowledge and opinion in the American electorate.* Cambridge, MA: Harvard University Press.

Postman, N. (1985). *Amusing ourselves to death: Public discourse in the age of show business.* New York: Viking Penguin.

Patterson, T. E. (1980). *The mass media election: How Americans choose their president.* New York: Praeger.

Patterson, T. E., & McClure, R. D. (1976). *The unseeing eye.* New York: Putnam.

Pomper, M. M. (Ed.). (1985). *The election of 1984: Reports and interpretations.* Chatham, NJ: Chatham House Publishers.

Ranney, A. (1983). *Channels of power: The impact of television on American politics.* New York: Basic Books.

Ranney, A. (Ed.). (1985). *The American elections of 1984.* Washington, DC: American Enterprise Institute Book published by Duke University Press.

Reilly, T. (1979). Lincoln-Douglas debates of 1858 forced new role on the press. *Journalism Quarterly, 56,* 734–743.

Robinson, M. J., & Sheehan, M. A. (1983). *Over the wire and on TV.* New York: Russell Sage.

Sabato, L. S. (1981). *The rise of political consultants: New ways of winning elections.* New York: Basic Books.

Sandoz, E., & Crabb, Jr., C. V. (Eds). (1985). *Election '84: Landslide without a mandate?* New York: New American Library.

Sparks, E. E. (Ed.). (1908). *The Lincoln-Douglas debates of 1858.* Springfield, IL: Illinois State Historical Library.

Tebbel, J., & Watts, S. M. (1985). *The press and the presidency: From George Washington to Ronald Reagan.* New York: Oxford University Press.

Trent, J. S., & Friedenberg, R. V. (1983). *Political campaign communication: Principles and practices.* New York: Praeger.

White, T. H. (1961). *The making of the president: 1960.* New York: Atheneum.

Wills, G. (1987). *Reagan's American: Innocents at home.* New York: Doubleday.

NAME INDEX

SUBJECT INDEX